GENERATION 2000

STUDENT'S BOOK 2

**COLIN GRANGER
DIGBY BEAUMONT**

Contents

Lesson	1 Missing	2 Twenty questions	3 London is a big city	4 Munch	5	6 New identity	7 My big ambition	8	9	10
Grammar	Have got Present simple Quite, very	Present simple Present simple passive Have got Made of Used for + -ing There is	There is, there are -ing clauses Present continuous Present simple What?	One (substitute word) -ing clauses What...like?	SKILLS: What's my job?	Present simple Past simple Present perfect simple For and since What? Where? How old? How long?	Would like to Hope to My big ambition is to	READING: The amazing life of the emperor penguin	PROJECT: Help save the planet	Consolidation A
Communication	Describing people's appearance (She's quite tall and slim. She's got dark, wavy hair and grey eyes. She wears glasses.)	Describing objects (Its a machine. It's made of metal and plastic. It's used for drying hair.)	Describing a street scene (There's an old woman sitting at a newspaper stand.) Saying what people are doing now (What's he doing at the moment? - He's eating a sandwich) Talking about everyday habits (What does he do in the club?-He takes the tickets)	Identifying (Tina is the one taking an order) Describing people's character (What's Tina like? - She's kind and friendly)		Asking for and giving personal and biographical information (What's your name? Where do you live? Where were you born? How long did you live in New York? How long have you lived in London?)	Talking about ambitions (Would you like to be famous? One day I hope to go to a Madonna concert. My big ambition is to speak perfect English.)			

Lesson	11 She's coming tomorrow	12 The future in your hands	13 An invitation	14 You must be home by eleven	15	16 They were the diamonds I was looking for	17 Friday the thirteenth	18	19	20
Grammar	Present continuous In, on, at, to, from, by, with Where? When? What time? How?	Will May	Would like to Have to Present continuous Go + -ing	Must Have to Can	SKILLS: I couldn't without...	Past continuous Past simple What? How many? Who?	Past continuous and past simple When (linking word) What?	READING: Stranger than fiction	PROJECT: Write a quiz	Consolidation B
Communication	Talking about future arrangements (Kay Sloane is coming to London tomorrow. She is travelling by train. When are Clay and Sloane meeting?)	Making predictions (She'll have a long life.) Express possibility (She my get married more than once)	Greeting someone (Hello. How are you? - I'm fine, thanks. And you? - I'm very well, thank you.) Inviting someone (Would you like to go to a disco this evening?) Accepting invitations (Yes, I'd love to./Yes, okay.) Refusing invitations (I'm afraid I can't./I'm sorry but I can't) Giving reasons for refusing invitations (I have to stay in and study tonight. I'm already doing something.) Talking about future arrangements (Are you doing anything on Tuesday evening?)	Talking about necessity or obligation (You must make your bed every morning. You mustn't leave your clothes on the floor. I had to clean my room every day when I was your age. Do you have to be home by a certain time? - Yes, I do. I don't have to do the washing up at home.) Talking about permission (Can you wear any clothes you like? - Yes, I can. I can't watch anything I like on TV.)		Describing a background scene (I was standing outside the Calypso Club. It was raining hard and I was getting wet, very wet.) Describing events and actions (Suddenly, a large black car came round the corner and stopped in front of the club.)	Talking about interrupted actions (I was running a bath when the telephone rang. What was Larry doing when the phone rang? What did he do then?)			

Lesson	21 Hope Street	22 Mick Malone's office	23 A great idea!	24 The barbecue	25	26 I know what we'll do!	27 Just a minute!	28	29	30
Grammar	There is, there are, there should be Too many, too much, not enough Not anywhere to Only one	Present perfect continuous For and since How long?	Shall we? Let's Why don't we? How about + -ing? When? Who? How many? Where? What?	Would you like? Would you like me to? Shall I? I'll	SKILLS: Are you a TV-addict?	Will Present simple for the future after when, as soon as and until	Present simple for the future after if If sentences (1st Conditional)	READING: The wildest woman in the West	PROJECT: The Good Guide	Consolidation C
Communication	Criticising (There are too many cars parked on the pavement. There aren't enough litter bins.) Making recommendations (There should be an underground car park. There should be more litter bins.)	Talking about duration (How long has he been playing the saxophone? - Since he was 14. I've been living in Barcelona for fifteen years.)	Asking for suggestions (When shall we have the barbecue?) Making suggestions (Let's have it on Sunday afternoon) Agreeing with suggestions (Yes, okay./all right.) Disagreeing with suggestions (No, not on Sunday. I'm going to the cinema then)	Offering things (Would you like a kebab?) Offering to do things (Would you like me to get you some more Coke? Shall I cut the bread? I'll help you carry those things.) Accepting offers (Yes, please./Yes, thanks./Yes. That would be great.) Refusing offers (No, thanks./No, I'm fine at the moment, thanks)		Talking about the future (When I get home, I'll do my homework. As soon as I finish school today, I'll walk home with my friends. I won't have anything to eat until I get home.)	Talking about future conditions (What if somebody sees us? / If somebody sees us, we'll say we're lost.)			

Lesson	31 Larry's perfect Saturday	32 Definitions quiz	33 What do you think I should do?	34 This is the nine o'clock news	35	36 Survival	37 Imagine	38	39	40
Grammar	Look forward to + -ing Want to, want someone to Can I? Could I? Do you think I could? Can you? Could you? Do you think you could?	Which, who, that, where (relative pronouns) Present simple active and passive Can	Should I would (if I were you) Why don't you?	Past simple passive	SKILLS: Choosing a pet	Conditional sentences (2nd Conditional)	If sentences (2nd Conditional)	READING: The Amish	PROJECT: If I had the power	Consolidation D
Communication	Expressing wants (She wants to leave the baby with Larry. He wants Larry to stir the soup.) Asking for permission (Do you think I could leave Tabatha with you? Could I have a look at your magazine? Can I borrow your pen?) Making requests (Can you stir it for me? Could you take her with you? Do you think you could lend me your bike this afternoon?)	Defining (A vegetarian is a person who doesn't eat meat.)	Giving advice (You should try counting sheep. I wouldn't drink so much coffee if I were you. Why don't you find a part-time job?)	Talking about the past (A security guard was shot and injured in a robbery at a bank in London early this morning.)		Talking about imaginary conditions (I'd try to put out the fire first. - Yes, so would I./No, I wouldn't. I'd set off the fire alarm first)	Talking about imaginary conditions (Where would you live if you could live anywhere in the world? - I'd live in India.)			

Lesson	41 Pen pals	42 Now and then	43 Someone had switched off the light	44 Eye-witness	45	46 Secret diary	47 Interview	48	49	50
Grammar	Both But	Present simple Used to	Past perfect simple Why? Because	Past perfect simple Past continuous	SKILLS: A ghost story	Reported statements Say something, tell someone something	Reported questions and statements	READING: The true story of a miracle	PROJECT: An interview with someone famous	Consolidation E
Communication	Letter writing Describing similarities and differences (They are both 17. She lives in the UK, but he lives in the USA)	Talking about present habits and states (I have to be careful about what I eat.) Talking about past habits and states (I used to eat a lot.)	Talking about the past (Somebody had opened the drawer of his desk.) Asking for and giving reasons (Why did you say 'I'm sorry.'? - Because I'd forgotten her birthday.)	Talking about the past (I was crossing the road. I'd just come out of the telephone box.)		Reporting statements (My optician said (that) my eyes were fine. He told me (that) I didn't need to wear glasses.)	Reporting questions (He asked him if his recent tour had been successful. I wanted to know if he had had a good time in the States.) Reporting statements (He said that it had been very successful. He told Larry that he had had a great time.)			

Pronunciation section	page 96
Information gap material	pages 99 and 108
Tapescripts	page 100
Reference Grammar	page 109
Wordlist	page 122

Missing

1

A

Look at the picture and answer the questions.

1 What is the man's name ?
2 What is his job ?
3 What is the time ?
4 What is the date ?
5 Who is Peter Cooper ?

🎧 01 Listen to the man introducing himself. Check your answers.

B

🎧 02 Look at the pictures and listen to the descriptions of the four young men. Match the descriptions with the pictures.

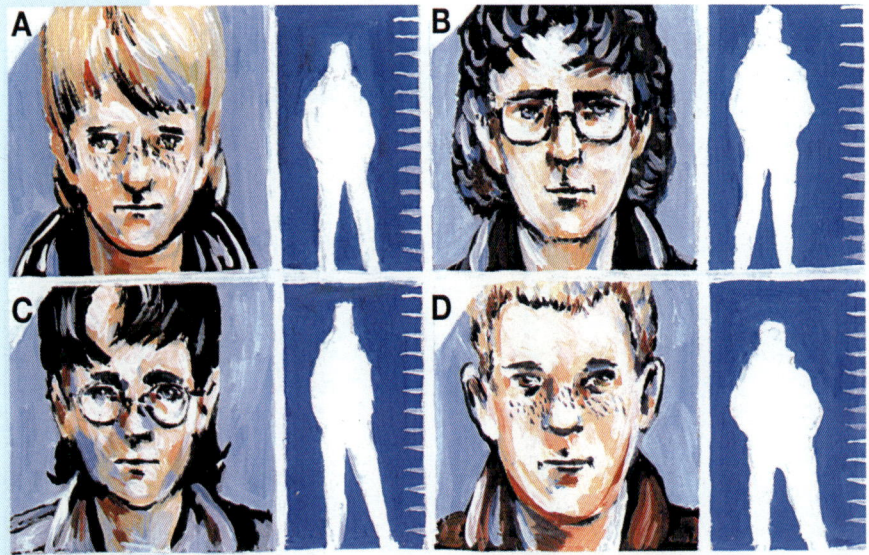

C

🎧 03 Listen to Mick Malone speaking to Peter Cooper's mother. Which of the four young men in the pictures in B is Peter ?

D

Make notes about a classmate.

Name	Ms X
Height	Quite tall
Build	slim

🎧 02 Copy the form below. Then listen again and make notes.

Name	D
Height	Quite short
Build	well built
Hair	very short, fair
Eyes	brown
Other features	freckles

Height – tall short
Build – well built slim
Hair – (1) long short
       (2) straight curly
       (3) dark fair
Eyes – brown blue green
Other features – freckles glasses

Then describe this student to your classmates. Can they guess who it is ?

Example
Ms X is quite tall and slim. She's got dark, wavy hair and grey eyes. She wears glasses.

E

Write a description of yourself.

I am	(quite/very)____ .
I have got	
I wear	____ .

Use your notes to make sentences about the four young men.

He **is**	(quite/very)____ .
He **has got**	
He **wears**	____ .

Example
D – He's quite short and well built. He's got very short, fair hair and brown eyes. He's got freckles.

Twenty questions

2

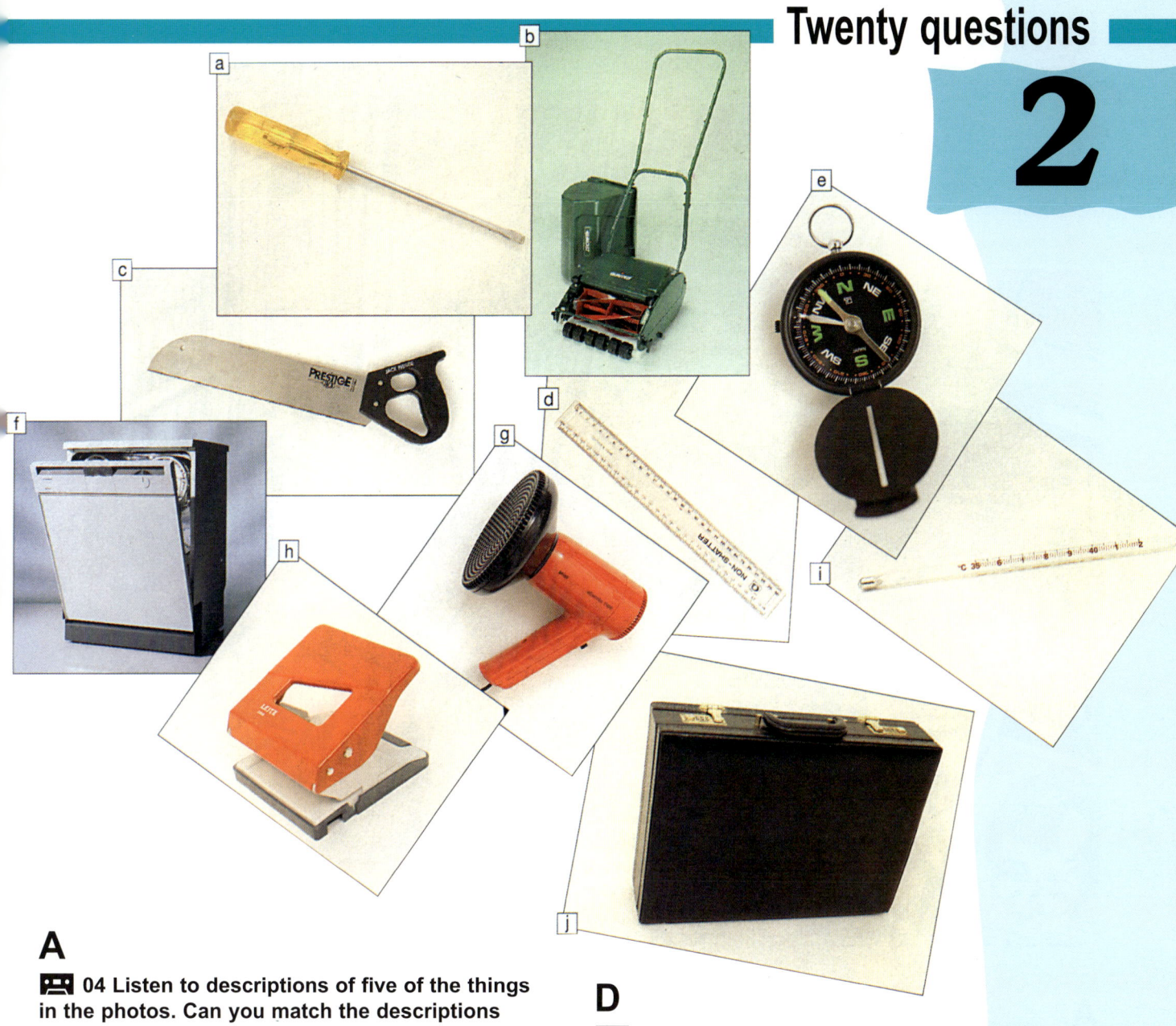

A

📼 04 Listen to descriptions of five of the things in the photos. Can you match the descriptions with the photos?

Example *1 g*

B

Describe one of the other things in the photos. Can your classmates tell you which thing you are describing? Use some of these words and structures to help you.

It's big/small/long/thin/flat/round.
It's made of metal/glass/wood/plastic/leather/rubber.
It's got a handle.
It's a machine/a tool.
It's used for measuring things/turning screws/ washing dishes/making holes in paper/ drawing lines/cutting grass.

C

Do you know the names of any of the things in the photos? You can find the names on page 107.

D

📼 05 Listen to some people playing *Twenty Questions*. What object are they talking about?

E

Now play *Twenty Questions*. Think of an object. Your classmates have to find out what the object is. They can ask you twenty *Yes/No* questions – questions which you can answer with *Yes* or *No*.

Example

Is it big/small/long/thin/flat/round/rectangular/ heavy/light?
Is it made of metal/glass/wood/plastic/leather/ rubber/wool?
Has it got legs/a handle/wheels?
Do you (normally) find it inside/outside/in a kitchen/ in a car?
Is it a machine/tool?
Is it used for ...-ing?
Is there one (of these things) in this room?

London is a big city

3

It's 6.20 pm on Friday, October 5th and I'm looking for a missing person – a young man called Peter Cooper. London is a big city and it's going to be very difficult to find him. A private investigator needs to be very observant. For example, look at the people in this street. Where are they and what are they doing?

A

🔊 Listen to Mick. Then make sentences about the people in the street. Use the words in the boxes.

There is a/an___			He/She is___-ing___.
___-ing___.			
There are two___			They are___-ing ___.

Examples

There's an old woman sitting at a newspaper stand. She's counting her money.
There are two young men waiting at a bus stop. They are looking at a magazine.

old woman	stand	at a bus stop	lock	a hamburger
young men	sit on	at a newspaper stand	look at	their guitars
old man	stand	on the pavement	light	their helmets
young women	wait	outside a café	put on	a magazine
man	sit	outside a café	eat	the door
young people	come out of	a motorbike	count	a cigarette
woman	kneel	a takeaway	put away	her money

🔊 Listen and check your answers.

B

🔊 06 Listen to Mick. Find the people he speaks about in the picture.

🔊 06 Listen again. Find the answers to these questions.
1 What are the names of the four people?
2 What do they do to earn money?
3 Why does Mick think they can help him?

Now make sentences about the four people.

Example

Her name is Meg. She sells newspapers in the street. She sees a lot of people every day.

C

🔊 07 Listen to Mick speak to the four people. Who can help Mick find Peter?

D

Look at the picture and answer the questions.
1 What time is it?
2 Who is Mick with?
3 Where do you think they are?
4 Who are they looking for?
5 Who do you think the other four people in the picture are? Are they customers or do they work at the Star Club?

 08 Listen to Mick and check your answers.

E

What do you think the four people do at the club? What are they doing at the moment? Ask and answer. Use the words in the boxes.

Example

1
A: *What **does** he **do** in the club?*
B: *He **takes** the tickets.*
A: *What**'s** he **doing** at the moment?*
B: *He**'s eating** a sandwich.*

comb	drinks
operate	people's coats and bags
eat	a plug
serve	his hair
read	the tickets
take	a magazine
change	the lights and sound
take	sandwich

Now match the people with their jobs.

Example
1 – He's the doorman.

technician
doorman
barmaid
cloakroom attendant

F

 09 Listen to Mick speaking to the four people. Who is he speaking to in each conversation? What do we find out about Peter? Make notes.

A – The technician - Peter never stops dancing.

 09 Listen and check your answers.

G

It's 10 o'clock at night and the doorman is opening the club. Find Peter in the picture.

Munch

4

A

Munch is the name of a TV soap. It's about a fast food restaurant. Read what these TV viewers think about the main characters in the programme. As you read, try to find the characters in the picture.

Example
Tina - g

❝ The character I like the best is **Tina**. She is very kind and friendly and laughs and smiles a lot. Everyone likes her. ❞

❝ I really like **Melanie**. She is really lazy and hates doing any work. She is also very funny and makes people laugh. ❞

❝ I don't like **Rupert** at all. He is really vain and likes looking at himself in the mirror all the time. He is also quite cruel and likes upsetting people. ❞

❝ The character I really don't like is **Kevin**. He is really insincere and he never says what he really thinks. He is also ambitious and wants to be assistant manager one day. ❞

❝ I feel very sorry for **Andy**. He is in love with Tina and is very jealous. He is really bad-tempered and can get very angry. ❞

❝ My favourite character is **Sabir**. He is hard-working and works a lot of hours because he has to earn money for his family. He is also very honest and always says what he thinks. ❞

❝ I really hate **Mrs Palmer**. She is the boss of the restaurant and is very rude to her staff. She is also mean and wants to save money all the time. ❞

❝ I feel very sorry for **Paul**. He is in love with Tina but is very shy and never asks her for a date. He is also a bit boring and always talks about things like the weather. ❞

B

What are the characters *Munch* like ? Read the descriptions in A again and find two adjectives for each person. Make notes.

Tina-kind, friendly
Melanie-lazy, funny

Work with a classmate. Close your books and ask and answer using your notes.

Example

A: *What's Tina like ?*
B: *She's kind and friendly. What's Melanie like ?*
A: *She's...*

Identify the characters in the picture and make sentences. Use the words in the box.

Example

| g - (I think) Tina is the one taking an order. |

holding a knife	combing his hair
reading a magazine	taking an order
looking at a hamburger	carrying a box
looking at a menu	writing something in a notebook

🎧 Listen and check your answers.

D

Associations
Are the adjectives in the box positive or negative? Make lists. Put any adjectives you think can be positive or negative in a separate list.

+	–	+/–
friendly funny	cruel	ambitious

ambitious bad-tempered boring cruel friendly
funny hard-working honest insincere jealous
kind lazy mean rude shy vain

Compare your list with a classmate's. Are there any differences?

E

What are you like? Are you ambitious, cruel, etc? Tick (✓) or cross (✗) the adjectives on your lists. Put a question mark (?) next to the adjectives you are not sure about.

+	–	+/–
friendly funny	cruel ✗	ambitious ✗

Show your list to a classmate. Do you agree with your classmate's ideas about himself/herself?

F

Choose three people: characters in TV soaps, film and pop stars, actors, actresses, sportsmen, sportswomen, politicians, etc. Write descriptions of them.

> I really like tennis star André Agassi. He is very sociable and funny and he makes people laugh. He's also a bit rebellious and sometimes does crazy things.

Then show your descriptions to a classmate and discuss. Do you agree with everything in your classmate's description?

C

Look at the picture. Who do you think is saying these things?

1 'It's a very nice day today, isn't it?'
2 'That's none of your business. Leave me alone.'
3 'Don't put too much salad in these hamburgers.'
4 'What do you think of my hair?'
5 'Shh! Don't say anything.'
6 'Hi. How are you today?'
7 'Are you hiding from Mrs Palmer?'
8 'I'll write that down in my notebook.'

▶ 10 Listen to the conversations and check your answers. Who is speaking in each conversation?
▶ 10 Listen again. Do you agree with the TV viewers in A?

9

What's my job?

SKILLS 5

SPEAKING

A

Match the photos with the names of the jobs.

| hairdresser   disc jockey |
| computer programmer   surgeon |

What do these people do?

Example
Hairdressers shampoo, cut and style hair.

READING

B

Work in groups of four. Choose a different Job file each and make notes about the good and bad points of the job.

hairdresser —

good   bad
You can talk to
the customers.   Salary

SPEAKING

C

Now ask your partners about the other Job files. Which job do you think is the best? Why?

JOB FILE 54

Name Marc Morris
Age 26
Profession Junior Surgeon
Job Description Marc assists senior surgeons with many different surgical operations. He examines patients in hospital before and after they have their operations. He also works in the outpatients clinic, where patients who have recently had operations are examined. In addition, he assists with emergency surgery at night or at weekends.
Hours Marc works very long hours - about 80 to 90 a week.
Salary The starting salary is £20,000 a year, increasing to £35,000 to 45,000. You can earn more if you work with private patients.
Qualifications You need good grades at 'A' Level in science subjects, such as biology, chemistry and physics.
Training Before you can become a junior surgeon you have to study for five years at medical school. Then you have to work in a hospital for one year spending a few months in each section of the hospital.
Getting started When you have got your science 'A' levels, apply to a medical school.
For more information Write to:
Career Opportunities (Junior Surgeon), Careers House, Crisp Road, London W6 9RL

JOB FILE 23

Name Anthony Simons
Age 22
Profession Hairdresser
Job Description Anthony has been a hairdresser for about four years and has done lots of training courses for cutting and styling hair. His day is very varied and depends on the requirements of the clients. He usually welcomes them as they arrive and talks to them briefly about what they want him to do to their hair. After that a trainee hairdresser washes the client's hair. Anthony then cuts, styles, colours or perms their hair. One evening a week, the hairdressing salon invites men and women to model for them. Anthony finds this the most enjoyable part of his job because he can try out new styles.
Hours Normally Monday to Saturday, 8.30am to 5.30pm.
Salary The starting salary for a hairdresser is probably one of the lowest! However, once you have done all the training, you can earn £200 a week. If you work for a very fashionable salon, you can earn a lot more.
Qualifications No formal qualifications are necessary. A good general knowledge of hair fashions is useful.
Training The training takes place mainly at the salon. Most good salons also send their trainees to college for one day a week to study for diplomas in cutting and styling.
Getting started Visit your local salons and ask about becoming a trainee. Alternatively, apply to the hairdressing department in a college.
For more information Write to:
Career Opportunities (Hairdresser), Careers House, Crisp Road, London W6 9RL

JOB FILE 32

Name Anna-Marie Bexford
Age 27
Profession Radio Disc Jockey
Job Description Anna-Marie does a two-hour show on Saturday mornings on national radio, but that doesn't mean she only works on Saturdays! She spends the rest of the week preparing the show - researching, interviewing and writing. She also does other work for the radio station, for example promotions and public relations. This means that occasionally she has to attend dinners and press conferences, or do interviews with music magazines.
Hours Anna-Marie works about 40 hours a week.
Salary An assistant DJ on a local radio station earns about £15,000 a year. A good national radio DJ can earn more than £100,000 a year.
Qualifications No qualifications are needed, but you have to have a good general knowledge of music. You also have to be flexible. If you only like pop music, you probably won't do very well.
Training Anna-Marie started with a local radio station making the tea! After a year, she got a job as an assistant to a DJ, helping to prepare a show. Then she applied for and got her present job.
Getting started The best thing to do is write to your local radio station and ask about voluntary work. Then try to get a job as an assistant DJ.
For more information Write to:
Career Opportunities (Radio DJ), Careers House, Crisp Road, London W6 9RL

JOB FILE 14

Name Anita Chang
Age 26
Profession Computer Programmer
Job Description Anita works for a large insurance company in Bristol. She spends most of her time meeting people in the company and talking to them about what they need their computers to do. She then designs new systems for them and programs the computers to suit their needs. Her job is often difficult because the computer system can't always do what people want it to do. She occasionally travels to other cities where the company has offices and meets other programmers to learn about their work.
Hours Generally Monday to Friday, 9am to 5pm. However, Anita works 'flexi-time' - she has to work 35 hours a week, but she can start and finish when she likes. If she needs to finish a programme she sometimes has to work very late.
Salary The starting salary for this job is about £14,000 a year, rising quickly to between £25,000 and £35,000.
Qualifications You must have a good degree in computer science or a computer-related subject.
Training After you have graduated from university, you can start applying for trainee jobs. The company will then train you for the specific job they want you to do.
Getting started Find out about computing courses at universities. You will need good 'A' levels (particularly maths) to be accepted for a course.
For more information Write to:
Career Opportunities (Computer Programmer), Careers House, Crisp Road, London W6 9RL

WRITING

D

Read Lina Lannis's letter to Career Opportunities. What career is Lina interested in?

> Career Opportunities
> (Hairdresser)
> Careers House
> Crisp Road
> London
> W6 9RL
>
> 12 Alexandra Court
> 53 Becklow Road
> London
> W12 9ER
> 14th May
>
> Dear Sir or Madam,
> I have read your Job file on hairdressing. Please send me more information about this career.
> I look forward to hearing from you.
> Yours faithfully,
> Lina Lannis

Read Lina's letter again. Notice:

1 where Lina writes her address, the date, and *Career Opportunities'* address;
2 how she begins the letter, says that she has read the *Job file,* asks for more information, and ends the letter.

Now write a letter to Career Opportunities similar to Lina's. Give your own name and address and today's date. Ask for more information about one of the other jobs in the *Job files*.

LISTENING

E

🎧 Listen to part of a radio quiz programme called *What's My Job?* What job do you think the guest does?

SPEAKING

F

Now play *What's My Job?* in groups of four.
Student A – Think of a job.
Students B, C, D – Ask *Yes/No* questions to find out A's job. Remember, you can only ask 20 questions!
Example questions
Do you work inside/outside?
Do you wear a uniform/special clothes?
Do you work on your own/with other people?
Do you work long hours/unusual hours/at nights
Is your job hard/dangerous/well-paid?
Do you have to have special training/special qualifications?

11

New indentity

6

A

 Look at the picture above. Bert and Harry are at an airport. They are going away on holiday. Read or listen to the conversation and answer these questions:

1 Why are they in a hurry?
2 Which flight are they catching?
3 Why is Harry worried?
4 Why isn't Bert worried?

Bert: Hurry, Harry. Look it's the final call for our flight.
Harry: Have you got your passport, Bert?
Bert: Yes, of course I've got my passport, Harry. Don't worry so much. Look here it is.
Harry: But that isn't your passport, Bert. Look at the name on it: Tom Barrymore.
Bert: I know it isn't my passport. I lost my passport so I borrowed this one from a friend of mine.
Harry: But that's very dangerous, Bert. The immigration officer is going to ask you questions. She's going to find out it's not your passport.
Bert: Don't worry so much, Harry. I know all about Tom Barrymore. Look, he gave me this information to memorise. I can answer any questions she asks. No problem.

B

12 Look at the picture above. The immigration officer is asking Bert some questions. Look at the information Tom gave Bert. Then listen to the conversation. Does Bert make any mistakes?

12 Listen again. What are Bert's answers to these questions?

1 What's your name?
2 Where were you born?
3 How old were you when you moved to Oxford?
4 How long did you live in Oxford?
5 Where do you live now?
6 How long have you lived in Brighton?
7 Where do you work?
8 How long have you had this job?
9 How long have you been married?
10 How many children have you got?

Then practise the questions.

C

Work with a classmate. Act out a conversation between the immigration officer (Student A) and Bert (Student B). Student A (with book open) – Ask Student B questions. Student B (with book closed) – Try not to make any mistakes.

A: What's your name?
B: My name's Tom Barrymore.
A: Where were you born?
B: ...

D

New identity game

Work with a classmate.

Student A – Learn this new identity.

Then change roles.

Student B – Learn this new identity.

Your name is John (♂)/Joan (♀) Morris. You were born in Sydney, Australia. Your family moved to New York when you were ten. You lived in New York for six years. You now live in London. You have lived in London since 1990. You work for the United Nations. You have had this job for three years. You have been married since last September.

Your name is Paul (♂)/Paula (♀) Paterson. You were born in San Francisco, USA. Your family moved to India when you were two. You lived in India for twelve years. You now live in Berlin, Germany. You have lived in Berlin since 1988. You work for Delta. You have had this job since last September. You have been married for eight years.

Student B – Prepare questions to ask Student A. Use the questions in the box to help you.

Student A – Prepare questions to ask Student B. Use the questions in the box to help you. Ask and answer. Student A – Open your book. Student B – Close your book and answer A's questions.

> What's your name?
> Where do you live now?
> Where were you born?

Ask and answer. Student B (with book open) – Write down any mistakes Student A makes. Student A (with book closed) – Try not to make any mistakes.

Example
B: *What's your name?*
A: *Joan Morris.*
B: *Where do you live now?*
A: *In New York. (Student B writes down New York.)*
B: *Where were you born?*

| What's your name? |
| Where do you live? |
| Where do you work? |
| |
| Where were you born? |
| How old were you when you moved to___? |
| How long did you live in___? |
| |
| How long have you lived in___? |
| How long have you had that job? |
| How long have you been married? |

E

Write a new identity for your classmate to learn. Then play the *New identity game* again.

Your name **is**___. You **were born** in___. Your family **moved** to___ when you **were**___. You **lived** in___ for___. You now **live** in___. You **have lived** in___ since___. You **work** for___. You **have had** this job for___. You **have been** married since___.

Note the difference:

| **for** | twelve years
six months
five days
ten minutes | **since** | 1988
last September
Saturday
2 o'clock |

My big ambition

7

A
Find a question for each picture.

Example
1 Would you like to get married before you are 20 ?

| Would you like to | live
travel
own
get
be
study | in a pop group ?
to be a 100 ?
to Nepal ?
at a university ?
a fast car ?
married before you are 20 ? |

Then work with a classmate. Ask and answer.

A: Would you like to ___ ?
B: Yes, I would. / No, I wouldn't.

Example
A: Would you like to get married before you are 20 ?
B: No, I wouldn't.

Tell your classmates what you have found out.

Example
Dominique would like to own a fast car, travel to Nepal and study at a university.

Finally, make a table of results for your class.

get married before 20 - 2 students
live to be 100 - 9 students
own a fast car - 12 students

B
Write three questions to ask your classmates.

Would you like to be famous ?
Would you like to travel in space ?
Would you like to earn a lot of money?

Ask and answer.

C

Speed reading

Work with a classmate. First, copy the chart below. Then read what these young people say and complete the chart as quickly as you can. Check your answers with your teacher as soon as you have finished.

Patrick Murdoch, 19, from Birmingham, is unemployed. He spends most of his time training as a long distance runner.

In a few weeks time I'm going to run in the London Marathon, which is one of the most important marathons in the world. This year there will be over 35,000 runners in the race - including some of the best international runners and I hope to be amongst the first hundred past the finishing line. My big ambition is to be chosen to run for Britain at the Olympics.

Mayank Patel, 21, works in a fashion store called Next. He has had this job for two years and is now assistant manager.

My ambition is to start my own business. I've been at Next for two years now and I'm going to stay for a couple more years to get more experience. By then I hope to have raised enough money to open my own clothes shop. Do you know anyone with £50 - 60,000 they don't need?

Rachel Kirby is a seventeen-year-old student from south London. Rachel's biggest interest is music. She can both sing and play the piano.

I've still got one more year at school, but when I leave, I'm going to start a band with some friends of mine. We're all good musicians and, of course, one day we all hope to make a record and become rich and famous! Whatever happens, I'd very much like to be a professional musician one day.

Name	Age	Occupation	Plans	Hopes / Ambitions
Patrick			He's going to run in the London Marathon.	
Mayank	21			His ambition is to start his own business. He hopes to open his own clothes shop.
Rachel		student		

D

Write about your hopes and ambitions. Write two sentences that are true and one sentence that is not true. Begin your sentences with:

> I'd very much like to___.
> One day I hope to___.
> My big ambition is to___.

Example
I'd very much like to live in Mexico.
One day I hope to go to a Madonna concert.
My big ambition is to speak perfect English.

Read your sentences to your classmates. Can they tell you which sentence is not true?

READING 8: The amazing life of the emperor penguin

A

Look at the map and the photos of the emperor penguins. Read the captions to the photos and look at the information on the map. Try to guess the meaning of any words you don't know.

1. A male emperor penguin feeding his chick
2. Emperor penguins walking across the ice to their breeding grounds
3. Emperor penguin families returning to the sea
4. Male emperor penguins incubating their eggs

B

Emperor penguins are different to most other birds and even to most other penguins. Read these facts:

- Emperor penguins don't build nests.
- The male emperor penguin incubates the egg, not the female.
- The male stands while it incubates the egg; it doesn't sit on the egg like most other birds.
- Emperor penguins breed in one of the most inhospitable places in the world - in an area where there is no food and no shelter.
- The female lays the egg in late autumn and the chick hatches in winter, the coldest time of the year, not in spring or summer like most other birds.

Look at the facts again and try to think why emperor penguins do or don't do these things. For example, why don't emperor penguins build nests ? Why does the male incubate the egg and not the female ? Try to guess the answers if you don't know.

C

Read the text. Find the answers to the questions you thought about in B.

Example
Why don't emperor penguins build nests?
Because there is no vegetation on the ice.

emperor penguins and their chicks in a snowstorm

emperor penguin lifting the egg onto his feet

In the early autumn the emperor penguins leave the sea and climb onto the ice. They then walk 50 - 60 kilometres to their breeding grounds close to the South Pole.

When they arrive at the breeding grounds in late March, the penguins choose a mate. They then wait five to six weeks until the female lays her egg. As soon as the female has laid the egg, the male lifts it onto his feet. The female then returns to the sea leaving the male to incubate the egg.

There is no vegetation on the ice so the emperor penguins do not build nests. Instead, the males stand with the eggs tucked away under their stomachs. They stand for nine to ten weeks hardly moving because the eggs must not fall onto the ice.

The chicks hatch in July. Antarctica is one of the coldest and most inhospitable places in the world. In the middle of winter it has temperatures of -70°C and there is no food and no shelter. But it has one important advantage: it is the safest place in the world for emperor penguins to breed as there are no predators. The emperor penguin is the only animal in the world that can survive such low temperatures. Their only enemy is the cold and the males and the chicks stand close together in big groups to protect themselves from the icy winds and storms.

When the chicks hatch, the males have not eaten for over two months. Even so the male finds some food in his stomach to feed the chick. He has to keep the chick alive until the weather improves and the female returns from the sea with food. In March the males weighed around 46 kilos, but now they only weigh 16 kilos. The smaller female emperor penguin would not have survived for so long without food.

After the females return in early August, the males walk 150 kilometres back to the sea for a short 'holiday' before returning with food. The male and the female then take it in turns to return to the sea for food. In the late spring, when the chicks are big and strong enough, the emperor penguin families return to the sea. The adults then have just the three summer months in the sea before returning to the breeding grounds once more.

D

Try to answer these questions. Discuss your ideas with your classmates.

1. *Lines 2 and 29* Why do the emperor penguins walk *50 - 60 kilometres* from the sea to their breeding grounds in March, but then have to walk *150 kilometres* back to the sea in August?
2. *Line 9* What kind of *vegetation* do birds normally use to build nests?
3. *Line 12* Why mustn't the eggs *fall onto the ice*?
4. *Line 17* There are no *predators* on the ice but there are predators when the emperor penguins are in the sea. What are they?
5. *Line 22* Male emperor penguins don't eat for *over two months*. What do they live on?
6. *Line 25* What is the *food* of a penguin?

E

Work with a classmate. Copy and then complete this calendar with the activities below. Use the text on page 17 to help you.

Activity	Month of year	Season
walking to the breeding grounds	March	
	April	Autumn

The Emperor Penguin Calendar

Activity	Month of year	Season
	March	
	April	Autumn
	May	
	June	
	July	Winter
	August	
	September	
	October	Spring
	November	
	December	
	January	Summer
	February	

females returning with food

incubating the eggs

living in the sea

returning to the sea

walking to the breeding grounds

egg hatching

choosing a mate

egg laying

Compare your completed calendars with your classmates'. Are they the same?

F

Question game
Are you now an expert on emperor penguins? Write questions about the text in C to ask your classmates. Make sure you know the answers to the questions you ask.

How many eggs do emperor penguins lay in a year? (one)
When do the chicks hatch?
(in July)

Then close your books and ask and answer.

Help save the planet

9

Aim:
To make a poster on environmental issues.

A
In class: Before you make your poster

1 Look at Amanda and Julian's poster. Read Part One. Which of their ideas do you think will save the most energy? Can you think of another way of saving energy?

2 Read Part Two. Does your family reuse plastic bags. If you do, where do you keep them?

3 Read Part Three. Can you recycle aluminium cans in your neighbourhood? Look at the photo of the rubbish dump. What else can be recycled?

Example
newspapers

B
Out of class: Make your poster

Make your poster with a classmate. Write about some ways you can help save the planet by reducing, reusing, and recycling – (see the ideas box below). Try to find pictures to illustrate your ideas. If you can't find pictures, make drawings.

> reducing packaging (eg cardboard boxes), reducing pollution, reusing containers (eg bottles, plastic cartons), reusing water, recycling glass, recycling paper

You need:
- Some paper
- Glue and scissors
- Some coloured pens

C
In class: Use your poster

Show your poster to your classmates. Give them more information about your ideas. Answer any questions.

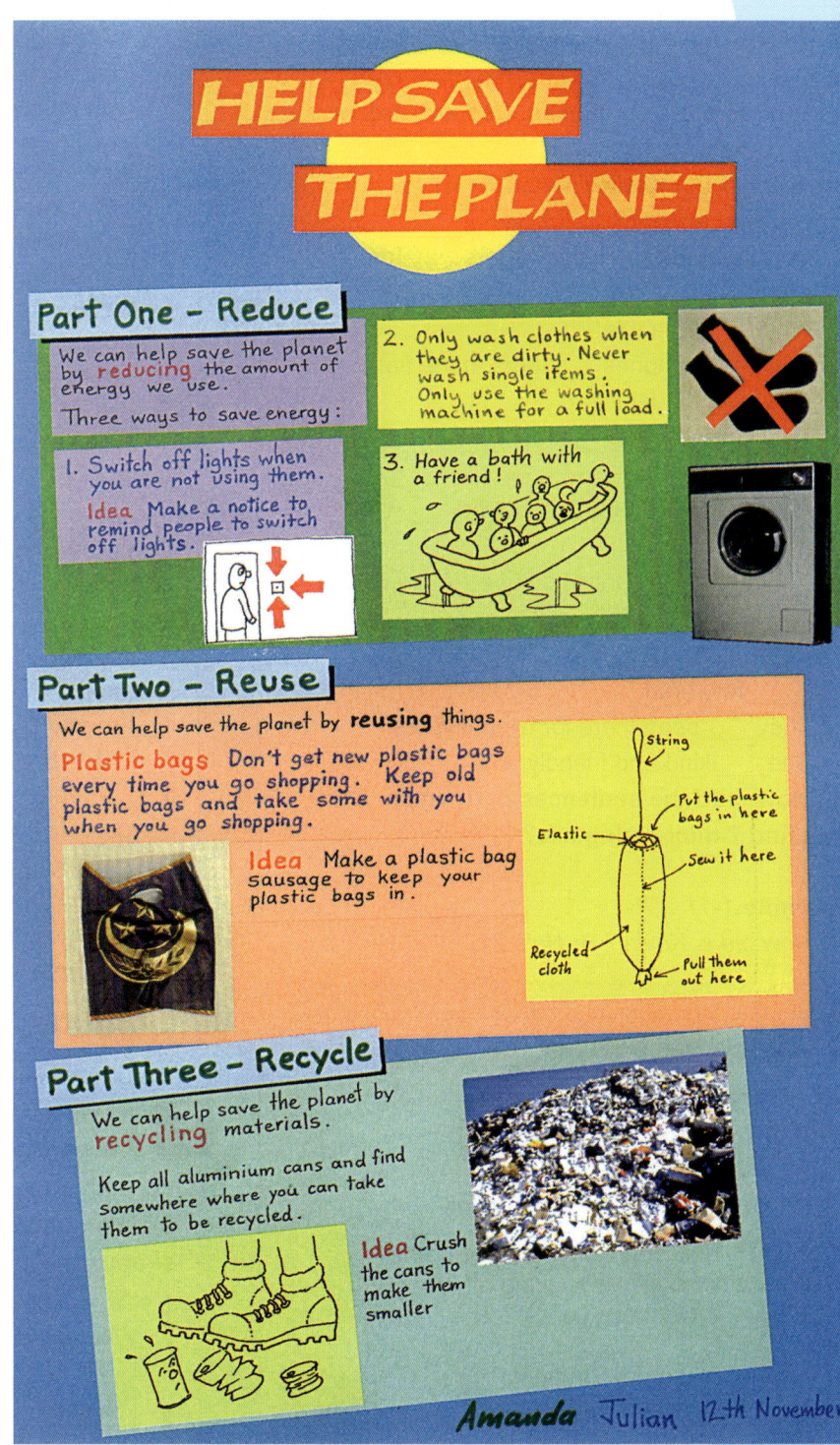

Consolidation A

10

A Be and have (Revision)

(i) Complete the sentences. Use *am, are, is, have* or *has.*

1 How old____Kevin?
2 ____you hungry?
3 How many brothers and sisters____Tom got?
4 What____Tina like?
5 How many phones____there in the flat?
6 How____you feeling?
7 How long____your grandparents lived in their flat?
8 He____got two brothers, but he____n't got any sisters.
9 No, we____n't hungry, but we____thirsty.
10 There____two.
11 He____21.
12 I____very tired.
13 They____been there for twenty years.
14 She____kind and friendly.

(ii) Now read the sentences in (i) again. Can you find 7 mini-dialogues?

Example 1-11
A: *How old is Kevin?* B: *He's 21.*

B -ing clauses (>GR A4)

Join these sentences. Use *-ing* clauses.

Example
That's my friend Max. He's waiting outside.
That's my friend Max waiting outside.

1 There's Tina. She's sitting in the corner.
2 Who's that boy? He's taking off his coat.
3 Do you know those people? They're waving at us.
4 Look at that man. He's standing on his head.
5 Can you see that woman near the bank? She's parking her car.
6 There are two men outside the shop. They're looking in the window.

C One, ones (>GR A7)

Use *one* or *ones* in place of a word or words in each sentence.

Example
Who's that girl, the girl with Paul?
Who's that girl, the one with Paul?

1 I like this jacket more than the other jacket.
2 Look at those people, the people at the bus stop.
3 Is that your car, the car outside?
4 I need a pen, but I haven't got a pen.
5 Whose are those socks, the red socks?
6 I'm making a cup of tea, would you like a cup of tea?

D Present continuous and present simple (>GR A6)

Complete the questions. Use the present continuous or the present simple. Give true answers.

Example
1 *Are you studying English at the moment?*
   – Yes, I am.

1 ____you____(study) English at the moment?
2 ____you____(study) English every day?
3 ____your teacher ever____(wear) glasses?
4 ____your teacher____(wear) glasses at the moment?
5 What____you usually____(wear) to school?
6 What____you____(wear) now?

E Present simple passive (>GR A2)

(i) Complete the questions. Use the present simple passive.

1 What/a compass/use/for?
2 What/a thermometer/make/of?
3 What/vacuum cleaners/use/for?
4 What/windows/make/of?
5 How often/the Olympic Games/hold?
6 How often/the soccer World Cup/play?

(ii) Now, can you answer the questions in (i)?

Example
1 *It's used for showing direction.*

F Past simple (>GR A8, A9)

(i) Ask someone about last Saturday.

1. What time____(you/get up) on Saturday ?
2. What____(you/have) for breakfast ?
3. What____(the weather/be) like ?
4. ____(you/go) out in the morning ?
5. ____(you/be) at home in the afternoon ?
6. What____(you/do) in the evening ?
7. What time____(you/go) to bed ?

(ii) Now answer the questions in (i). Give true answers.

Example
1. *I got up at 9 o'clock.*

G Present perfect simple with *for* and *since* (>GR A10, A11)

Complete the sentences. Use the present perfect simple with for or since.

1. Antonella____(live) in Rome____two years.
2. George____(have) a job in a sports shop ____January.
3. We____(be) on holiday____Sunday.
4. Sarah____(not/be) to Greece____1991.
5. My parents____(toe) married____thirty years.
6. You____(be) here____2 o'clock.
7. My video____(be) broken____over a week.
8. I____(not/work) in this office____very long.
9. Paul____(know) Stefanie____he was a child.
10. ____you____(speak) to your friend____last Saturday ?

H Infinitive (>GR A13)

Complete the sentences. Use suitable verbs in the correct form.

1. When I leave school I'd like____to university.
2. One day I hope____a doctor.
3. Would you like____a lot of money ?
4. One of my ambitions is____to New York.
5. Do you hope____your own business one day ?
6. I wouldn't like____in a foreign country.
7. My ambition is____a long and happy life.

I Present simple, past simple and present perfect simple (>GR A12)

(i) What is Richard saying ? Choose the correct form.

> My name is Richard McGregor. I live in Bristol in the south-west of England. I don't come from Bristol. I____*(am/was/have been)* born in Scotland. I____*(live/lived/have lived)* in Bristol for a year now. Before I____*(come/came/have come)* to Bristol I____*(live/lived/have lived)* in London. I____*(am/was/have been)* there for three years. I____*(work/worked/have worked)* in a bank there. I____*(work/worked/have worked)* for an insurance company now. I____*(have/had/have had)* this job for six months. My best friend is my wife Maggie. We____*(know/knew/have known)* each other since we were children.

(ii) What about you ?

1. Where were you born ?
2. Where do you live ?
3. How long have you lived here ?
4. Where do you go to school ?
5. How long have you been a student at this school ?
6. Which school did you go to before this one ?
7. How long were you there ?
8. Think of a friend. How long have you known him or her ?

Give true answers to the questions. Make sentences.

Example
1. *I was born in Madrid.*

11 She's coming tomorrow

A

Private investigator, Mick Malone, is working on a new case. There was a big diamond robbery in Manchester last week. Mick thinks that Ron Clay, a well-known London criminal, wants to buy the diamonds from the thieves.

Today is Thursday, 1st November. Mick is in a house opposite Ron Clay's flat in London. He has hidden a microphone in Clay's telephone. He is waiting for the thieves to contact Clay.

▣ 13 Listen. Clay's phone is ringing now. Is this the call that Mick is waiting for?

B

▣ 13 What have Ron Clay and Kay Sloane arranged to do? Listen again. Then complete Mick's notes.

> Date: Thursday, 1st. November
> Kay Sloane is coming to_____tomorrow.
> She is travelling by_____. She is leaving_____
> at_____ in the_____. Ron Clay is getting the_____
> from his_____ in_____ tomorrow_____
> and_____ are meeting at the_____ on_____
> morning. They are meeting at_____ is
> bringing the_____ with her.

Example

> Kay Sloane is coming to London tomorrow. She is travelling by train.

C

What have Clay and Sloane arranged to do? Write questions to ask each other.

Where is ...-ing?   Where are ... -ing?
When is ...-ing?   When are ...-ing?
What time is ... -ing?   What time are ... -ing?
How is ... -ing?   Are...-ing?
Is ... -ing?

Example

> Where is Kay Sloane going tomorrow?
> Is she leaving in the morning?
> When are Clay and Sloane meeting?

Work with a classmate. Student A – Keep your book open and ask Student B your questions. Student B – Close your book and answer A's questions.

Example

A: *Where is Kay Sloane going tomorrow?*
B: *To London.*

D

What about you? Have you made any arrangements for the future? Are you doing these things?

  going out this evening
  playing volleyball this week
  going to a disco this weekend
  visiting relatives this weekend
  going to a foreign country this summer

Example

>   *I'm going out this evening.*
> Or   *I'm not going out this evening.*

E

Ask about your classmate's arrangements for this evening, tomorrow evening and this weekend.

Example

> A: *Are you doing anything this evening?*
> B: *Yes, I'm meeting some friends./No, nothing special.*
> Or A: *What are you doing this evening?*
> B: *I'm meeting some friends./Nothing special.*

The future in your hands

12

A

Discuss these questions first.
1. What do you know about palmistry? Have you ever been to a palmist?
2. Do you believe it is possible to tell a person's future by studying his or her hands?

B

Do you know how to read your palm? Look at the palm of your left hand. Then look at the picture of the palm with the article *Reading your palm* opposite. Can you find the five important lines shown in the picture on your palm? A palmist believes that each of these lines tells us something different about our future. What do the lines mean? Read the article and find out.

C

Study the lines on Judy Carter's palm. Make sentences about her future.

She	will may	have ___ be ___ get ___ become ___

Example
She'll have a long life and good health.

Reading your palm

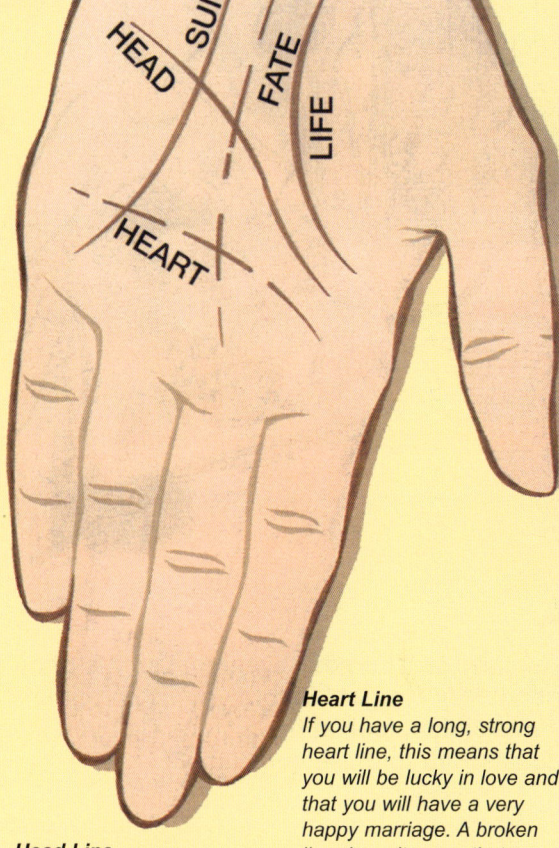

Life Line
If you have a long, strong life line, this means that you will have a long life and good health. A line which is weak near the top means that you will have a very busy life when you are young, but that you will have a much quieter time as you get older.

Fate Line
A long, strong fate line means that you will have a happy and successful future. If you have a short fate line, this shows that you will have an exciting life, but that you will never be rich. A broken line means that you will have many different jobs in your life. It also means that you will have a lot of children.

Sun Line
The sun line is often difficult to see on many palms. If you have a long sun line, this shows that you will be lucky in your life: the sun will always shine on you! A sun line which starts in the middle of the palm means that you will be very successful when you are middle-aged. A line which starts nearer the top of the palm means that you will be very happy later in your life.

Head Line
The length of this line shows intelligence. The longer the line is, the more intelligent you are. If you have a curved head line, this means that you may become a good musician, artist or writer. A straight line shows that you may become a scientist.

Heart Line
If you have a long, strong heart line, this means that you will be lucky in love and that you will have a very happy marriage. A broken line doesn't mean that you will be unlucky in love. It shows that you will have a lot of friends in your life. You may also get married more than once. A short or weak line means that you may find it difficult to make friends, but that when you do they will always be very good friends.

D

Work with a classmate. Study the lines on your classmate's palm. Make notes. Then write about his or her future.

He She	will ___ may ___

E

Exchange papers around the class. Then read about another student's future to the class. Don't say the student's name. See if the class can guess who it is!

An invitation

13

A

It is early on Thursday evening. Larry is phoning a friend, May Morgan. Before you listen to the conversation, look at the picture. Can you guess the answers to these questions?

1 Where does Larry invite May to go to this evening?
2 Why can't she go out with him this evening?
3 So when does Larry invite her to go out with him?
4 Why can't May go out with Larry then?
5 So what do they decide to do?

14 Now listen to the conversation. Check the answers to the questions. Also, find out where and what time Larry and May are meeting.

B

Practise these ways of greeting people.

A:	Hello. Hi.	How are you?	
B:	I'm	fine, very well,	thank you. thanks.	And you?
C:	I'm	fine, very well,	thank you. thanks.	

C

Notice this way of inviting someone to do something.

> **Would you like to** go to a disco this evening?

Invite your classmates to do some of these things at different times this week.

> go to a disco/a concert/a party/the cinema
> go swimming/windsurfing/dancing/shopping
> go for a coffee/a walk
> play tennis/video games

Accept or refuse your classmates' invitations.

Accepting an invitation	Refusing an invitation
Yes, I'd love to. Yes, okay.	I'm afraid I can't. I'm sorry, but I can't.

Example
A: Would you like to go windsurfing on Saturday?
B: Yes, okay.
A: Would you like to play tennis tomorrow?
B: I'm afraid I can't.

D

When we refuse an invitation, we often give a reason. For example:

I have to stay in and study.   *I'm going* to the cinema.
I have to clean my room.   *I'm meeting* a friend.
I have to wash my hair.   *I'm* already *doing* something.

Think of more reasons like these.

| I have to ___ . | I'm ___ -ing. |

E

Write your diary for next week. Decide what you *have to do* on *two* evenings, and what you *are doing* on *one* evening. Write these things in your diary.

Example

Now make conversations. Your classmates will invite you to do things on different evenings next week. Use your diary to find an evening when you can go out together.

Example

A: Would you like to go to the cinema on Monday evening?
B: I'm sorry, Eva, but I can't. I'm playing tennis with Mario on Monday evening.
A: Are you doing anything on Tuesday evening?
B: No, nothing special.
A: Would you like to go on Tuesday evening, then?
B: Yes, I'd love to.

If you agree to go out, write the arrangement in your diary.

F

Now look at your diary and write about what you *are doing* and what you *have to do* next week.

Example

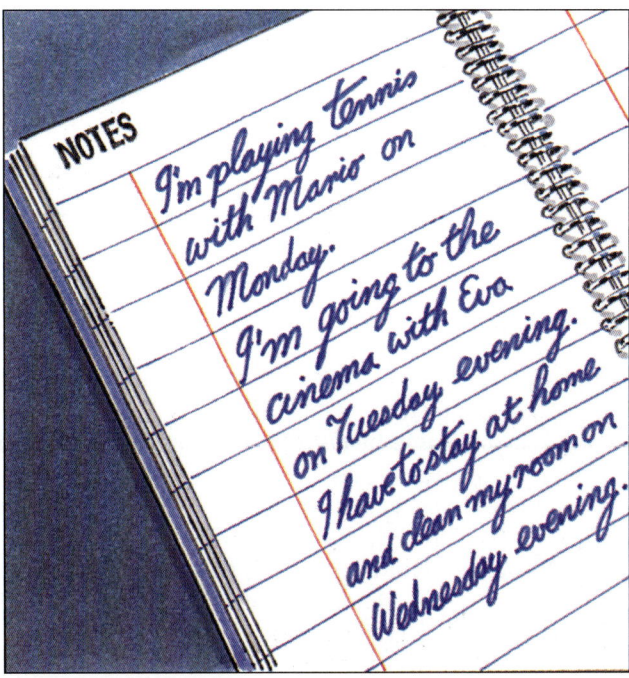

You must be home by eleven

14

A

These are the eleven most common topics British teenagers argue about with their parents or guardians.

> chores   clothes and appearance   coming home late   friends
> getting up in the morning   going out at night   homework   money
> music   politeness and good manners   TV and video

Are they the same things teenagers argue about with parents or guardians in your country? Can you think of any other topics to add to the list?

B

Look at the picture. Judy Carter is arguing with her parents about five things in the list. Read or listen to the conversation. What are the five things?

Mother: Where are you going, Judy?
Judy: Out.
Mother: Yes, but where?
Judy: I'm going to see some friends. Okay?
Mother: But you've got school tomorrow and it's late.
Judy: It's not late. It's 9.30.
Mother: It's late to go out. And anyway, what about the story you have to write for English?
Judy: I've written it.
Mother: Are your sure? I don't think you do enough for school. Well, anyway, you can't go out like that.
Judy: Why not?
Mother: Your skirt is far too short.
Judy: Oh, okay. I'll put my jeans on.
Mother: And you must be home by eleven.
Judy: By eleven! But mum, it's 9.30 now.
Mother: Well, as I say, you've got school tomorrow. I had to be home by ten when I was your age, so you've got nothing to complain about.
Judy: That was hundreds of years ago. Things are different now.
Father: Don't be rude, Judy! You mustn't speak to your mother like that. Go on, apologise.
Judy: Oh, okay. I'm sorry. Is that okay? Can I go now?
Father: Yes, you can go out but remember, no later than eleven and put something else on.
Judy: Oh, okay.

What do you think? Listen again and discuss these questions.

1 *You've got school tomorrow and it's late.* – Is 9.30 late to go out?
2 *You can't go out like that./ Your skirt is far too short.* – Look at the picture. Is this true?
3 *You must be home by eleven.* – Is eleven too early to ask Judy to come home?
4 *I had to be home by ten when I was your age.* – How old do you think Judy is?
5 *Don't be rude, Judy! You mustn't speak to your mother like that.* – What did Judy say to make her father so angry? Was she rude?
6 *Oh, okay. I'm sorry.* – Is this a real apology?

C

Role play

Look at the list in A again. Choose a topic (eg chores) and write some sentences a parent or guardian might say. Use:

> You must___.
> You mustn't___.
> I had to___when I was your age.

> You must make your bed every morning. You mustn't leave your clothes on the floor. I had to clean my room every day when I was your age.

Work with a classmate. A is a parent or guardian, B is a teenager. Role play your topic.

Example

A: Your room is very dirty and untidy. You must make your bed every morning.
B: Oh, okay.
A: And you mustn't leave your clothes on the floor.
B: Why not? It's my room.
A: *I had to clean my room every day when I was your age.*

Then change roles.

D

Read through this survey.

Part A Can you ___ ?	Part B Do you have to ___ ?
1 wear any clothes you like	1 be home by a certain time
2 have a boyfriend/girlfriend	2 tidy and clean your room
3 go to late-night parties	3 do the washing up at home
4 stay out all night	4 do some homework every day
5 stay in bed late at the weekend	5 tell your parents where you are going
6 go out anytime you like	6 tell your parents what you spend your money on
7 listen to any kind of music	7 be polite to your parents
8 watch anything you like on TV	8 eat food you don't like
9 use bad language at home	9 go to bed at a certain time

Complete the survey about a classmate. Ask and answer.

> A: Can you wear any clothes you like?
> B: Yes, I can. / No, I can't.
>
> A: Do you have to be home by a certain time?
> B: Yes, I do. / No, I don't.

Make notes of your classmate's answers. Don't write his/her name.

> Part A
> 1-✓   2-X

Make a table of results for your class.

	Number of students	
	Yes	No
Part A		
wear any clothes you like	17	6
have a boyfriend/girlfriend	13	10

E

Choose some topics in the survey to talk about with your classmates. Give more details if possible.

> I can___. /I can't___.   I have to___. /I don't have to___.

Examples

A: I don't have to do the washing up at home.
B: I do. I have to do it every day.
C: So do I.

A: I can't watch anything I like on TV. My parents don't like me to watch horror movies, for example.
B: I can't watch late-night movies.
C: I can watch anything I like.

SKILLS 15 — I couldn't live without...

SPEAKING

A

Here is a newspaper headline.

SIX MONTHS COMMUNITY SERVICE FOR TEENAGE SHOPPING ADDICT

Work with a classmate. Can you guess what the news story is about?

LISTENING

B

15 Listen to the radio news report of the same story. Were you right?

This is a police report about the teenager in the story, but parts of it are missing. Listen again and complete the report.

> Family name: Thom
> First Name: K
> Age:
>
> Thomas stole his father's
> He used the card to buy comp
> CDs, a new watch, cloth
> trainers. He spent over L
> month before his father found ou
> took away the card. After tha
> stole money from other pu
> until his teacher caugh h
> stealing money fr

READING

C

Work in groups of four. How fast can you read? This is a reading race!

Look at the magazine article *I couldn't live without...* opposite. Read the article quickly, looking for answers to these questions. The first group to finish is the winner!

1. How old is Viv?
2. Who loves chocolate?
3. Does Martha wear make-up at school?
4. Who couldn't Lynnette live without?
5. Who sent Viv a present from the USA?
6. What does Lynnette do for two hours every day?
7. Who gave Viv his Walkman?
8. Who likes making her friends look horrible?
9. Why is Viv saving money?
10. What sports does Martha do?
11. Who is cuddly?
12. Who enjoys being frightened?

WRITING

D

Work with the same group as in C. Tell the other students about three things you couldn't live without, and why. Then design and write a magazine page like the one in this lesson for your group.

I couldn't live without...

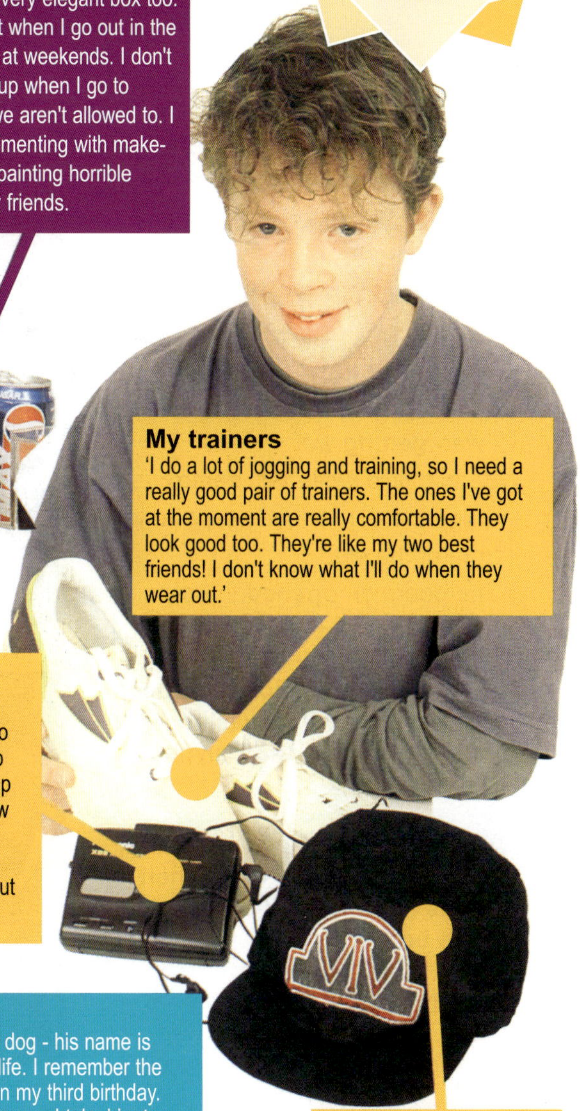

17-year-old Viv Lennox loves sport. He's a very keen football fan and follows his team, Manchester United, round the country. What couldn't Viv live without?

My rucksack
'I use my rucksack everyday. I need it for my school books. I also use it to carry my sports kit - I play basketball twice a week and do aerobics once a week. It's a great bag. It's brightly-coloured and it holds a lot of things. I've had it for a couple of years now and it has lasted really well. Before I had it, I carried all my things in plastic carrier bags - ugh!'

My make-up set
'I don't wear a lot of make-up, but all the colours I like are in this set. It's in a very elegant box too. I often use it when I go out in the evenings or at weekends. I don't wear make-up when I go to school, as we aren't allowed to. I enjoy experimenting with make-up and like painting horrible faces on my friends.'

16-year-old Martha Seyka loves horror films and collects posters of the most frightening ones! Her ambition is to work in the film industry. What does Martha say she couldn't live without?

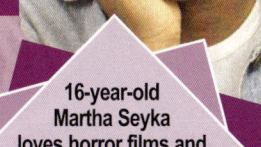

Pepsi Max
'Our fridge at home is absolutely full of Pepsi Max. I have always drunk a lot of soft drinks, since I was a small child. I drank a lot of Pepsi when I was younger. Then they started making Diet Pepsi, which tasted great, but this is even better and isn't fattening, as it hasn't got any calories.'

My trainers
'I do a lot of jogging and training, so I need a really good pair of trainers. The ones I've got at the moment are really comfortable. They look good too. They're like my two best friends! I don't know what I'll do when they wear out.'

My Walkman
'I love listening to it all the time when I'm out. I don't ever take it off, even when I go jogging. I like lots of different kinds of pop music. I don't really have a favourite group at the moment. The Walkman I've got now is very trendy. It was a present from my Dad. The one I had before was stolen at school and I was so upset that he went out and bought me a new one.'

14-year-old Lynnette O'Deil is a big pop music fan. She collects CDs and pop magazines. What are some of the special things that Lynnette couldn't live without?

My cuddly toy
'I've had my lovely toy dog - his name is Fozzie - almost all my life. I remember the day I got him. It was on my third birthday. My parents gave him to me. I take him to bed with me every night. He's so cuddly! He's a great comfort if I feel sad. I couldn't live without him, I'll love him forever!'

My baseball hat
'My aunt lives in the USA and she bought me this wonderful hat from Disney World. She bought it for me because it says Viv, my first name, on the front. She sent it to me for my seventeenth birthday. I've never been to the United States, but I'd love to go there one day. I've been saving money from the job I have, working at my local supermarket two evenings a week. Hopefully I'll save enough to go and visit my aunt next summer.'

Computer games
'I'm mad about computer games and couldn't live without them. I've been playing for several years now. I had my first computer when I was six years old. I usually play for about two hours every day. Some computer games are quite expensive and I can't always afford to buy the ones I want, so I often swap games with my friends. I also play in computer games competitions from time to time.'

Snickers chocolate bars
'I think I'm probably the worst choc-aholic in my school. And Snickers are my very favourite chocolate bars. They're delicious! The only problem is they're very fattening, so when I go past the sweet shop, I always try to look the other way and stop myself from going in. Sometimes it's difficult though!'

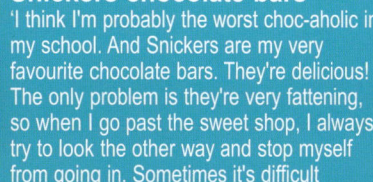

16 They were the diamonds I was looking for

A

 Look at the picture and listen to Mick Malone. What was the date yesterday?

Saturday 3rd November

Sometimes the life of a private investigator isn't easy. Take yesterday, for example. It was 11.45 at night and I was standing outside the Calypso Club...

1   11.45 pm Friday 2nd November

2   5 am Saturday 3rd November

B

Look at the pictures. Which pictures are these sentences about?

Example
It was raining hard. – Picture 1

> It **was raining** hard.
> It **was getting** light.
> I **was getting** wet.
> Suddenly, a white taxi **came** round the corner and **stopped** in front of the club.
> The doorman **opened** the car door and a man **got out**.

 16 Listen to Mick and check your answers. Why was he standing outside the Calypso Club last night?

 16 Look at the two pictures and listen to Mick again. Then tell his story using the language in the box.

Example
It was 11.45 at night and I was standing outside the Calypso club. It was...

> It was____ and I was____ outside the Calypso Club. It was____ and I was____, very ____. Suddenly, a____ round the corner and____ in front of the club. The doorman____ the car door and a____. He/She was____, very____. He/She was the____ I was____.

Do you know the names of the two people? Look back at Lesson 11 if you can't remember.

C

Find out what your classmates were doing at different times last night. Make notes of your classmates' answers.

> A: What were you doing at + *time*?
> B: I was____-ing.

Example
A: *What were you doing at 9.45?*
B: *I was watching TV. What were you doing at 7.30?*
A: *I was having dinner. What were you doing at...?*

Make sentences about your classmates using your notes.

Example
Dimitris was watching TV at 9.45.

D

Look at the picture and answer these questions. When Mick went into the club...

1 Where were Ron Clay and Kay Sloane standing?
2 What was Sloane wearing?
3 What was Clay wearing?
4 What was Clay taking out of his briefcase?
5 What was Sloane showing Clay?

🎧 17 Now listen to Mick and check your answers.

E

Memory game

🎧 18 Look at the picture again. Then listen and find the people Mick is describing.

Test your memory. Look at the picture and write five questions to ask your classmate. Make sure you know the answers to the questions you write.

Examples

> When Mick went into the club...
>
> How many people were sitting at the table?
> What was the woman wearing?
> What was the man smoking?
> What were they drinking?
> Who was the other man looking at?

Work with a classmate. Close your books and ask and answer.

Friday the thirteenth

17

A
Look at the picture. Today is Saturday, 14th December and Larry is telling his friends about what happened to him yesterday. What do you think they are laughing about?

B
These pictures show what happened to Larry yesterday. Find a sentence in the box below for each of the six pictures.

Example
Picture 1a – *I was running for the bus when I dropped my bag.*

I **was running** a bath		the telephone **rang**.
I **was running** for the bus	**when**	I **dropped** my bag.
I **was playing** basketball		I **collided** with another player.

I **missed** the bus and **was** late for school.
I **went** to answer it and **forgot** all about my bath.
I **had** to have first aid and **couldn't** play anymore.

How do you think Larry felt yesterday? Again find a sentence in the box below for pictures 1b, 2b, and 3b.

He felt embarrassed/nervous/angry.

🔊 19 Listen to the conversation and check your answers.

C
Memory game
Study the pictures in B again. Then work with a classmate.

Student A – Turn to page 99. Ask your classmate the questions. Check his/her answers.

Student B – Close your book and answer your classmate's questions.

What **was** Larry **doing** when_____?
What **did** he **do** then?

Examples
A: What was Larry doing when the phone rang?
B: He was running a bath.
A: That's right.
A: And what did he do then?
B: He went to answer it and forgot all about his bath.

D

Unlucky things often happen to Larry. Look at the pictures. These things happened to him in the past. Make sentences.

| He was | | | |
| They were | ____-ing____ | when___. |

| He | |
| They | felt very/really____. |

Example

1 He was swimming in the sea when his shorts fell off in the water. He felt very embarrassed.

swim	on a computer	it	press the wrong button
go down	in the sea	he	attack him
run	in a lift	a dog	fall off in the water
work	in a park	his shorts	stop between the third and second floor

| scared | angry | embarrassed | depressed |

E

What about you?
Think of an occasion in the past when you felt angry, embarrassed, scared or depressed. Then write about it. Use the questions to help you.

1 How old were you? / When did it happen?
2 Were you alone or were you with someone?
3 Where were you?
4 What were you doing and what happened?
5 How did you feel?
6 What did you do afterwards?

> This happened two years ago. I was cycling in the town when I had an accident. I wasn't hurt but I felt very depressed because my bike was damaged. I had to take it to a repair shop.

🎧 20 Listen to Larry and check your answers.

🎧 20 Listen again. Then look at the pictures and tell the full story.

Example

Picture 1 – This happened when Larry was ten. He was swimming in the sea when his shorts fell off in the water. He felt really embarrassed. He had to find his shorts and put them on under the water.

Stranger than fiction

18

A
Can you do any of these things?

Can you stop a watch just by holding it in your hand?

Can you predict accurately what will happen in the future?

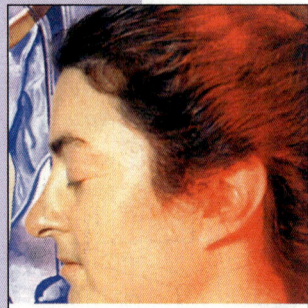
Can you know what someone is doing when you can't see or hear this person?

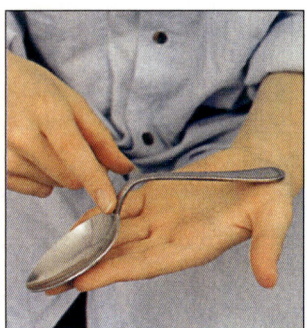
Can you bend a spoon just by touching it with one finger?

Can you hold a pen on a piece of paper and not control what the pen writes?

Some people believe that the three people you are going to read about in this lesson have extraordinary psychic powers which make it possible to do these things.

B
Look at the two photos in the article about Morgan Robertson and discuss these questions.

1. What do you think is the connection between Morgan Robertson and the Titanic?
2. Do you know what happened to the Titanic?

Read Part One and check your ideas.

Part One

Morgan Robertson

Morgan Robertson (1861-1915), author of 'The Wreck of the Titan'

In 1898, the American writer, Morgan Robertson, wrote a story called *The Wreck of the Titan*. In his story, a large passenger ship called the *Titan* sails from England on its maiden voyage to New York. The ship has the very latest technology and everyone on board believes it is unsinkable. A few nights later the *Titan* hits an iceberg and sinks. Because there are not enough lifeboats on the ship, many passengers – including many rich and famous people – die in the icy water of the North Atlantic. Not many people read *The Wreck of the Titan* – the only unusual thing about the story was that Morgan Robertson claimed that he wrote it in a psychic trance.

Fourteen years later, on April 9th, 1912, a large passenger ship called the *Titanic* left Southampton, England on its maiden voyage to New York. The ship was of the very latest design and it was described as being 'unsinkable' by its engineers. Five nights later the *Titanic* hit an iceberg and sank. There were not enough lifeboats on the ship and 1,513 people – including many rich and famous passengers – died in the icy water of the North Atlantic.

The Titanic (1912)

C
Try to find words or phrases in the first paragraph of the article on Morgan Robertson which mean:

1 the first journey on the sea or ocean
2 the most recent, modern
3 impossible to sink
4 small boats carried on a ship and used when the ship sinks
5 a large piece of ice floating in the sea
6 people who travel on a ship, on a plane, in a car, etc.
7 to say something – when we are not sure it is true
8 a kind of sleep where you can see and hear things

Example
1 maiden voyage

A
Read Part Two. Then decide whether these sentences are true or false.

1 Uri Geller is dead.
2 Geller says he bends spoons and stops clocks using the power of the mind.
3 Everyone believes him.
4 James Randi tried to do the same things as Geller with magic tricks but failed.
5 Scientists don't believe Geller has any psychic powers.
6 Geller's drawings were very much the same as the scientist's.

Example
1 – false

Part Two

Uri Geller

Uri Geller is the most famous modern psychic. He has appeared on television all over the world and millions of people have seen him bend spoons by touching them with just one finger and stop clocks and watches just by holding them in his hand. Geller claims that he can do these things using the power of the mind. However, many people don't believe him and an American magician, James Randi, showed a group of scientists that he could do the same things as Geller using simple magic tricks.

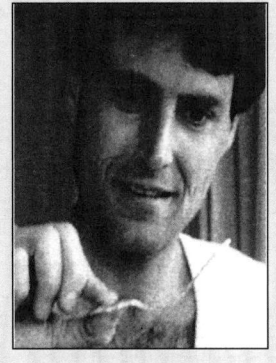
Uri Geller - Born in Israel in 1947

However, in a number of tests Geller proved to scientists that he had another remarkable psychic power. In these tests Geller sat in a special room where the scientists could see him, but he couldn't see them. A scientist then drew pictures and Geller - who could not see what the scientist was drawing - tried to draw the same pictures. In many of these tests Geller's pictures were remarkably similar to the pictures drawn by the scientist.

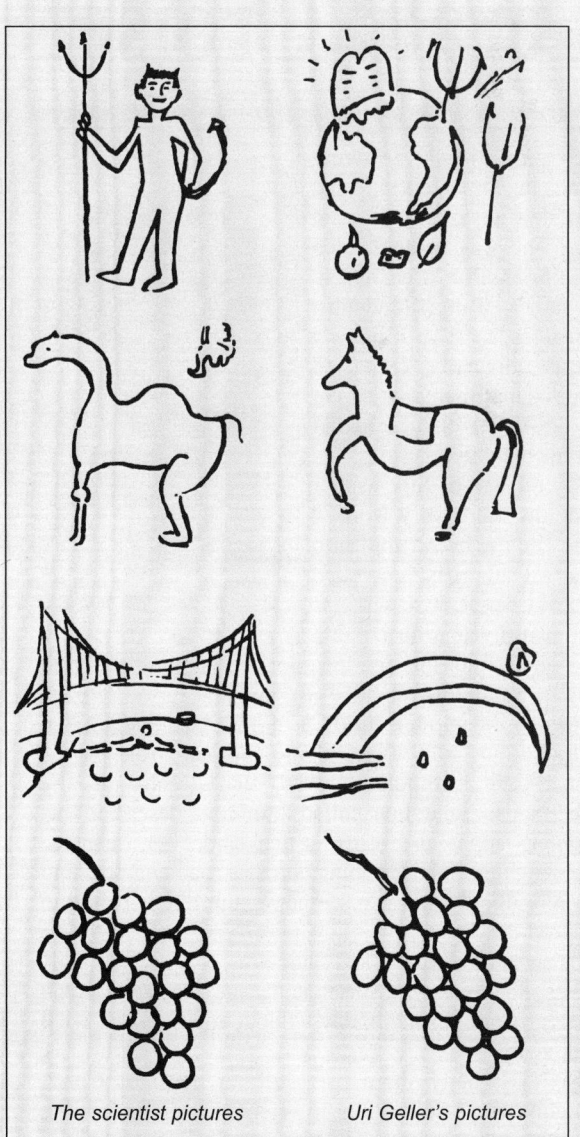
The scientist pictures   *Uri Geller's pictures*

C
Read Part Three and answer these questions

1. Where was Carol Sandelius when she disappeared?
2. Why was Walter Sandelius so worried at the end of July?
3. How did Sandelius find out about Gerald Croiset?
4. Where was Sandelius when he telephoned Gerald Croiset for the first time - in Kansas or Utrecht?
5. Why did Croiset tell Sandelius that he needn't worry?
6. What did Croiset predict?
7. Why was Sandelius astonished when he telephoned Croiset for the second time?

Part Three

Gerald Croiset

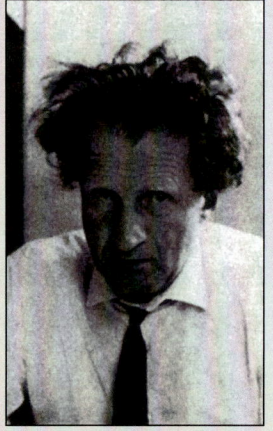

Gerald Croiset (1909-1980)

In July, 1967, a young American woman disappeared from the Kansas City hospital where she was being treated for injuries after a car crash. Her father, Walter Sandelius, a professor of politics at Kansas university, contacted police departments all over the USA but they couldn't find his daughter.

By the end of July, Walter Sandelius was a very worried man. Then a friend told him about a Dutch psychic called Gerald Croiset. Croiset was famous in Europe for helping the police find missing people and solving difficult crimes. Sandelius decided to contact him. Perhaps Croiset could help him find Carol, his missing daughter. He found out Croiset's telephone number. Croiset lived over 8,000 kilometres away in Utrecht in the Netherlands. Sandelius called him and described his daughter's appearance. Croiset then said, 'Yes, I can see your daughter. She is running across a road and crossing over a bridge. Now I can see her again. She is riding in a big red car.'

'Is she still alive?' asked Sandelius.

'Yes, don't worry,' Croiset said, 'She is alive and you will hear from her in six days. Phone me then and we'll speak again.'

Six days later there was still no news of Carol. Sandelius went downstairs to telephone Croiset in the Netherlands. As he picked up the phone, he was astonished to see his daughter sitting on the sofa in the living room.

F
Read about these four kinds of psychic phenomena. Then find examples of them in the three articles.

Automatic Writing - a process where the writer holds a pen on a piece of paper and writes in a trance-like state without any control over what he or she is writing.

Clairvoyance - 'seeing' or knowing things, not with the eyes, but with the mind.

Extra-sensory perception (ESP) - the ability to get information without using the five ordinary senses of sight, hearing, taste, touch and smell.

Psychokinesis (PK) - the ability to move or change objects with the power of the mind.

Example
Automatic writing - how Morgan Robertson wrote 'The Wreck of the Titan'

G
Discuss these questions with your classmate.

1. Which article do you find the most interesting? Why?
2. Whose powers do you find the most impressive - Robertson's, Geller's, Croiset's?
3. Is there one article you find less believable than the others?

H

How strong is your extra-sensory perception? With a classmate, carry out the test the scientist used with Uri Geller in the article in Part Two.

Student A - Turn round facing away from Student B.
Student B - Draw a picture. Think very hard about what you are drawing.
Student A - Concentrate very hard. Draw a picture.
Compare pictures and change roles.
Report back to the class.

Examples
*Our drawings were completely different.
There were some things the same.
They were very similar.*

Write a quiz

19

Aim:
To write a quiz about a topic you know a lot about.

A

In class: Before you write your quiz

Work with a classmate. Write the answers to Mike and Karen's quiz about sport. Guess if you don't know. Then compare your answers with your classmates'.

B

Out of class: Write your quiz

Work with a classmate. Choose a topic. The topic should be one your classmates know something about. (See the ideas box below.) Then write questions for your quiz. Try to write different types of quiz questions (eg *Look at the pictures; Choose the correct answers; Are these sentences true or false?*) Make sure you know the answers. Find some pictures to illustrate your quiz. If you can't find the right pictures, make drawings.

> art, cars, a city/town, a country, famous places, films, games, literature, music, TV

You need:
- Some paper
- Glue and scissors
- Some coloured pens

C

In class: Use your quiz

Show your quiz to your classmates. Tell them to write the answers. Then give your classmates the answers and tell them any additional information you know.

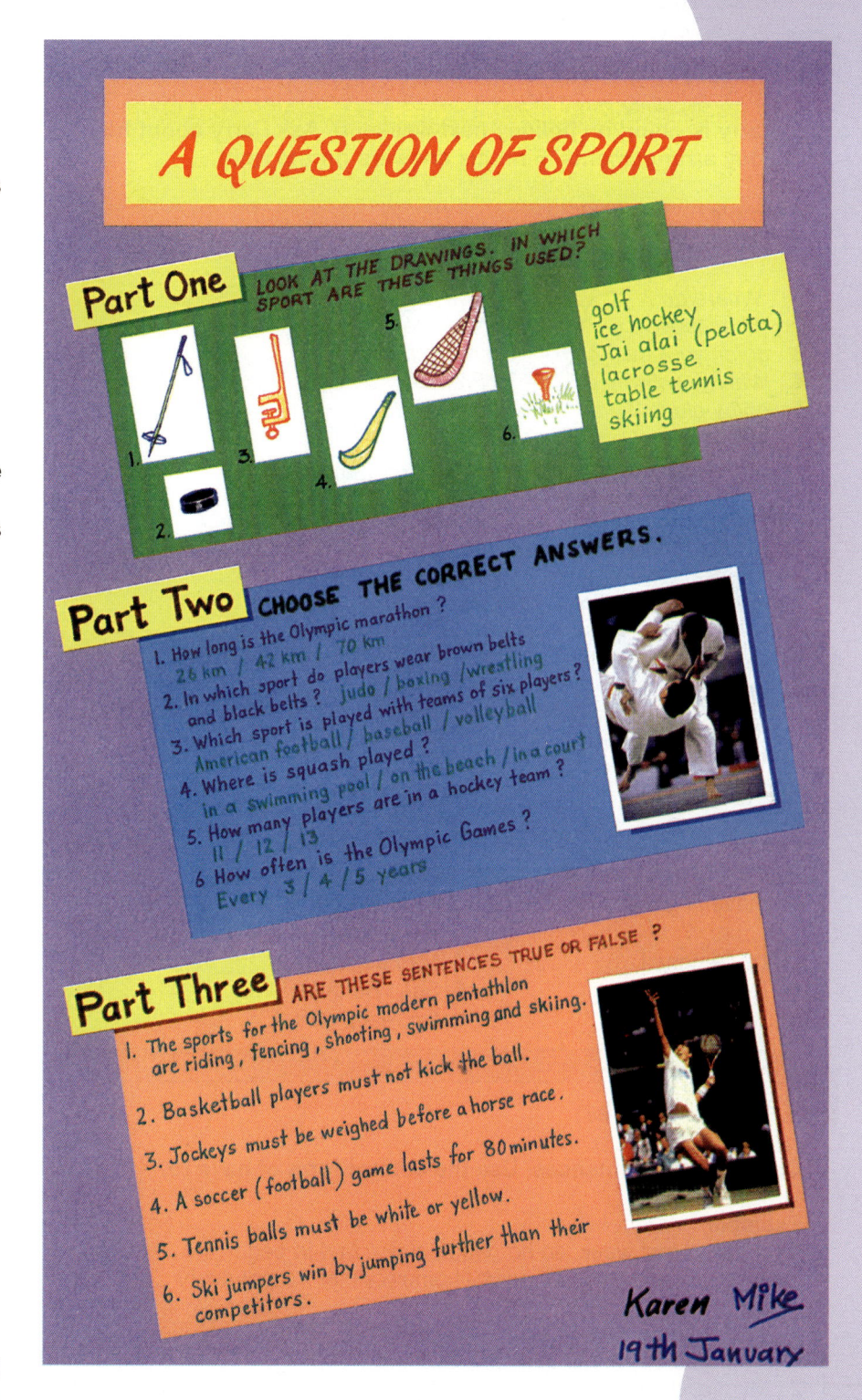

A QUESTION OF SPORT

Part One LOOK AT THE DRAWINGS. IN WHICH SPORT ARE THESE THINGS USED?

golf
ice hockey
Jai alai (pelota)
lacrosse
table tennis
skiing

Part Two CHOOSE THE CORRECT ANSWERS.

1. How long is the Olympic marathon?
   26 km / 42 km / 70 km
2. In which sport do players wear brown belts and black belts? judo / boxing / wrestling
3. Which sport is played with teams of six players? American football / baseball / volleyball
4. Where is squash played?
   in a swimming pool / on the beach / in a court
5. How many players are in a hockey team?
   11 / 12 / 13
6. How often is the Olympic Games?
   Every 3 / 4 / 5 years

Part Three ARE THESE SENTENCES TRUE OR FALSE?

1. The sports for the Olympic modern pentathlon are riding, fencing, shooting, swimming and skiing.
2. Basketball players must not kick the ball.
3. Jockeys must be weighed before a horse race.
4. A soccer (football) game lasts for 80 minutes.
5. Tennis balls must be white or yellow.
6. Ski jumpers win by jumping further than their competitors.

Karen Mike
19th January

Consolidation B

20

A Present continuous for the future (>GR B1)

(i) Larry is going on holiday next weekend. Ask Larry about his holiday arrangements. Find his answers on the right.

Example
1 *Where are you going ? - To France.*

1	Where/go ?	No, we're going by car.
2	When/leave ?	For two weeks.
3	go/on your own ?	On a camp site.
4	Who/go with ?	To France.
5	go/by plane ?	Next Saturday.
6	Where/stay ?	No, I'm not.
7	How long/go for ?	I'm going with my family.

(ii) Now write about Larry's holiday arrangements.

Example
Larry is going to France. He's leaving next...

B Must (>GR B6)

Think of a way to complete each sentence. Use *must...* or *mustn't...*

Example
I haven't got any money. I *must ask my parents for some.*
or I haven't got any money. I *must go to the bank.*

1 I'm hungry. I____.
2 It's late. We____.
3 You're tired. You____.
4 My hair is dirty. I____.
5 Ssh ! Be quiet ! We____.
6 I'm really unfit. I____.

C Have to (>GR B7)

Complete the sentences. Use the correct form of have to.

Example
Paul was ill last week, so he <u>had to stay</u> (stay) in bed.
<u>Does Jane have to do</u> (Jane/do) homework for school every evening ?

1 ____(you/be) home early this evening ?
2 My grandfather____(go) into hospital next week.
3 I____(get up) very early yesterday morning.
4 ____(you/wear) glasses when you were a child ?
5 Jane can't stay in bed today. She____(go) to school.
6 Jane____(not/go) to school tomorrow. It's a holiday.
7 Bob is a postman. - What time____(he/start) work every morning ?

D Mustn't and don't have to (>GR B6, B7)

Complete the sentences. Use *mustn't, don't have to* or *doesn't have to*.

1 You____eat too many sweets. They're bad for your teeth.
2 You can pay me the money later. You____pay me now.
3 It's Bob's birthday soon. We____forget to send him a card.
4 Kate____wear a uniform at her school. She can wear what she likes.
5 You____lie in the sun for too long. It's dangerous.

E Will (>GR B3)

What will you do in your life ? Look at these questions.

1 Will you travel a lot in your life ?
2 Will you live in a foreign country ?
3 Will you get married ?
4 Will you have children ?
5 Will you be rich ?

What do you think ? Make sentences: *I think I'll...* or *I don't think I'll....*

Example
1 *I think I'll travel a lot in my life, or I don't think I'll travel a lot in my life.*

F May (>GR B4)

What do you think life may be like in the year 2050 ? Give one or two of your own ideas using *may*.

Example
In 2050 people may live on other planets.
There may be factories in space.
Children may not go to school.

G Past continuous (>GR B9, B10)

You had a bad day yesterday! This is what happened:

1. You hurt your foot.
2. You dropped your camera.
3. You fell off a ladder.
4. You burnt yourself.
5. You got your clothes dirty.
6. Your TV broke down.

Think of what you were doing when these things happened. Make sentences. Use the past continuous.

Example
I hurt my foot when I was playing tennis.
or *I hurt my foot when I was running for a bus.*

H Past simple and past continuous (>GR B10)

First, read these situations.

1. Mick was walking in the park when he saw an old friend, Sue. When Mick saw Sue, he stopped and talked to her.
2. Tina was waiting at a bus top when she saw an accident. When Tina saw the accident, she phoned the police.
3. Bert and Harry were driving home when their car broke down. When their car broke down, they walked home.

Now ask and answer: *What was/were... doing when... ?* and *What did... do when... ?*

Example
1. *What was Mick doing when he saw Sue? - He was walking in the park.*
What did he do when he saw her? - He stopped and talked to her.

I Infinitive and -ing form (>GR B3, B4, B6, B7, B8, B11)

Complete the sentences. Use suitable verbs in the correct form.

1. Would you like____to a disco tomorrow?
2. I'm tired. I must____to bed.
3. We may____tennis tomorrow.
4. Do you like____computer games?
5. Tomorrow will____warm and sunny.
6. Rachel wants____a professional musician one day.
7. Larry hates____to the dentist.
8. Do you have____to school on Saturdays?
9. We sometimes go____on the river.
10. Can you____a boat?

J *Like* and *would like* (>GR B11)

(i) Complete the questions: *Do you like... ?* or *Would you like... ?*

1. ____to speak perfect English?
2. ____speaking English?
3. ____being a student?
4. ____to be famous one day?
5. ____to be in a famous pop group?
6. ____playing computer games?

(ii) Which of these questions mean: (a) Do you enjoy this, in general? (b) Do you want to do this?

(iii) Now answer the questions in (i). Give true answers.

Example
1. Yes, I would, or No, I wouldn't.
2. Yes, I do. or No, I don't.

K Question words (Revision)

| What   Where   Who   Why   When   Whose |
| How   What time   What kind   Which sport |
| How old   How tall   How much   How many |
| How often   How long |

Look at the answers and complete the questions. Use the question words in the box.

1. ____are you? - I'm 17.
2. ____is your birthday? - On 3rd May.
3. ____do you live? - In Manchester.
4. ____have you lived there? - For two years.
5. ____do you do? - I'm a student.
6. ____brothers and sisters have you got? - I've got one sister.
7. ____are you? - I'm 1 metre 65.
8. ____do you weigh? - About 58 kilos.
9. ____of sports do you like? - Football, tennis and golf.
10. ____do you prefer, tennis or golf? - Tennis.
11. ____is your favourite tennis player? - Andre Agassi.
12. ____do you like him? - Because he's funny.
13. ____do you usually get up? - At 7.30.
14. ____do you come to school? - By bus.
15. ____do you go swimming? - Once or twice a week.
16. ____is this book? - It's mine.

Hope Street

21

A

🎧 The people living in Hope Street have got a lot of problems. Listen to what they say. Find some of the things they talk about in the picture.

Example
A - 6 There aren't enough litter bins so people throw their rubbish on the pavement.

> There aren't enough litter bins so people throw their rubbish on me pavement. There should be wore litter bins.

A / **B**

> There are too many cars parked on the pavement and pedestrians have to walk on the road. There should be an underground carpark so people don't have to park in the street.

C / **D**

> There isn't enough street lighting and some of the lights in the doorways of the houses are broken. It's really dangerous to go out at night. There should be a lot more street lights.

> There isn't enough public transport in this area. The buses are full and they're nearly always late. There should be a lot more buses.

> There's too much noise and there are too many young people with nothing to do. There should be a club or a café.

> There isn't anywhere to play. We have to play in the street. There should be a park.

E / **F**

> There's too much traffic and people drive too fast. There should be a pedestrian crossing so we can cross the road safely.

G / **H**

> There's only one small shop and everything in it is very expensive. There should be a supermarket and more shops.

B

What problems have the people in Hope Street got? Look at the picture again and make a list.

There are too many___.	There isn't enough___.
There aren't enough___.	There isn't anywhere___.
There is too much___.	There is only one___.

Examples
There aren't enough litter bins.
There are too many cars parked on the pavement.

D

Think about a place you know which has a lot of problems. What are the problems? What improvements would you recommend? Make true sentences. There are some ideas in the box to help you.

Examples
There are too many cars. There should be a pedestrian zone. There is too much pollution. There isn't enough entertainment. There is only one good disco. There isn't anywhere to meet friends after school.

bottle bank   car   car park
cinema   club   cycle lane
disco   entertainment   graffiti
litter bin   noise   park
pollution   pedestrian crossing
pedestrian zone
public transport   rubbish
shop   sports centre
street lighting   swimming
pool traffic   tree

E

Is there anything wrong with your school? Work with a classmate. Make notes about the problems and any ideas you have for improving your school.

Problems
There are too many students.
There isn't anywhere to sit and relax.
There's only one basketball court.
There aren't enough books in the library.

Improvements
There should be more classrooms.
There should be more books in the library.

C

The people in Hope Street want a number of improvements to be made in the area where they live. Find their ideas in the texts in A and add them to the problems on the list you made in B.

> There aren't enough litter bins. There should be more litter bins.

The council can only afford to pay for three of these improvements. Work with a classmate. Make a list of the three you think are the most important. Compare your ideas with the rest of the class.

Compare your ideas with your classmates'. Vote on the best three ideas in the class.

Mick Malone's office

22

A

Work with a classmate. Look at the picture of Mick Malone's office. Are these sentences true or false? Correct the sentences that are false.

Example
1 True.
2 False. He was born in Dublin.

1 His office is in Soho, London.
2 He was born in London.
3 He got his licence to be a private investigator in 1991.
4 Mick lives in his office.
5 Mick sleeps on the sofa.
6 He has got eight goldfish.
7 He plays the saxophone.
8 He got a provisional driving licence in 1992.

🎧 21 Compare your answers with your classmates'. Then listen to Mick talking about his life and check your answers.

B

🎧 21 When did Mick do these things? Listen again. Make notes.

> 1 when he was 14

1 He bought his first sax.
2 He got a provisional driving licence.
3 Mick moved to London from Ireland.
4 He got his licence to be a private investigator.
5 A friend of his gave him two goldfish.
6 He moved out of his flat and came to live in the office.

in 1990	three weeks ago
when he was 14	two months ago
in 1992	in 1991

Now make sentences.

Example
1 He bought his first sax when he was 14.

🎧 21 Listen to Mick again and check your answers.

C

Find the questions about Mick's life.

Example
1 How long has he been playing the saxophone?

How long has he been	(1) playing	in London?
	(2) learning	as a private investigator?
	(3) living	goldfish?
	(4) working	to drive?
	(5) breeding	in his office?
	(6) living	the saxophone?

A: How long has he been _____-ing_____?
B: For two/three____.
   Since____/he was____.

Example
A: How long has he been playing the saxophone?
B: Since he was 14.

Listen and check your answers.

42

D

What about you?
Work with a classmate – but not with someone you know very well. Ask and answer.

> What musical instruments/sports/games do you play?
> What hobbies have you got?

Examples
A: *What musical instruments do you play?*
B: *I play the piano. What musical instruments do you play?*
A: *I don't play any. What hobbies have you got?*
B: *I collect postcards from different countries and I take photos. What hobbies have you got?*

Make a list of your classmate's free-time activities.

Musical instruments	Sports	Games	Hobbies
piano	volleyball	cards	collecting postcards
			taking photos

Then find out how long your classmate has been doing the activities on your list. Ask and answer.

> **A:** How long have you been ____-ing?
> **B:** For/Since____.

Examples
A: *How long have you been playing the piano?*
B: *Since 1991.*
A: *How long have you been playing volleyball?*
B: *For six years.*

Note down your classmate's answers.

Musical instruments	Sports
piano (1991)	volleyball (6 years)

Make sentences about your classmate.

> He/She has been ____-ing ____ for/since ____.

Example
Paula has been playing the piano since 1991.

E

What about you?
Write four true sentences about yourself.

> I've been ____-ing ____ for/since ____.

Examples
I've been learning English since 1991.
I've been writing to my penfriend for two years.
I've been living in Barcelona for fifteen years.
I've been going to discos since I was fourteen.

A great idea!

23

A
Sabir, Melanie and Kevin work in a fast food restaurant called Munch. The boss of the restaurant, Mrs Palmer, has just given them a coffee break.

🎧 22 It's Friday afternoon. Listen. What do Sabir, Melanie and Kevin decide to do this weekend?

B
🎧 22 Listen again and answer these questions.
1. What will the weather be like this weekend?
2. When are Sabir, Melanie and Kevin going to have the barbecue?
3. Who are they going to invite?

C
🎧 22 Listen again. Sabir asks Melanie and Kevin for suggestions about two things. What does he say?

Asking for suggestions

| _____ shall we _____ ? |

Sabir, Melanie and Kevin all make suggestions. What do they say?
Making suggestions

| Let's _____. |
| Why don't we _____ ? |
| How about _____ -ing ? |

D
Sabir asks for more suggestions about the barbecue.
1. How many people/invite?
2. Where/have the barbecue?
3. What/have to eat?
4. What/have to drink?
5. When/buy the food and drink?

Complete what Sabir says. What suggestions could Melanie and Kevin make about these things?

Example
1. **A:** How many people shall we invite?
   B: Let's invite about fifteen, or Why don't we invite around ten? or How about inviting twenty?

🎧 23 Listen. Check what Sabir, Melanie and Kevin actually say.

E
Work in groups of three or four. You are planning a barbecue. Ask for and make suggestions about it. Decide when and where to have it, how many people and who to invite, what to have to eat and drink, etc.

Example
A: When shall we have the barbecue?
B: How about having it on Sunday afternoon?
A: No, not on Sunday. I'm going to the cinema then.
C: Let's have it on Saturday afternoon, then.
A: Okay.
B: Yes, all right.

Make notes of your decisions. Then look at your notes and explain what you have decided to do.

Example
We're going to have our barbecue on Saturday afternoon.

WHEN?	Saturday afternoon
WHERE?	
HOW MANY PEOPLE?	
WHO?	
WHAT TO EAT?	
WHAT TO DRINK?	

The barbecue

24

A

🎧 24 Listen to the conversations at the barbecue. Who is speaking?

Example 1 j-k

B

🎧 24 Listen again. What offers do the different people make?
Offering things

Would you like	a(n)_____?
	some_____?

Offering to do things

Would you like me to_____?
Shall I_____?
I'll_____.

How is each offer accepted or refused?

Example
Girl: I'll help you carry those things, Andy.
Andy: No, it's okay. I can manage, thanks.

C

Work with a classmate. Student A - Keep your book open. Read B the problems and offers. Which offers does B choose? Make a note. Student B - Close your book. Listen to the problems and offers. Which offers do you make?

How kind and helpful are you?

Your friend tells you his or her problems. Which offers do you make - a), b) or c)?

1. **It's cold in this room.**
   a) I'll open the window.
   b) Would you like me to lend you a sweater?
   c) Shall I switch on the light?

2. **I'm thirsty.**
   a) Shall I give you a hand?
   b) Would you like something to do?
   c) Would you like me to get you a drink?

3. **I can't do this exercise.**
   a) Shall I show you my answers?
   b) Would you like me to explain it to you?
   c) I'll do it for you.

4. **These bags are very heavy.**
   a) I'll carry you if you like.
   b) Would you like me to carry them?
   c) Shall I throw them away for you?

5. **I haven't got much money.**
   a) Would you like me to show you mine?
   b) Shall I carry it for you?
   c) I'll lend you some if you like.

6. **I'm bored.**
   a) Would you like a glass of water?
   b) Shall I get you some aspirins?
   c) I'll play you my new CD if you like.

D

Your classmate will tell you his or her problems. Offer to help.

Example
A: *I've got a terrible headache.*
B: *Would you like me to get you some aspirins?*
A: *Oh, yes please.*

Suggested problems
*I've got a terrible headache.
It's too dark in this room.
I'm hungry.
That music is too loud.*

Think up some more problems like these. Tell your classmate and see if he or she offers to help you.

45

SKILLS 25 — Are you a TV-addict?

SPEAKING

A

Are you or any of your classmates TV-addicts? What types of TV programmes do you like watching?

Work with a classmate. Ask each other these questions.

1. How many hours a week do you watch TV?
2. What types of TV programmes do you like watching?

Tell the class about your classmate. Find out:

1. Who is the biggest TV-addict in your class?
2. What are the most popular programmes in the class?

READING

B

What would life be like without TV? During an experiment last year, the Albert family's TV was taken away from them. Fifteen-year-old Chris Albert wrote an article about Life without TV for his school magazine. Read Chris's article and answer these questions.

1. How did Chris spend his spare time during the experiment?
2. Has the experiment changed Chris's attitude to TV?

Here are some adjectives that describe people's feelings.

| bored | pleased | angry | interested |
| impressed | confused | lonely | awkward |

Find these words in Chris's article. Put them in the same order in which they appear in the article and explain what they describe.

Example
1 confused - Chris felt quite confused when the TV was first taken away.

Life without TV
by Chris Albert

When our TV was first taken away, I felt quite confused. I really didn't know what to do. I tried to keep busy, to stop myself thinking about TV, but my sister kept coming into my room and asking me stupid questions. I ended up getting angry and shouting at her. The evenings were the worst because we usually watch TV from about seven until we go to bed.

Then I started going to my friend Mark's house in the evenings. We spent most of our time watching TV. However, after about a week, I felt awkward about spending so much time in someone else's house, so I decided that I had to think of something else to occupy my time.

It wasn't easy at first, because I didn't really have any hobbies. I listened to all my CDs and played all my computer games, but I soon got bored and wanted other things to do. I spoke to my Mum about it and she suggested that I should go to the library. I thought it was a really boring idea, but I went anyway.

I found some books on computer programming at the library and took them home with me. The more I read, the more I could do with my computer, and the more interested I became. My sister even started to join in!

One of the main problems I found with not having a TV was that when all my friends talked about the programmes that I couldn't watch, I felt lonely and left out, because I didn't have anything to say. However, when I told my friends about computer programming, they were very impressed. They started coming to my house in the evenings so that I could show them things on my computer. It felt good to know something that they didn't.

When our TV was returned to us, I was very pleased and I started watching it again, but I don't watch it as often as I did before. Nowadays I spend more and more time working on my computer.

LISTENING

C

🔊 25 As part of the same experiment, the Alberts' TV was given to another family, the McDonalds. The McDonalds were chosen for the experiment because they were a very unusual family - they had never had a TV before! Listen to what sixteen-year-old Rosa McDonald says about the experience. Then say if these sentences are true or false.

1 Rosa started watching the TV when it first arrived.
2 Rosa's parents have always wanted a TV.
3 Rosa had a busy life before the family had a TV.
4 Rosa's friends thought Rosa was very strange.
5 Rosa's family found the TV guide very useful.
6 Rosa watches some TV programmes now.
7 Rosa's father wants to buy a TV.
8 Rosa thinks TV is boring.

Compare your answers with a classmate's.

Rosa McDonald

WRITING

D

Read Chris's article again. Write a similar article yourself. Pretend that your TV was taken away from you for a month. Write what you did and how you felt about Life without TV.

When the TV was first taken away...

I know what we'll do!

26

A

Look at the picture below. Bert and Harry are at home. What is Harry worried about?

Read or listen to part one of the conversation. Then answer the questions.
1. Why do Bert and Harry need money?
2. What is Bert's idea?

Harry: This is terrible, Bert. We owe over £500.
Bert: Don't worry so much, Harry.
Harry: But how are we going to pay these bills? We haven't got any money.
Bert: Umm. Let me think. Ah, I've got an idea. I know what we'll do. Look at this story in the newspaper. We'll kidnap Red Runner. She's worth over a million pounds.
Harry: But we don't know where Buttercup Farm is, Bert.
Bert: Oh yes, we do, Harry. The address is here in the newspaper. Look: 'Buttercup Farm, Chestnut Lane, Cowslip.' We'll drive down to Cowslip and kidnap Red Runner straight away.
Harry: Just a minute, Bert. We can't kidnap Red Runner in our car. Our car is much too small.
Bert: Umm. You're right, Harry. Let me think. Umm. I know! Listen, Harry, this is what we'll do...

B

These pictures show the rest of Bert's idea. Match the pictures with the sentences in the box.

Example 1 - c

a When we get home, we'll phone Red Runner's owners.
b We'll go and find Red Runner and bring her back to the van.
c We won't go in bur car. We'll hire a van.
d I'll say, 'We won't give you Red Runner back until you send us £500,000.'
e When we get to Cowslip, we'll park in a quiet place near Buttercup Farm.
f As soon as she's in the van, we'll drive back to London.

Listen to Bert and check your answers.

C

Work with a classmate. What is Bert's idea? Take it in turns to be Bert. Use the pictures in B to help you.

Example
This is what we'll do. We'll drive down to Cowslip. We won't go in our car. We'll hire a van. Then ...

D

Look at the picture and read what Bert and Harry say. Harry can see a possible problem with Bert's plan. What is the problem?

Look at the pictures below and complete what Bert says with the words in the box.

Example
1 As soon as we **find** a quiet place, we'**ll stop** and **put** Red Runner into a field.

> Just a minute, Bert. How are they going to send us the money? We can't give them our address, can we?
>
> Umm. You're right Harry. We can't. Let me think. Umm. I know! This is what we'll do....

We'll drive into the country. As soon as we ____ a quiet place, we __ and ___ Red Runner into a field. Then we __ there until it __ dark. When it __ dark, we __ a tree. As soon as we __ in the tree, I ___ Red Runner's owners and ___ them where to bring the money. We __ in the tree until they ____ with the money. When they ___, we __ the tree and ___ the money. Then we __ home in the van. We __ the money as soon as we __ home. Then we __ the owners again and __ them where Red Runner is.

arrive be climb down climb up count drive find get leave phone pick up put stay stop tell wait

Listen to Bert and check your answers.

E

What will you do? Write two true sentences and one sentence which is not true. Begin the sentences as follows:

> When I get home, I'll __.
> As soon as I finish school today, I'll __.
> I won't have anything to eat until __.

Examples
When I get home today, I'll do my homework.
As soon as I finish school today, I'll walk home with my friends.
I won't have anything to eat until I get home.

Read your sentences to your classmates. Can they tell you which sentence is not true?

Just a minute!

27

A

Harry is very worried about Bert's plan to kidnap Red Runner. Look at the pictures. What do you think Harry asks Bert? Match the pictures with the questions in the box.

Example
1 What if somebody sees us?

What if they see us in the tree?
What if we can't climb it?
What if it's not all there?
What if a neighbour hears her?
What if somebody sees us?
What if she won't get into the van?

📼 26 Listen to part one of the conversation and check your answers.

B

Role play
Look at the pictures in A again. How does Bert answer Harry's questions? Ask and answer.

A: What if __ ?
B: If __ , we'll __ .

Example
1
A: *What if somebody sees us?*
B: *If somebody sees us, we'll say we're lost.*

📼 26 Listen to part one again and check.

C

27 Harry is still very worried about Bert's plan. Look at the picture. What do you think he is worried about? Listen to part two of the conversation and find out.

D

Look at the picture again and ask Harry's questions. Find the words in the box.

Example
a - What if she gets hungry?

get	eating the furniture
need	ill
come	kicking us
start	hungry
start	round to our flat
get	some exercise

Can you remember Bert's replies? Ask and answer.

Example
A: *What if she gets hungry?*
B: *If she gets hungry, we'll...*

27 Listen to part two again and check your answers.

E

28 Harry is worried about one final thing. Listen to part three of the conversation and find out what it is.

F

Role play
Work with a classmate.

Student A - Your classmate is going camping. Turn to page 99. Ask your classmate the questions.
Student B - You are going camping. Turn to page 108. Answer your classmate's questions.

Examples
A: What if it rains all the time?
B: If it rains all the time, I'll go to a hotel.
A: Okay. What if you can't find a camp site?
B: If I can't find a camp site, I'll camp in a field.
A: Okay. What if... ?

The wildest woman in the West

28

A
Look at the first picture and discuss these questions.
1. What kind of town was Deadwood in 1880?
2. What kind of woman was Calamity Jane?

Then read paragraphs 1-2 and check your answers.

B
Now read paragraphs 3-7, looking for answers to these questions.
1. What was Calamity Jane's real name?
2. Where and when was she born?
3. What did Jane's family do in 1863?
4. Did Jane get married when she was a young girl?
5. What did Jane do in 1886?
6. What kind of work did she do?
7. Why was working on the Deadwood Stage so dangerous?
8. How did Jane get her nickname?

Part One

Calamity Jane in Deadwood, South Dakota, 1880

1 In 1875 gold was discovered near the small town of Deadwood, South Dakota. Not long after, there were hundreds of gold miners in the town. Where the gold miners went, gamblers and gunfighters quickly followed. Soon there were many wild people in Deadwood. And one of the wildest of all was a woman - Calamity Jane.

2 Calamity Jane was an excellent horse rider. And she could use a gun as well as most of the gunfighters in the West. She was also well-known in the saloon bars of Deadwood, where she had a reputation for drinking whisky and making trouble.

3 Calamity Jane's real name was Martha Jane Canarray. No one is really sure where or when she was born. Most historians think that she was probably born in Missouri in 1849. As a child, she lived with her family on a farm there.

4 In 1863 the family left the farm and travelled west. Nobody is really sure what Jane did during the next few years. Some people say that she got married and lived in Virginia City for a time.

5 Then, around 1866, Jane started travelling. She went from town to town and from job to job. And she wasn't afraid of hard or dangerous work. She was a labourer with the Union Pacific Railroad for a time. Then she worked as a mule driver. After that, she became a scout with the United States Cavalry.

6 Jane also worked on the famous Deadwood Stage, which travelled between Deadwood and Cheyenne. This was very dangerous work because the stage coach was often attacked by bandits. On one journey, it was even attacked by a mountain lion. But as the lion jumped onto one of the horses, Jane quickly took out her gun and killed the wild animal with a single shot.

7 It was in Deadwood, around this time, that Jane got her famous nickname 'Calamity Jane'. When she walked into a saloon, the other customers used to shout, 'Here comes Calamity!' In other words, 'Here comes trouble!' Jane enjoyed her reputation. She used to fire off her guns in the saloons and break mirrors and bottles. The customers loved it. And so did the saloon keepers. Jane was an entertainer. She was good for business!

C
Now read Part Two of Calamity Jane's story.
Read paragraphs 1-5 and look at pictures a-e. Can you find the pictures which go with the paragraphs?
Example *1 - d*

Part Two

1 It was in the early 1870s that Jane's reputation really started to grow. And it was during this time that she met the famous 'Wild Bill Hickok'. Hickok was one of the most dangerous gunfighters in the West and had a lot of enemies. There were many stories about him in books and magazines.

2 Calamity Jane admired Hickok's reputation. When she met him, she also found that she liked the man. Soon they were very good friends. The times Jane had with Wild Bill were very happy ones. They were perhaps the happiest days of her life.

3 Then, on 2nd August 1876, the happy days came to a sudden end. Wild Bill was murdered; shot by a man named Jack McCall. At the time, Hickok was playing poker in Deadwood's Carl Mann Saloon. McCall came into the saloon and walked quietly up behind Hickok. Then he drew his gun and shot him in the back. Wild Bill started to get up. Then he fell across the table - dead.

4 Hickok was buried in Deadwood. After his death, Jane was a very sad and lonely woman. She spent her time in the saloons, drinking heavily and telling stories of her days with Wild Bill.

5 Some years later, there was a smallpox epidemic in Deadwood and Jane worked as a nurse for a time. It was very dangerous work; Jane risked her life to look after the sick. One child she nursed was a small boy called Robinson. He lived through the epidemic and came into Jane's life again years later.

Now read paragraphs 6-10 and look at pictures f-j. Can you find the pictures which go with these paragraphs?

6 In 1896 Jane got a job with a travelling stage show. On stage, she told stories of her life in the Wild West. She toured Chicago, St. Louis and Kansas City with the show. But, because of her drinking, she soon lost the job.

7 In July 1903 Jane arrived at the Galloway Hotel in Terry, near Deadwood. After the years of drinking and wild living, she was now very ill. She was fifty-five years old, but she looked seventy.

8 A few weeks later, she was dying. She opened her eyes and whispered, 'What's the date?' Someone told her it was 2nd August. She said, 'It's the twenty-seventh anniversary of Bill's death... bury me next to Bill'. Those were her last words. She died a short time after.

9 Calamity Jane was buried in the Mount Moriah Cemetery, Deadwood. Her funeral was one of the largest in the history of the town. The man who closed the coffin was C H Robinson, the rector of the cemetery. And he had good reason to remember Jane well. He was the small boy who Jane had nursed during the smallpox epidemic years before.

10 Jane got her last wish. She was buried next to Wild Bill Hickok. And there she lies today - Calamity Jane, the wildest woman in the West.

D

Now read Part Two of the story again.
Write questions about it to ask each other.

Who...?	What...?	Where...?
When...?	How...?	Why...?
Was...?	Were...?	Did...?

When did Jane meet Wild Bill Hickok?
Who was Wild Bill?

The Good Guide

29 PROJECT

Aim:
To write a guide to your neighbourhood.

A
In class: Before you write your guide

1 Read Part One and Part Two of Tina and Bipasha's guide. Can you think of somewhere in your neighbourhood which is good for bike repairs, trainers, a haircut, etc?

2 Read Part Three. Is there a restaurant, a street, a disco, a river in your neighbourhood that you would recommend people to avoid? Would your reasons be the same as Tina and Bipasha's?

B
Out of class: Write your guide

Write your guide with a classmate. Imagine you are writing it for a new student to your neighbourhood. Write about the best and the worst places. See the ideas box below. Include a map (draw a map if you can't get a photocopy) and some pictures. If you can't find pictures, make drawings.

> amusement arcades, cafés, cinemas, discos, hairdressers, parks, restaurants, shops, sports centres, supermarkets, swimming pools

You need:
- Some paper
- Glue and scissors
- Some coloured pens

C
In class: Use your guide

Read your classmates' guides. Did you choose the same places? Did you write similar things about these places?

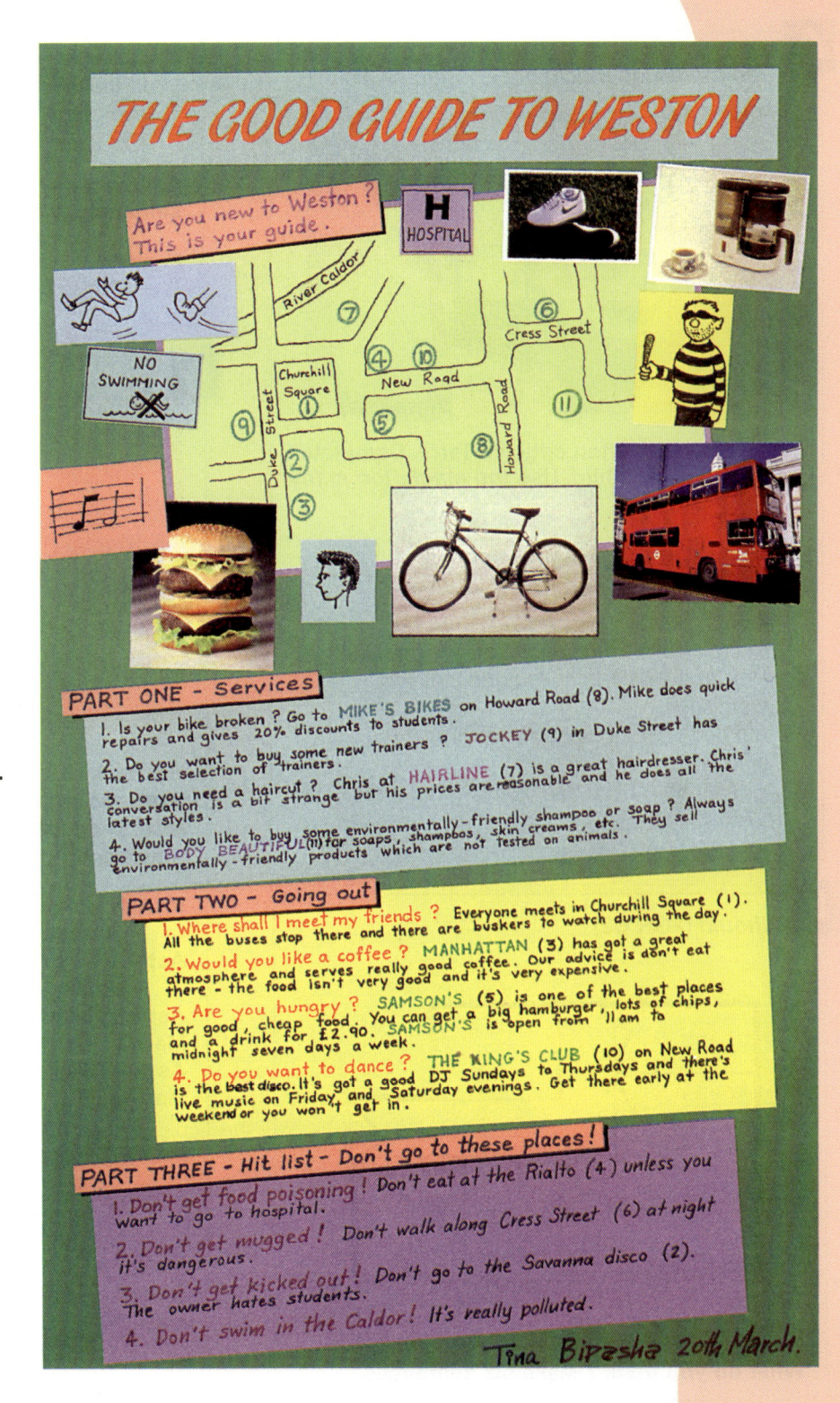

THE GOOD GUIDE TO WESTON

Are you new to Weston? This is your guide.

PART ONE – Services

1. Is your bike broken? Go to MIKE'S BIKES on Howard Road (8). Mike does quick repairs and gives 20% discounts to students.
2. Do you want to buy some new trainers? JOCKEY (9) in Duke Street has the best selection of trainers.
3. Do you need a haircut? Chris at HAIRLINE (7) is a great hairdresser. Chris' conversation is a bit strange but his prices are reasonable and he does all the latest styles.
4. Would you like to buy some environmentally-friendly shampoo or soap? Always go to BODY BEAUTIFUL (11) for soaps, shampoos, skin creams, etc. They sell environmentally-friendly products which are not tested on animals.

PART TWO – Going out

1. Where shall I meet my friends? Everyone meets in Churchill Square (1). All the buses stop there and there are buskers to watch during the day.
2. Would you like a coffee? MANHATTAN (3) has got a great atmosphere and serves really good coffee. Our advice is don't eat there - the food isn't very good and it's very expensive.
3. Are you hungry? SAMSON'S (5) is one of the best places for good, cheap food. You can get a big hamburger, lots of chips, and a drink for £2.90. SAMSON'S is open from 11am to midnight seven days a week.
4. Do you want to dance? THE KING'S CLUB (10) on New Road is the best disco. It's got a good DJ Sundays to Thursdays and there's live music on Friday and Saturday evenings. Get there early at the weekend or you won't get in.

PART THREE – Hit list – Don't go to these places!

1. Don't get food poisoning! Don't eat at the Rialto (4) unless you want to go to hospital.
2. Don't get mugged! Don't walk along Cress Street (6) at night it's dangerous.
3. Don't get kicked out! Don't go to the Savanna disco (2). The owner hates students.
4. Don't swim in the Caldor! It's really polluted.

Tina Bipasha 20th March.

Consolidation C

30

A Too many, too much, not enough (>GR C1)

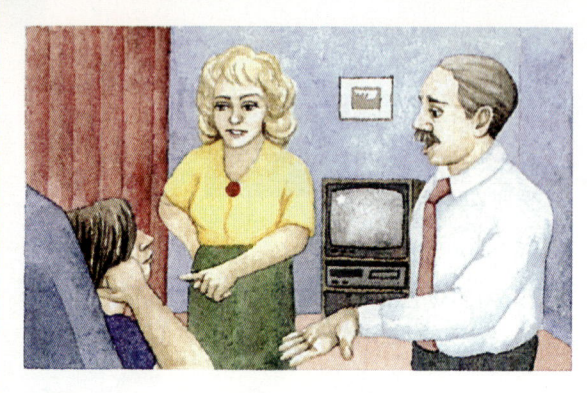

Terry's parents often criticise Terry. Complete what they say to him. Use *too much*, *too many* or *enough*.

1. You watch ____ TV. It isn't good for you.
2. And you're really lazy. You don't do ____ school work.
3. You're always tired. You have ____ late nights.
4. And you're very unfit. You don't take ____ exercise.
5. You don't eat the right things. You eat ____ junk food.
6. And another thing! You spend ____ money on computer games.

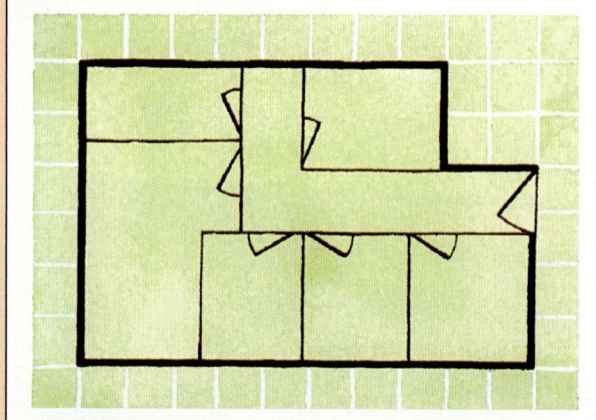

B Should (>GR C2)

What should there be in the perfect home? What do you think? Make six sentences.

Example
There should be one room for each person.
There should be a TV and video in every room.
There should be a robot to do all the housework.

C Present perfect continuous (>GR C3)

(i) Complete the questions. Use the present perfect continuous.

1. How long/you/study/English?
2. How long/your teacher/teach/English?
3. How long/you and your family/live/in your flat or house?
4. How long/Mick Malone/live/in London?
5. How long/you/use/this English book?

(ii) Now answer the questions in (i). Make true sentences with *for* and *since*.

Example
I've been studying English for five years.

D Suggestions (>GR C4)

Marina and Astrid are going to spend this weekend together. They are trying to decide what to do. What are the missing words in the conversation? Can you guess?

Marina: So, what ____ do this weekend? Any ideas?
Astrid: Well, I haven't got much money. Marina: No, neither have I.
Astrid: I know! ____ go camping?
Marina: Camping! Yes, that's a good idea.
Astrid: Right, then. So, where ____ go?
Marina: ____ going to Brighton? There are some good camp sites there.
Astrid: Yes, all right. Brighton is fine with me. How ____ get there? We can't use my motorbike. There's something wrong with it at the moment.
Marina: ____ go by train?
Astrid: It's cheaper by coach.
Marina: ____ go by coach, then.
Astrid: Okay.

Here are the missing words. Where do they go in the conversation?

| Why don't we | shall we | How about |
| shall we | Let's | Why don't we | shall we |

E Offers (>GR C5)

> Would you like _____ ?

> Would you like me to _____ ?
> Shall I _____ ?
> I'll _____ .

What are these people offering to do?

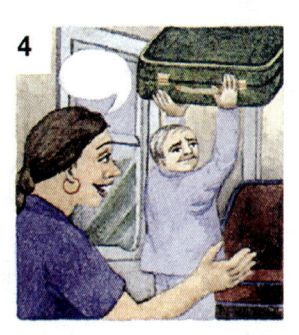

Find and complete the offers for the pictures.

Example
1 <u>Shall I</u> take your coat?
   or <u>Would you like me</u> to take your coat?

- Can you manage? Or _____ give you a hand?
- You can't go out there like that. _____ lend you an umbrella if you like. Or _____ phone for a taxi?
- I'm going out. _____ anything from the shops?
- _____ switch off the light? Or _____ leave it on?
- _____ take your coat?
- Sit down, _____ make you a cup of tea. Or _____ something else?

F Present simple for the future after *when, as soon as, until, if* (>GR C6)

Complete the sentences about Paul. Use the correct form of the verbs; the present simple or *will/won't*.

Paul is a college student. He is leaving college next year. What _____ (*he/do*) when he _____ (*leave*) college? He is taking some important exams next summer. As soon as he _____ (*finish*) the exams, he _____ (*try*) to find a summer job. He isn't sure what he _____ (*do*) after that. It depends on the results of the exams. If he _____ (*pass*) them, he _____ (*go*) to university. He _____ (*not/know*) what he _____ (*do*) if he _____ (*not/pass*). He _____ (*not/think*) about that until he _____ (*know*) the results.

G When, if (>GR C7)

Join a clause from A with a clause from B using *if* or *when*. Put the verbs into the correct form: the present simple or *will/won't*.

Example
1 I'll switch off the TV when this programme finishes.

A	B
I (*switch off*) the TV	I (*fail*) it the first time.
Bob and Eva (*get*) married	the weather (*be*) fine.
I (*not/have*) lunch today	this programme (*finish*).
I (*take*) my driving test	I (*not/feel*) hungry.
I (*take*) the test again	they (*be*) older.
We (*have*) breakfast outside	I (*be*) 18 years old.

H If sentences (>GR C8)

Think of a way to complete each sentence.

Example
If you're cold, <u>I'll close the window.</u>
Or If you're cold, <u>I'll lend you a sweater.</u>

1 If you're hungry, _____ .
2 If it rains tomorrow, _____ .
3 I'll lend you some money if _____ .
4 If we don't hurry, _____ .
5 We'll go to the cinema if _____ .
6 Tina will be surprised if _____ .
7 Paul won't pass his exams if _____ .
8 If it's sunny at the weekend, _____ .

Larry's perfect Saturday

A

It's Saturday and Larry doesn't have to go to school today. Look at the picture below. What is Larry looking forward to? Make sentences using words in the box.

Example
1 He's looking forward to getting up late.

He's looking forward to	meeting his friends. buying a CD. having a quiet breakfast. watching basketball on TV. looking around the shops. getting up late.

A

Look at the pictures. Who do you think Larry is speaking to? Match the pictures with the people in the box.

Example
1 - his older sister

his mother	his little sister	a neighbour
his father	his older sister	his grandfather

All the people in the pictures want something to happen. Can you guess what they want? Use the words in the boxes.

Examples
1 She wants to leave the baby with Larry.
2 He wants Larry to stir the soup.

He/She	wants to ___ wants Larry to ___ .

leave	channels
borrow	the baby with Larry
stir	some shopping for her
do	his sister with him
change	some money
take	the soup

🎧 29 Now listen and check your answers.

58

C

🔊 29 Listen again. What requests do the different people make? How does Larry agree to their requests?

Example
Sister: Do you think I could leave Tabatha with you for five minutes?
Larry: Well, er, yes, that's fine.

Asking for permission to do things

| Do you think I could__ ? |
| Could I__ ? |
| Can I__ ? |

Asking other people to do things

| Do you think you could__ ? |
| Could you__ ? |
| Can you__ ? |

Which of these forms do you think is

(a) the most polite?
(b) the least polite?

D

What do you think these people are saying? Can you make a short conversation for each picture?

🔊 30 Listen. Find the conversations for the pictures and check what the people are saying.

E

Make a list of three things that you would like to borrow from your classmate.

pen
bicycle
dictionary

Work with a classmate. Ask and answer.

Do you think	I could	borrow__ ?
		use__ ?
	you could lend me__ ?	

Could	I	borrow__ ?
		use__ ?
Can	you lend me___ ?	

Examples
A: Can I borrow your pen for a moment?
B: Sure. Here you are.
A: Thanks.

A: Do you think you could lend me your bike this afternoon?
B: I'm sorry, but I'm using it myself this afternoon.
A: Oh, right. Well, thanks anyway.

Definitions quiz

32

A

Complete the quiz with a classmate. Make a note of your answers.

B

Tell your classmates your answers. Make sentences. Do you agree with each other?

Example
A: *I think a vegetarian is a place where vegetables are grown.*
B: *Yes. Me, too.*
C: *No, it isn't! It's a person who doesn't eat meat.*

🎧 Then listen and check the correct answers.

C

Work with a classmate.
Student A – Ask B the questions on page 99. Then answer B's questions.
Student B – Answer A's questions. Then ask A the questions on page 108.

D

Work with a classmate. Write some *Definitions quiz* questions for your other classmates to answer.

What is a wardrobe?
a) a person who makes filings from wood
b) a person who loves clothes
c) a thing which is used fix hanging clothes in

---

1 What is a vegetarian?
a) a place where vegetables are grown 
b) a person who looks like a vegetable 
c) a person who doesn't eat meat 

2 What is a chatterbox?
a) a small box which is used for carrying teeth in  
b) a person who talks a lot 
c) an old car which makes a lot of noise

3 What is a pensioner?
a) a house where people can stay as paying guests 
b) a person who is extremely happy 
c) a person who doesn't work any more 

4 What is a teetotaller?
a) a person who doesn't drink alcohol 
b) a person who only drinks tea 
c) a machine which is used for adding up numbers 

5 What is a briefcase?
a) a person who has a very bad memory 
b) a thing which is used for carrying banknotes, credit cards, tickets, etc.  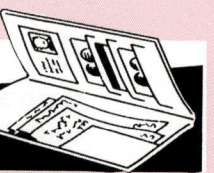
c) a thing which is used for carrying books and papers 

6 What is a professor?
a) a person who does something for money 
b) a person who has a high position as a teacher in a university 
c) a person who teaches in a school 

7 What is a library?
a) a shop where books are sold 
b) a person who sells books 
c) a place where you can look at or borrow books 

---

a person / a man / a woman etc	who_____
a place / a house / a shop etc	where_____
a thing / a tool / a machine etc	which_____

We can also use *that* instead of *who* and *which*.

| a person / a man / a woman etc | that_____ |
| a thing / a tool / a machine etc | that_____ |

60

What do you think I should do?

33

A

Look at the pictures. What advice are the people giving Larry? Match this advice with the pictures.

a   You should go to bed earlier.
b   Why don't you try drinking from the other side of the glass?
c   I wouldn't wear that shirt.

📻 31 Listen to the conversations and check your answers.

📻 31 Listen again. What other advice do the people give Larry?

You should/shouldn't ___.

I'd/I wouldn't ___ (if I were you).

Why don't you ___?

B

What do you think? Discuss these questions.

1   *Brown doesn't go with blue.* - Is this true in your opinion? What colours go with blue?
2   *People need eight hours sleep every night.* - Do they? How many hours do you need?
3   *Breakfast is the most important meal of the day.* - What do you think is the most important meal of the day?
4   *Hic... hic* - What do you think is the best way of stopping hiccups?

C

Find the advice for these problems.

Example *1 - f*

Problems

1   I haven't got any money.
2   I've got ink on my white T-shirt.
3   I've got a very bad memory.
4   I'm always tired.
5   I'm really unfit.
6   I can't sleep at night.

Advice

a   You should write things down.
b   You shouldn't work so hard.
c   Why don't you run to school every day?
d   I'd try putting it in milk.
e   I wouldn't drink so much coffee, if I were you.
f   Why don't you find a part-time job?

📻 Listen and check your answers.

Work with a classmate. Can you think of alternative advice for any of the problems? Choose your best idea and act out the situation for your classmates.

Example

A: *I can't sleep at night. What do you think I should do?*
B: *You should try counting sheep.*
A: *Umm, that's a good idea. Thank you.*

D

Write a problem on a piece of paper. Fold your paper and write a pseudonym on the front. Give it to your teacher to 'post' to a classmate.

Write some advice for the problem you receive. Fold your paper and write the sender's pseudonym on the front. Then give it to your teacher to 'post' back.

Read the advice to your problem. Is it good advice?

Rocky

I'm in love with someone but this person doesn't love me. What do you think I should do?

Rocky

I would be cool with this person. Perhaps this will make him or her love you.

This is the nine o'clock news

34

A

There are three main stories on the nine o'clock news this evening. Look at the pictures. What do you think the stories are about?

Which story are these sentences from - Story 1, Story 2 or Story 3?

- a A large chemical factory was burnt down in a fire in Liverpool this afternoon.
- b A security guard was shot and injured in a robbery at a bank in London early this morning.
- c Hundreds of houses were damaged and thousands of square kilometres of farmland were flooded after a storm in the south-west of England last night.
- d A safe was blown open and over £800,000 was stolen.
- e Hundreds of people were evacuated from their houses because of poisonous fumes and six firefighters were taken to hospital.
- f Twenty-five people were rescued from their houses by helicopter and a number of main roads were closed.

🎧 Listen to the news and check your answers.

🎧 Listen again. Then tell the news.

Example

Good evening. This is the nine o'clock news. A security guard was shot and injured in a robbery at a bank in London early this morning....

B

Memory game
Work with a classmate. Ask and answer about the three news stories. Student A - Keep your book open and ask questions 1-5. Student B - Close your book and answer your classmate's questions. Then swap roles. Student B ask questions 6-10.

Example

A: *Who was shot in the robbery?*
B: *A security guard.*

1 Who/shoot/in the robbery?
2 What/blow open?
3 How much money/steal?
4 How many houses/damage/in the storm?
5 What/flood?
6 How many people/rescue/by helicopter?
7 What/close?
8 What/burn down/in the fire?
9 How many people/evacuate from their houses?
10 Where/the six firefighters/take?

Story 1

Story 2

Story 3

C
Look at the picture. What is this news story about?

Work with a classmate. Can you guess what the missing words are? Choose from the verbs in the box.

Example
*Over twenty vehicles **were involved** in an accident on the M11 this morning.*

Over twenty vehicles____in an accident on the M11 this morning. A car driver____in the accident when his car____into the back of a van. Emergency services____twenty minutes to get to the scene of the accident because of heavy rush hour traffic. Over fifty people____and the police____the motorway for four hours while the road____.

cleared/was cleared	closed/was closed	crashed/was crashed
injured/were injured	involved/were involved	killed/was killed
took/was taken		

Listen to the news story and check your answers.

D
Think about a news story you have read or heard lately. Work with a classmate. Ask and answer about your news stories.

Example
A: *This story is about a robbery.*
B: *What was stolen?*
A: *Money.*
B: *Where did the robbery take place?*
A: *In a post office.*
B: *How many robbers were there?*
A: *There were four.*
B: *Were they caught?*
A: *Yes, they were.*

Write this story and then tell it to your classmates.

SKILLS 35 Choosing a pet

SPEAKING

A
Can you match the names of these pets with the photos?

Example
1 a budgie

| budgie | cat | dog | hamster | horse | mouse |
| parrot | rat | snake | stick insect | tropical fish | |

Now discuss these questions with your classmates.
1. Have you got a pet? If you have, what is it? Have you or your friends got any of the animals above?
2. Which pets are the easiest to look after? Which are the most difficult? Why?
3. Before you buy a pet, you need to be sure that you can look after it properly. What questions do you think you need to ask yourself? Make a list of questions.

> How much exercise will the pet need?
> Can I pay for a vet if the pet is ill?
> Who will look after the pet when I'm on holiday?

READING

B
Now read this advice to people who are thinking of buying a pet. How many of your questions in A are the same as those here?

The RSPCA
Helping you take care of your pets

Before you buy a pet, ask yourself these questions:

- How much will the pet cost?
- How much will its food cost?
- Will I have enough time to look after it properly?
- Who will look after it when I'm on holiday?
- Is there enough space for the pet where I live?
- How much exercise will it need?
- How much noise will it make?
- Will I be able to train it?
- How often will I have to clean its bedding?
- Will everybody in my family enjoy having a pet?

For more information, please write to:
RSPCA,
PO Box 1475,
London N12.

READING

C

Dr Desmond Lewis believes that people often choose pets which are not suitable for them. Dr Lewis uses a psychological test to find out which pet is the right one for a person's personality type.

Do the test yourself. Find out what kind of pet is right for you. First, look quickly at these four shapes and choose the one you like best.

○   ▲   ≈   ■

Now find your shape below. Read about your personality type and find out which pet is best for you.

▲ You are a leader. You are also an ambitious person. You want to be successful in everything you do. You can be impatient. You are not very good at waiting for things to happen. You are unhappy if you are not doing something active.

You love activity, so your ideal pet is one who will keep you busy. An animal which needs a lot of exercise, such as a large dog, would be an excellent choice. A horse would also give you a lot to do and would therefore make a good pet for you. Because you enjoy leading others, an independent animal, such as a cat, would not be a suitable choice.

■ You have a logical and practical approach to life. People who are good at maths and computing often prefer this shape. It is also the shape chosen by cautious people, people who like to think carefully before doing anything.
You like to use your brain, so you need an intelligent pet. Some people do not like rats, but you would probably find them very interesting. They are very clever animals. Another possibility is tropical fish. They would be a good choice for you as you could learn about how to look after them and the way they live. However, it is not as easy as you think to look after these beautiful creatures.

○ You are the kind of person who likes to be with others all the time. You are warm and sociable, so you find it easy to meet new friends and make people feel happy and relaxed. You enjoy talking. In fact, some people think you can be too talkative.

You should not choose an animal which lives outside. You need a pet which will be near you as much as possible. A good choice would be a small dog. You could take the dog everywhere and people would stop and talk to you about it. The perfect pet for you, however, is a budgie. If you had a budgie, you could teach it to talk and you would never be lonely!

≈ You like to be different to everyone else. You enjoy your own company. You are artistic and creative. You like having lots of hobbies - a different one every day! You get bored quickly and like constant change.
Snakes are quite unusual pets, but, because they don't move very often in cold weather, you would probably find them boring. A beautiful, colourful parrot would be a good choice for your artistic personality. However, the perfect pet for you is a cat. Cats are like you. They are independent, think for themselves and are happy alone.

SPEAKING

D

Discuss these questions with your classmates.
1. How many of your classmates chose the same shape as you?
2. What does the test say about your personality and the type of pet which is best for you? Do you agree with the test?

LISTENING

E

📼 32 You are going to hear descriptions of four people: Guido, Martina, Emmy and Imran. What are these people like? As you listen, choose adjectives from this list to describe each person.

ambitious artistic bad-tempered
cautious creative friendly funny
helpful impatient independent
logical popular quiet reserved
serious shy

Example
Guido - popular, friendly...

READING

F

Look at Dr Lewis's personality test in C again. Which shape do you think each of the four people in E would choose? According to the test, what would be the best pet for each person?

WRITING

G

Here is some advice about how to look after a small dog, but some of the words are missing. Can you complete the advice with suitable words?

Looking after your small dog

A small _dog_ needs regular exercise, but _it_ cannot go _for_ long walks. You should take your dog____ short____ two____ three times____ day.

A dog____ to have____ regular feeding routine. You____ feed____ dog at the same time____ day. But____ must____ careful not____ feed it too much. One tin____ dog food____ day____ enough. You____ also make sure____ dog always ____ enough water____ drink, especially____ summer.

When____ first get____ dog, take____ to the vet____ a general check-up. After that____ need____ take____ there regularly ____ vaccinations ____ further check-ups.

Now write some advice about how to look after another pet.

Survival

36

1 You find a fire in a corridor of the building. There is a fire extinguisher and a fire alarm on the wall. What would you do?
a   I would try to put out the fire first,
b   I would set off the fire alarm first.

2 You are in a room on the second floor when you hear the fire alarm. You open the door and see there is already some smoke outside in the corridor. What would you do?
a   I would go out into the corridor and try to go downstairs,
b   I would close the door and stay in the room.

3 You have to get to the end of a corridor, but the corridor is full of smoke. What would you do?
a   I would run along the corridor,
b   I would crawl along the corridor.

4 You have to leave the floor you are on because the fire is getting closer, but you cannot go down the stairs because of the smoke and the flames. What would you do?
a   I would go down in the lift.
b   I would go up the stairs to the roof.

5 You are trapped in a room on the fourth floor. The room is full of smoke and you cannot get out of the door because of a fire in the corridor. What would you do?
a   I would open the window and jump to the ground,
b   I would open the window and shout for help.

6 You are now out of the building, but you see somebody shouting for help from a first floor window. What would you do?
a   I would go back into the building to help this person,
b   I would tell someone from the emergency services.

A

Imagine that you are in a building that is on fire. Would you survive the fire? Study the six situations and note down your answers - a or b.

Compare your answers with your classmate's. Say what you would do in the situations in A.

> **A:** I'd ___.
> **B:** Yes, so would I./No, I wouldn't. I'd ___.

Examples
1
A: *I'd try to put out the fire first.*
B: *No, I wouldn't. I'd set off the fire alarm first.*
2
A: *I'd close the door and stay in the room.*
B: *Yes, so would I.*

🔊 33 Now listen to an expert and check your answers.

B

🔊 33 Listen again. What would the expert do in the situations in A? Make sentences.

Example
1 She'd set off the fire alarm first because the most important thing to do is to warn other people in the building.

C

Survival quiz
Read through the situations and think about what you would do.

Work with a classmate.
Student A - Turn to page 99. Ask your classmate the questions. Write down his or her answers - a or b. Then tell your classmate the correct answers.
Student B - Look at pictures 1-4. Listen to the questions and say what you would do.

1 You are walking alone on a beach when you see someone in the water. This person is calling out for help. What would you do?

2 You are walking in the forest when you meet a bear. The bear begins to run towards you. What would you do?

3 Your plane has crashed high in the mountains. You are hundreds of kilometres from civilisation. What would you do?

4 You are lost in a snow storm. You don't know in which direction to walk. What would you do?

Student B - Now turn to page 108. Ask your classmate the questions. Write down his or her answers - a or b. Then tell your classmate the correct answers.
Student A - Look at pictures 5-8. Listen to the questions and say what you would do.

5 You are lost in the jungle and are trying to find a village or a town. You come to a river. What would you do?

6 You are in a lifeboat in the middle of the ocean. You have got some food but you haven't got any water. You are very thirsty. What would you do?

7 You have been bitten on the leg by a poisonous snake. You are a long way from the nearest hospital. What would you do?

8 You see somebody getting a powerful electric shock from a hairdryer. You want to help this person. What would you do?

Now say what you would do in the eight situations.

Example
1 I'd try to find some other people to help.

Imagine

37

A

🔊 34 Musician, Hanna Caine is being interviewed on a TV programme called Imagine. First, read the questions the interviewer asks her. Then look at the pictures. They are connected to Hanna's answers to four of the questions. Match the pictures with the questions. Listen to the interview and check your answers.

1. Where would you live if you could live anywhere in the world?
2. Who would you meet if you could meet a famous perso from the past?
3. What would you change about the world if you had the power to change something?
4. What would you change about your personality if you could change something?
5. What would you change about the way you look if you could change something?
6. What would you buy if you had a lot of money?

🔊 34 Listen again. What would Hanna do?

Example

> 1 She'd live in San Francisco.

B

First, think about how you would answer the six questions in A. Then work with a classmate. Interview each other. Ask the questions and make a note of your classmate's answers.

Example

> **A:** Where would you live if you could live anywhere in the world?
> **B:** I'd live in India.

> 1 - India
> 2 -

Choose three things from your notes and tell the rest of the class about your classmate.

> If he/she ___, she'd/he'd ____.

Example

If Helena could live anywhere in the world, she'd live in India.
If she could meet a famous person from the past, she'd meet James Dean.
If she could change something about the world, she'd make the rich countries give more aid to the poor countries.

C

Dilemmas
Imagine you are in these situations. Think about what you would do and then tell a classmate.

Examples
1
A: *I'd tell my friend. What about you?*
B: *So would I.*
2
B: *I wouldn't say anything to the manager of the shop. I'd do nothing.*
A: *I wouldn't. I'd tell the police.*

1 You are in a disco. What would you do if you saw a friend's girlfriend kissing another boy. Would you tell your friend?

2 You are in a shop. What would you do if you saw someone shoplifting? Would you say something to the manager of the shop?

3 You are watching some friends play cards. What would you do if you saw someone cheating? Would you say something to that person?

4 You are walking in the street. What would you do if you found a purse? Would you keep it?

D

Write some *What would you do?* situations for a classmate to answer.

You are doing an examination. What would you do if you saw another student cheating? Would you tell the teacher?

E

Choose two of these situations to write about.
1 If I didn't have to go to school, I'd____.
2 If I could be really good at any school subject, I'd____.
3 If I could meet a famous person, I'd____.
4 If I could have a holiday anywhere in the world, I'd____.

Example
If I didn't have to go to school, I'd stay in bed until about 11. Then I'd get up and have something to eat. In the afternoon I'd meet my friends and we'd play video games or go to the cinema. I wouldn't get bored. I'd be really happy.

If I could have a holiday anywhere in the world, I'd go to India. I'd travel from the south of India up to the Himalayas and I'd visit all the famous places.

The Amish

READING 38

A

The photograph above does not show a scene from the past. It shows an Amish family in the USA today. From the photograph:

1. What kind of people do you think the Amish are?
2. What kind of lives do you think they lead?

Would you like to know more about the Amish people? Work with your classmates. Write some questions you would like answers to.

> Are the Amish people farmers?
> Do they drive cars?
> What language do they speak?
> Do they have TVs?

Now read the article and note down answers you find to any of your questions.

> A lot of Amish people are farmers.

Did you learn any other interesting things about the Amish from the article?

1 This photograph shows a family in one of the many Amish communities in North America today. Like a lot of Amish people, the family in the photograph are farmers. They farm land in Lancaster County, Pennsylvania, USA. The Amish have been farming land there for over three hundred years. The first Amish families came to the USA and Canada in the early 1700s from Switzerland and Germany. They came to escape from religious persecution in their own countries.

2 In nearly every way, life for Amish people today is the same as it was for their ancestors three hundred years ago. They wear the same traditional clothes. They speak to each other using their own special German dialect. They live in large family groups, with two or three generations under the same roof. They live in simple wooden houses without mains water and mains electricity. The water they need is taken from wells and the houses are lit by oil lamps. They have no telephones, no dishwashers and no TVs. They do not drive cars. They travel in horse-drawn buggies.

3 Neighbourliness is extremely important to the Amish. They spend a lot of time visiting their neighbours and helping each other. It is very common in Amish communities for friends and neighbours to come together to build new barns for each other. Everyone helps on these occasions - men, women and children. Amish people also love social events. They have huge wedding celebrations, and they have 'sisters' days', when all the married sisters from a family bring their own husbands and children together.

Building a new barn

4 Amish communities have their own schools. Schooling ends after the eighth grade, at the age of 13 or 14, because the Amish do not believe in higher education for their children. In Amish schools, there is usually only one teacher who teaches all the children together in one room. The older children help to teach the younger ones. An Amish education is very practical. Children are taught, for example, arithmetic, religious songs and how to earn a living from the land.

5 Amish people all have a strong belief in God. They have no churches. Instead they meet every Sunday in each other's homes to worship together. They have a large number of rules about how to live their lives. All Amish people promise to obey these rules when they are adults. If people break the more important rules, the rest of the community will not speak to them or have anything to do with them until they are ready to say they are sorry for their mistakes.

Inside an Amish school

6 Today there are about 100,000 Amish people living in North America. They try to keep their traditional way of life in the middle of a very different modern American society. The Amish do not believe that modern technology is evil. But they are afraid that if they allowed it into their lives, it would destroy many important things. They say that if they had cars, they would live further apart. They think that if they had TVs, there would be less time for conversation. They believe that if they had telephones, they would stop speaking face-to-face. And they are afraid that if they had tractors, they would become greedy and want more land than they really need.

A traditional way of life in the middle of modern American society

B

Here are eight words from the article. Can you guess what they mean ? First, find them in the article and decide what kind of word each one is - a noun, an adjective or a verb.

Paragraph 1: escape   persecution
Paragraph 2: horse-drawn   mains
Paragraph 3: neighbourliness   huge
Paragraph 5: worship
Paragraph 6: greedy

Example
escape - a verb
persecution - a noun
horse-drawn - an adjective

Now find the words above which mean:

friendliness and kindness   very big   pulled by a horse   very bad or cruel treatment   wanting too much   have religious services   get away   coming from the main system

Example
friendliness and kindness - neighbourliness

Now find these eight words in the article. Are they verbs, nouns or adjectives ? Can you explain what they mean ?

Paragraph 2: ancestors   dialect   wells   buggies
Paragraph 5: obey   adults
Paragraph 6: destroy   tractors

C

Work with a classmate. Choose one of these topics.

- Amish schooling
- the Amish and modern technology
- where the Amish live now and why they live there
- Amish religion and rules
- Amish neighbourliness and social events
- Amish life now and three hundred years ago

Look through the article and find the paragraph which deals with your topic.

Read the paragraph and make notes about the topic. Then, with your books closed, explain all you can about the topic to your classmates.

D

Read the article again and note down the most important differences between Amish life and life in your country.

Then work with your classmates. Make a list of the differences.

Examples
They wear traditional clothes.
They travel in horse-drawn buggies.
They don't have cars.

E

Look back at the questions you wrote in A. Are there any of your questions which the article does not answer ? There is more information about the Amish in the Teacher's Book. See if your teacher can answer your other questions.

If I had the power

39

Aim:
To make a poster about something you would stop if you had the power.

A

In class: Before you make your poster

1 Look at Justin's poster. Read Part One. Match the pictures to the points he makes about smoking.

Example A - 4

2 Read Part Two. Can you think of any other reasons why people smoke?

3 Read Part Three. What do you think of Justin's ideas - would they stop people smoking? What is his best idea? Can you think of other ideas which would stop people smoking?

B

Out of class: Make your poster

Think of something you would stop if you had the power - see the ideas box below. Try to follow the same format as in Justin's poster, eg *Part One - Why drugs are bad for you; Part Two - Why people take drugs; Part Three - What I would do to stop people taking drugs.* Find pictures to illustrate your ideas or make drawings. Write captions for the pictures.

> drugs, nuclear weapons, racism, sexual discrimination, unemployment, vivisection

You need:
- Some paper
- Glue and scissors
- Some coloured pens

C

In class: Use your poster

Show your poster to your classmates. Answer any questions.

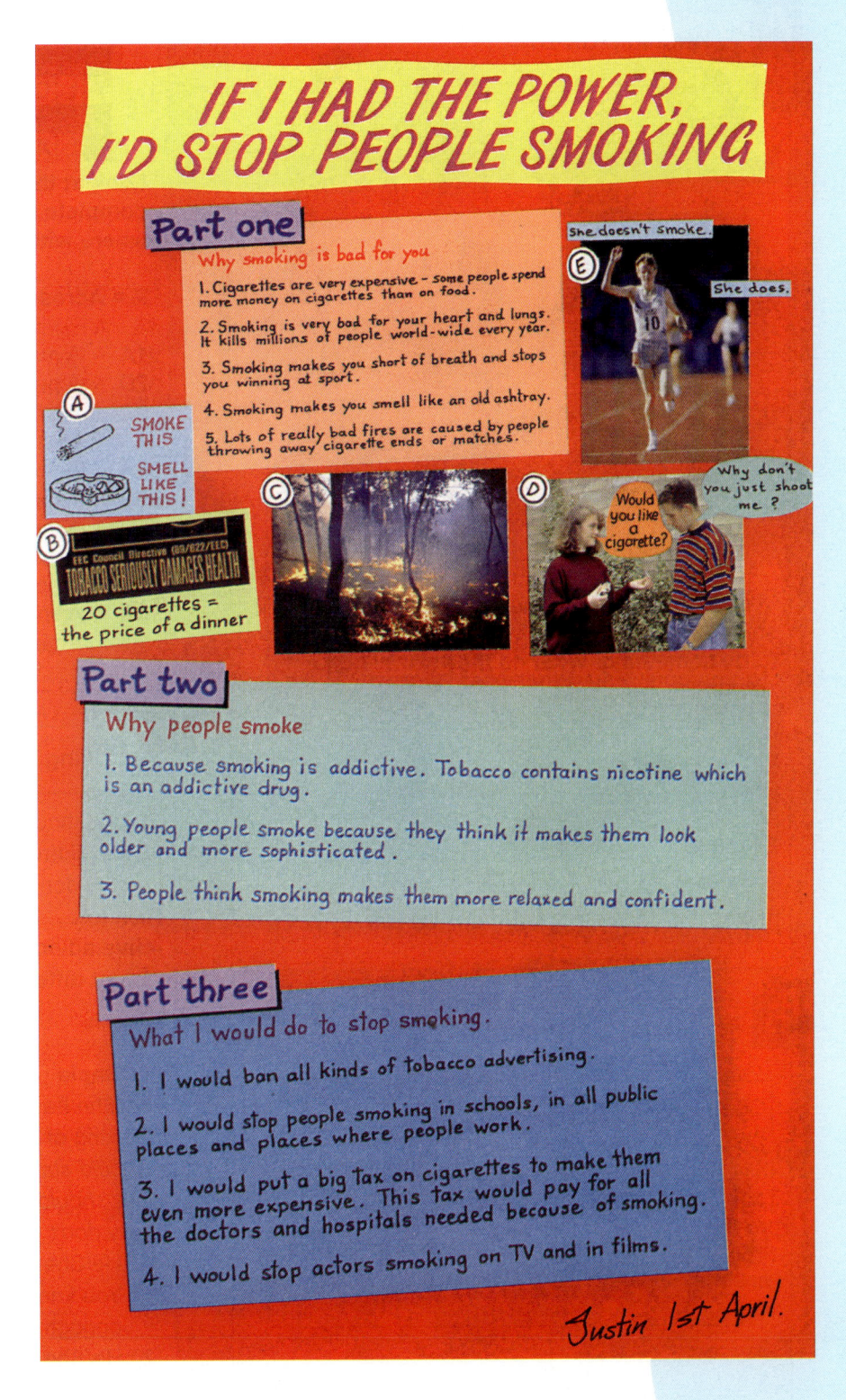

IF I HAD THE POWER, I'D STOP PEOPLE SMOKING

Part one

Why smoking is bad for you

1. Cigarettes are very expensive - some people spend more money on cigarettes than on food.

2. Smoking is very bad for your heart and lungs. It kills millions of people world-wide every year.

3. Smoking makes you short of breath and stops you winning at sport.

4. Smoking makes you smell like an old ashtray.

5. Lots of really bad fires are caused by people throwing away cigarette ends or matches.

(A) SMOKE THIS SMELL LIKE THIS!

(B) EEC Council Directive (89/622/EEC) TOBACCO SERIOUSLY DAMAGES HEALTH
20 cigarettes = the price of a dinner

(E) She doesn't smoke. She does.

(D) Would you like a cigarette? Why don't you just shoot me?

Part two

Why people smoke

1. Because smoking is addictive. Tobacco contains nicotine which is an addictive drug.

2. Young people smoke because they think it makes them look older and more sophisticated.

3. People think smoking makes them more relaxed and confident.

Part three

What I would do to stop smoking.

1. I would ban all kinds of tobacco advertising.

2. I would stop people smoking in schools, in all public places and places where people work.

3. I would put a big tax on cigarettes to make them even more expensive. This tax would pay for all the doctors and hospitals needed because of smoking.

4. I would stop actors smoking on TV and in films.

Justin 1st April.

Consolidation D

40

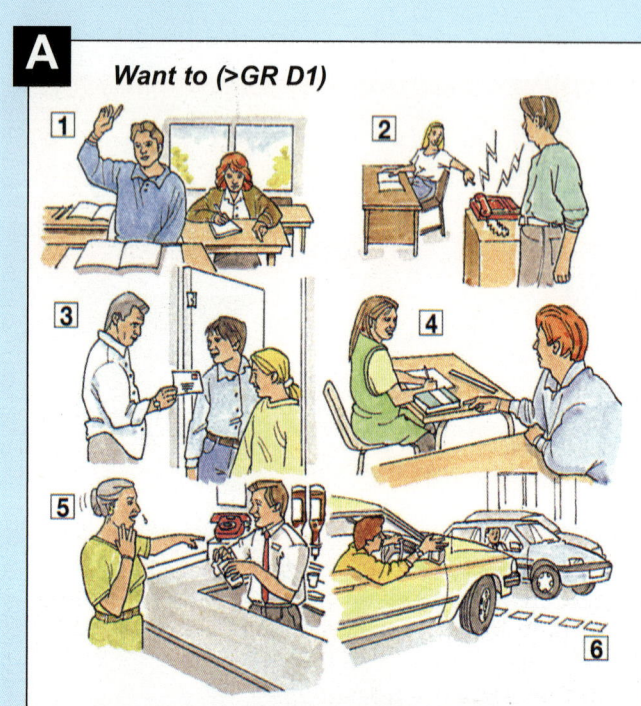

A Want to (>GR D1)

In each picture someone wants to do something or someone wants another person to do something. What do they want? Make sentences.

| He | wants | to____. |
| She | | him/her/them to____. |

Example
1 He wants to ask a question.
move use answer post ask borrow

B Requests (>GR D2)

Can I/you____?
Could I/you____?
Do you think I/you could____?

Look at the people in the pictures in A. What are they asking?

1 Could / ask a question, please!
2 _____?
3 _____?
4 _____?
5 _____?
6 _____?

C Which, who, where (>GR D3)

Crossword answers:
1A HAIRDRYER
2D AUSTRALIAN
3D RULER
4A SURGEON
5D SAW
6D TIE
7D OFFICE
8A WORKAHOLIC
9A FLORISTS
10A LAUNDERETTE

Look at the crossword answers above and complete the clues below. Use which, who or where with suitable verbs.

A = Across   D = Down

1A   A machine *which is used* for drying hair.
2D   A person____from Australia.
3D   A thing____for drawing lines and measuring things.
4A   A doctor____on people.
5D   A tool____for cutting things.
6D   A thing____round the neck.
7D   A place____business____.
8A   A person____working.
9A   A shop____flowers.
10A A place____people____clothes in machines.

D Giving advice (>GR D4)

You should(n't)____.
I would(n't)____if I were you.
Why don't you____?

Give advice to a friend in these situations. How many different pieces of advice can you think of?

Example
He/She has got a very bad cold, but he/she is thinking of going out to a disco this evening.
I would stay at home if I were you.
You shouldn't go out.
Why don't you take some aspirin and go to bed?

1 He/She feels very unfit and has a bad cough. You know he/she smokes a lot and doesn't take enough exercise.
2 He/She has lost his/her cheque book and credit cards.
3 He/She bought a new CD yesterday. Now he/she finds there is something wrong with it.
4 It is late at night. He/She is thinking of riding home on a bicycle without lights.

E Past simple passive (>GR D5)

Complete these news reports. Use the past simple passive.

A helicopter____(call) in yesterday to rescue two seventeen-year-old sailors who were lost at sea. The teenagers____(later/fly) to hospital.

A waiter____(attack) in a fight at the Calypso Club in the town centre late last night. Three men ____(later/arrest) by the police.

Two houses in North Street____ (completely/destroy) by fire last night. Luckily, the houses were empty at the time and no one____ (injure).

Jamie Charles, the Welsh international footballer, ____(transfer) from Brighton to Liverpool for £5 million yesterday. Charles____(buy) by Brighton three years ago for just £50,000 from Manchester City.

F Past simple active and passive (>GR D5)

Complete the text. Use the past simple, active or passive

On 26th April, 1986, a terrible accident____ (happen) at a power station near Chernobyl, 600 km south-west of Moscow. When the accident ____(happen), radiation____(release) from inside a nuclear reactor. The radiation____ (contaminate) the area and over 100,000 people ____(evacuate) from their homes in and around Chernobyl. Radiation____(also/carry) by the wind to other parts of Europe. In many places, people____(tell) not to drink milk or eat vegetables, and children____(keep) indoors.

G If sentences (>GR D6)

This man's car has got a puncture. He would like to change the wheel, but he hasn't got a spare wheel. He hasn't got a car phone and he doesn't know there is a garage nearby either!

(i) Complete the questions.

1   What would the man do if he had a spare wheel?
2   What____he____if he____a phone?
3   What____he____if he____there was a garage nearby?

(ii) Now think of ways of answering the questions. Make sentences: If...

Example
1 If he had a spare wheel, he would change the wheel.

H Review of if sentences (>GR C8, D6)

There are mistakes in some of these sentences. Find the mistakes and correct them.
1   You would do better in your exams if you studied harder.
2   If it will be sunny tomorrow, we will go swimming.
3   We won't go to the concert if we don't get a ticket.
4   If I would be older, I would buy a car.
5   You're tired. I will go to bed if I will be you.
6   If I have all the money in the world, I give it away.

Pen pals

41

A
Look at the picture and read the article in the magazine. What is Anna Jones doing?

Pen Pals Worldwide

Would you like a pen pal in another country? All you have to do is fill in the questionnaire about yourself and enclose it with a letter giving some information about the age, sex and nationality of the person you are looking for. Then post it to Sue Collins, Pen Pals, Young World, P.O. Box 112, London, SE18 8HG.

Pen Pals *Worldwide*

Name (BLOCK CAPITALS) _____
1 Age _____

B
Read Anna's letter to Sue Collins. Find out the age, sex and nationality of the pen pal Anna would like to write to.

C
Look at Anna's letter again and answer the questions using the diagram.

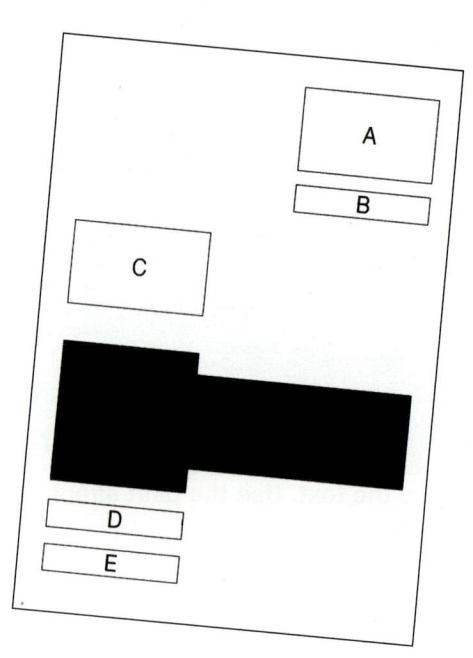

---

19 Cristal Way
Blaby
Leicestershire
LE15 4BR

15th June

Sue Collins
Pen Pals
Young World
P.O.Box 112
London SE18 8HG

Dear Ms. Collins,

I am writing to you regarding your article 'Pen Pals' in last week's Young World magazine.

I would be grateful if you could put me in touch with a pen pal in either the United States or Canada. I would like to write to a boy between 17 and 20 years of age.

I enclose the questionnaire. Thank you for your help.

Yours sincerely,

Anna Jones

Anna Jones

Example 1 - E

1 Where does Anna type her name?
2 Where does she sign her name?
3 Where does she put the date?
4 Where does she put the name and address of the person she is writing to?
5 Where does she put her address?

D
Write a letter to Sue Collins similar to Anna's using your own name and address and with information about the pen pal you would like.

E

Read Anna's questionnaire. Then compare it with the pen pal letter Anna received a few weeks after writing to *Young World*. How are Anna and Tim (a) similar, (b) different?

Examples

> They are both 17.
> She lives in the UK, but he lives in the USA.
> She's English, but he's American.
> They both live at home.

---

n Pals Worldwide

(BLOCK CAPITALS) ANNA JONES
17
dress (BLOCK CAPITALS) 19 CRISTAL WAY,
BY, LEICESTERSHIRE, LE15 4BR, UK
tionality   British
o you live at home?   Yes
ave you got any brothers and sisters?   No
Are you a student?   Yes
yes, what do you study?   English, Art, Computer Science, Biology
Can you speak another language?   I can speak a little French
Have you got a part-time job?   Yes
yes, what do you do?   I work in a supermarket
What do you like doing in your spare time?   I like going out with friends, going to discos, listening to music, reading, talking about politics, photography.
10 Can you play a musical instrument?   No
11 Are you interested in sport?   Yes
What sports do you play?   tennis, hockey
12 Have you visited other countries?   Yes
If yes, which countries have you visited?   France, Switzerland and Austria
Which countries would you like to visit?   USA, India, Brazil, Mexico

---

P.O Box 584
Orange Grove
California 93572
USA
July 8th

Hi Anna!

My name's Tim and I'd like to be your pen pal.

I'm 17 and I live in Napa Valley, California. I live at home with my mom and younger brother and sister. My parents are divorced, but I see my dad a lot. He lives in Los Angeles.

I'm a high school student and I'm taking English, math, physical education, US history, biology and music. I can speak Spanish because lots of my friends do.

I have an after-school job as a mechanic at a garage. I really like my job and I get paid $5 an hour.

In my spare time I enjoy going out with my friends. We go to the beach a lot and to the movies. My favorite movies recently are Jurassic Park and Terminator 2. I play the clarinet and I also like listening to music. I play on the basketball and football (American football!) teams at school.

I haven't visited any other countries but I would like to go to Europe one day. I'd love to visit Spain, Greece, and England, of course!

Well, that's enough about me for the moment. Please write soon.
Bye,

Tim

F

Anna's letter to *Young World* in B is an example of a formal letter and Tim's letter to Anna in E is an example of an informal letter. Compare the two letters. How are they different? Look at:

- the address(es) at the top of the letters
- how Anna and Tim begin their letters
- how they end their letters

Example

Anna writes the name and address of the person she is sending the letter to as well as her own address at the top of her letter. Tim only writes his address.

Note:

American English	British English
mom (mother)	mum
math	maths
favorite	favourite
movies	films
play on a team	play for a team

G

Look at Tim's letter in E again. In which paragraphs does he write about these things?

> sports   home and family   languages
> spare time activities   his age   school subjects
> other countries   musical ability

Example

sports - paragraph 5

Write a pen pal letter about yourself. Include information about all the topics in Tim's letter (sports, home and family, etc). Send the letter to a classmate or a student in another class.

77

Now and then

42

A

Look at the photos. They show what Carolina Kay and Peter Howard look like now and what they looked like when they were children. How old do you think they are now? How old were they then? Read or listen to the texts and find out.

Now

This photo was taken just a few weeks ago. I'm nineteen and work as a fashion model. My appearance is very important for my job and I have to be careful about what I eat. I love eating junk food but I don't eat chips any more because I don't want to put on weight. I also have to wash my hair every day. Can you see in the photo that I'm not showing my hands? That's because I bite my nails and I think my hands look really horrible.

Then

This photo was taken when I was nine. As you can see from the photo, I used to eat a lot. I loved eating junk food and I used to eat things like hamburgers and chips all the time. Doesn't my hair look terrible? I remember I never used to like washing it. I did have nice hands, however, because I didn't use to bite my nails at that time.

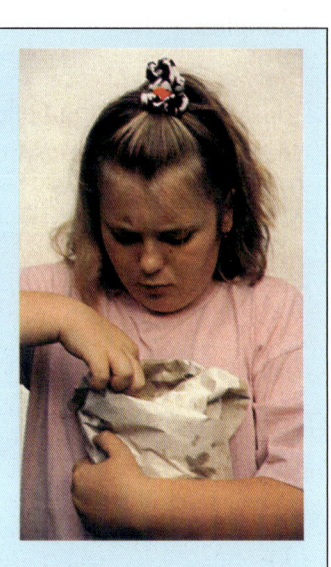

Now

This photo was taken this year in Crete. I'm twenty-two years old and really like my work as a travel guide. I like meeting people and I love travelling. Some people don't like coach travel but I never get travel sick. Languages are very important for my job. I like learning languages at night school. I can speak French and German and I also know some Spanish and Greek.

Then

This photo was taken at school when I was eleven. I didn't use to like school and the only things I liked were French and German. As you can see from the photo, I used to be really shy. I used to hate travelling and I sometimes even used to get travel sick going to school on the bus.

B

Carolina and Peter are very different today to when they were children. Work with a classmate. Read the texts again and find four differences for each person.

Example

> Now
> I have to be careful about what I eat.
> Then
> I used to eat a lot.

Afterwards, compare your answers with your classmates'.

C

What about you?
Look through the two Then texts again. Try to find three things that were true about you when you were a young child. Make notes.

Examples

> I used to be really shy.
> I didn't use to like school.
> I never used to like washing my hair.

Then compare your sentences with a classmate's. Did you write the same sentences?

D

Look at the photo. Does it show Alexander as he is now or as he was a few years ago? Find three 'clues' in the questionnaire.

CHANGING TASTES

How have your tastes changed over the last few years?

A few years ago — **Now**

Clothes
I used to wear tracksuits and trainers nearly all the time. I didn't use to like dark colours.

Now I wear denim most of the time.
I like wearing dark blue or black at the moment.

Food
I used to eat a lot of junk food like hamburgers and chips. I used to eat meat.

Now I don't.
Now I'm a vegetarian (except for the occasional fish).

Drink
I never used to drink coffee.
I used to drink a lot of coke.

Now I like it a lot.
Now I hardly drink any.

Music
I used to listen to heavy rock most of the time.
I never used to listen to classical music.

Now I listen to a lot of salsa.
Now I do.

Books/Magazines
I used to read a lot of science fiction.

Now I like reading writers like Borges and Allende.

Films
I used to see every horror movie on TV.

Now I find them boring.

Going out
I didn't use to go out very much.
My friends used to come round to to my home.

Now I go out all the time.
We usually meet in café's nowadays.

Sports/Leisure
I didn't use to play basketball.
I used to watch TV for hours every day.

Now it's my favourite sport.
I don't watch it so much anymore.

Read Alexander's answers again. Is there anything he writes which is also true for you? Make notes and then tell your classmates.

Examples

> He never used to drink coffee. I never used to drink coffee either.
> He finds horror movies boring. I find horror movies boring too.

E

How have your tastes changed over the last few years? Copy the questionnaire and write about yourself.

Afterwards, exchange questionnaires with a classmate and read about each other. Ask questions about things you want more information about.

Someone had switched off the light

43

> I had a shock when I got back to my office late last Monday night. When I switched on the light I knew somebody had been in my office while I was out.

A

🔊 Look at the two pictures and answer the questions.
1 What time did Mick leave the office last Monday morning?
2 What time did he get back at night?
3 Why did Mick have a shock when he switched on the light?

B

Compare the two pictures. How did Mick know somebody had been in his office? Find eight differences in picture B. Then make sentences using the words in the box.

Examples

> 1 Somebody had opened the drawer of his desk.
> 2 Somebody had emptied the wastepaper bin.

1	open	a note on the screen of his computer
2	empty	the three mugs on his desk
3	switch off	the poster off the wall
4	close	the aquarium from the top of the filing cabinet
5	wash	the drawer of his desk
6	take	the light in the bathroom
7	steal	the wastepaper bin
8	leave	the window

🔊 35 Listen to Mick and check your answers. Who do you think had been in Mick's office? Why had they done such strange things? Look at page 107.

80

C

> Next morning I decided to give my office a good clean. I thought I could finish everything by the time Mrs Parker arrived at 1.00 but at 12.55 I still had a lot of things to do.

🎧 Listen to Mick. Then look at the picture. What jobs had Mick done at 12.55 last Tuesday afternoon? What jobs had he still to do? Ask and answer.

1
A: *Had he cleaned the window?*
B: *No, he hadn't.*
2
A: *Had he made the bed?*
B: *Yes, he had.*

1 clean the window
2 make the bed
3 wash the dishes
4 tidy the desk
5 vacuum the carpet
6 mend the chair
7 pick up the newspapers from the floor
8 put the books onto the shelves

Now make sentences about what Mick had or hadn't done at 12.55 last Tuesday afternoon.

1 He hadn't cleaned the window.
2 He had made the bed.

D

Imagine you saw a friend with his/her mother in the street yesterday. You heard your friend say a number of things. Now you want to find out why your friend said them.

Work with classmate. Student A - look at page 99. Student B - look at page 108. Ask and answer.

Examples

A: *Why did you say 'I'm sorry.'?*
B: *Because I'd forgotten her birthday.*

Then change roles.

Think of some questions of your own to ask your classmate.

Example
Why did you say 'Be careful.'?

Eye-witnes
44

A

🔊 This accident happened at twenty-five past five yesterday afternoon. Read or listen to an eyewitness' statement about the accident. Whose statement is it? Find the person in the picture.

POLICE STATEMENT

NAME:_____ DATE:_____

TIME:_____ REF No.:_____

I had just got out of my car and was putting money into a parking meter. A young woman on a cycle was turning left into North Street when she was knocked down by a lorry. The lorry was turning right into South Street. It was the girl's fault. The traffic lights were red for her and green for the lorry driver.

🔊 Look at the picture. Read or listen to the statement again. What mistakes does the eyewitness make?

Example
The young woman wasn't turning left into North Street.

B

🔊 36 Listen to the statements of three more eyewitnesses. Who is speaking? Find the people in the picture. Say who they are, using the descriptions in the box.

The woman in the blue coat
The young man in the grey raincoat
The man wearing a brown hat
The young man with the dog
The teenager with dark hair
The young woman in the green dress
The man with the umbrella
The woman with the pram
The man wearing a black suit
The jogger in the pink tracksuit
The old lady with the bag
The girl in the yellow sweater

🔊 36 Listen again. Then answer these questions about the three eye-witnesses.

1. What had they just done?
2. What were they doing?

Only one of the eye-witnesses' statements is correct - which one is it? Say what happened in the accident.

C

Choose one of the eye-witnesses from the list in B. Say what you were doing or what you had just done at twenty-five past five yesterday afternoon. Get your classmates to guess who you are.

Examples

> **A:** *I was crossing the road.*
> **B:** *You're the woman with the pram.*
> **A:** *That's right.*
>
> **A:** *I'd just come out of the telephone box.*
> **B:** *You're the girl in the yellow sweater.*
> **A:** *That's right.*

D

Memory game
Work with a classmate. Who is the best eye-witness? Take it in turn to close your books and answer your classmate's questions about the picture. See how many questions you can answer. Change roles when you make a mistake or can't answer.

Example

> **A:** *What was the woman with the pram doing?*
> **B:** *She was crossing the road.*
> **A:** *What had the girl in the yellow sweater just done?*
> **B:** *She'd just come out of the telephone box.*

83

A ghost story

SKILLS 45

SPEAKING

A

Discuss these questions with your classmates.

1. Do you believe in ghosts?
2. Have you or any of your friends ever seen a ghost?
3. What would you do if you saw one?
4. What makes you feel frightened?

READING

B

You are going to read a ghost story. Below is the first part of the story, but the paragraphs are in the wrong order. Can you put them in the right order?

a One evening, when Mrs Baxter was in her bedroom brushing her hair, she suddenly felt icy-cold fingers on her shoulders. She looked in the mirror. There was no one behind her. She screamed and ran downstairs to the dining room, where she found her husband. Before she could say anything, all the lights went out and she felt something warm and wet on her face. Then the lights came on again. She looked up. There, on the ceiling, was a large, red mark. Blood was dripping from it.

b Ten years later, a young man called Andrew McStay was telling his friends about the house.
' It's been empty for the past ten years,' he said. 'People say there's a ghost there. But I don't believe in ghosts.'
'I bet you wouldn't go and stay there,' said one of his friends.
'Yes, I would. Why not?' Andrew replied.
'All right then,' said his friend, 'I'll bet you £50 you won't spend one night there.'
Andrew thought for a moment. He didn't really want to go and stay in the house, but he didn't want to look foolish in front of his friends. 'All right,' he said, 'I'll do it.'
And so it was that Andrew McStay went to the old house one cold winter's evening ...

c One day, soon after they had arrived in the house, the Baxters' dog, Rex, started barking angrily in the dining room. Mr Baxter rushed into the room to see what was wrong. Rex was jumping up at the wall as if he was trying to catch something. Then the dog fell and lay motionless on the floor. Mr Baxter looked at the wall. He couldn't see anything there. Just then, he felt very, very cold. He knelt down to look at Rex. The dog was dead.

d The Baxters moved out of the house the next day.

e This is a true story. It happened a long time ago in Scotland. A young couple, Duncan and Janet Baxter, and their two children moved in to an old house in the country, not far from Edinburgh.

f After that, the noises started. Every night was the same. First, the windows started shaking and the doors started banging. Then there was a terrible scream, followed by the sound of a man laughing. It was a cruel and horrible laugh. Soon the family couldn't sleep at all.

LISTENING

C

Now listen and check the correct order.

READING

D

Work with a classmate. Read the first part of the story again, with the paragraphs in the correct order. Find these words. Are they verbs, nouns or adjectives? What do they mean?

barking	rushed	motionless	shaking	banging
scream	cruel	icy-cold	shoulders	ceiling
mark	dripping	bet	foolish	

84

WRITING

E

What happened next in the story? Work with a classmate. Talk about the pictures. Then write about what happened.

> When Andrew arrived at the house...

SPEAKING

G

Discuss these questions with your classmates.

1. Where had the coins come from? Who had put them inside the wall?
2. Who was the ghost in the old house?

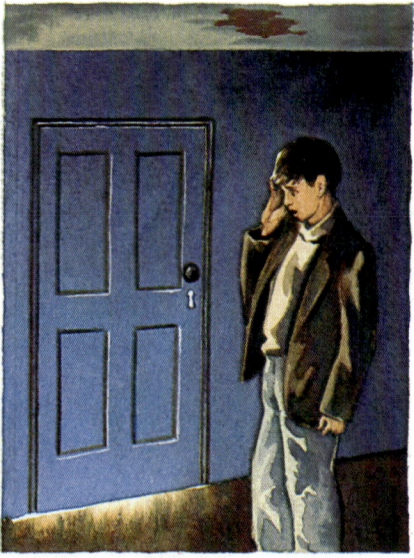

LISTENING

F

37 Listen to what happened. Underline the parts of your story which are the same as the one on the tape. Whose story is most like the one on the tape?

LISTENING

H

38 Listen to the final part of the story and find out the answers to the questions in G.

Can you think of a title for the story?

Secret diary

46

A

It's a quarter to eleven at night and Judy Carter is in her room at home. She is writing in her diary about some of the people she spoke to today. Who do you think V, W, X, Y and Z are? Match them with the people in the box.

Isabella - a girl Judy doesn't like
Glen - a boy Judy likes
Judy's mother
Dominique - Judy's best friend
Mr Winters - a teacher at Judy's school

Today started really badly! I was really angry with X at breakfast-time. She told me I couldn't wear my new top to school. She said it was cold. She told me that I would be too cold.

Z looked really unhappy at school today. She said that she had finished with Peter. She told me she had seen him kissing another girl.

We had V this morning and he was very angry with us. He told us we were the worst class in the school. He said we had to work harder.

I met W outside the school at lunchtime! He said that he might have a party at the weekend. He told me he would phone me about it on Thursday.

Y saw me speaking to W and wanted to speak to me afterwards, but I told her I was in a hurry. I said I had to catch a bus.

X looked at me when I got home. She said I looked very happy. I said I was going to my room. I told her that I had a lot of homework to do.

B

Find the reported speech. What do you think the five people actually said to Judy?

Examples
She told me I couldn't wear my new top to school.
– 'You can't wear your new top to school.'
She said it was cold.
– 'It's cold.'
She told me that I would be too cold.
– 'You'll be too cold.'

🔊 39 Listen to the conversations Judy had with the five people today and check your answers.

Note:

Direct speech	Reported speech
You **can't** wear your new top to school.	She told me (that) I **couldn't** wear my new top to school.
It **is** cold.	She said (that) it **was** cold.
You **will** be too cold.	She told me (that) I **would** be too cold.

C

Good news, bad news
Judy spoke to these people recently. Who said what? Match the speech balloons with the people. Was the news Judy heard good or bad?

Example
1 - an optician - c, good

[b] Your grandmother is very ill. She has had to go into hospital. She may have to have an operation.

You've got an ear infection. You must take antibiotics three times a day.

[d] I've marked your examination! You did very well. You got 92%.

Your eyes are fine. You don't need to wear glasses.

[f] I can't come to the disco with you on Friday. I have to go out with my parents.

[e] You play very well. I'm putting you into the school team.

[g] You need a filling. It won't hurt.

1 - an optician
2 - Judy's dentist
3 - Judy's doctor
4 - Judy's sports teacher
5 - Judy's grandfather
6 - Judy's maths teacher
7 - Judy's best friend

Judy is telling a friend what the people said. What do you think she says? Make sentences.

Example

> 1 My optician said (that) my eyes were fine. He told me (that) I didn't need to wear glasses.

🎧 40 Listen to Judy and check your answers.

D

Write down the names of five people you have spoken to recently on a piece of paper. Then write something they said to you. Write statements only. Don't write questions.

1 My brother - You can't borrow my Walkman.
2 Mrs Ramos (my English teacher) - You must do your homework.
3 Pablo (my best friend) - I played football yesterday.
4 My grandmother - I've lost my glasses.
5 My father - I'm angry with you.

Work with a classmate. Report what was said to you. Can your classmate guess who said what?

Examples
A: He said I couldn't borrow his Walkman.
B: Was it your father?
A: No.
B: Was it your brother?
A: Yes, it was.
She told me that I had to do my homework.
B: Was it...?

E

Memory game
Say something interesting to your classmates. It could be something personal, something in the news, something about a famous person, etc.

Example
André Agassi won the French Open tennis tournament last week.

Listen carefully to your classmates. Then try to remember what they said.

Examples
Felipe told us that Andre Agassi had won the French Open tennis tournament last week.
Teresa said she didn't like politicians.
Paulo said that he had gone to bed at two o'clock last night.

Interview

47

A

🎧 41 Larry is a reporter for his school radio station. Yesterday he interviewed rock star Johnny Guitar. Johnny didn't like four of the questions Larry asked. Read Larry's notes about the interview. Which four questions do you think Johnny didn't like? Listen to Larry telling his producer about the interview. Find out if you were right.

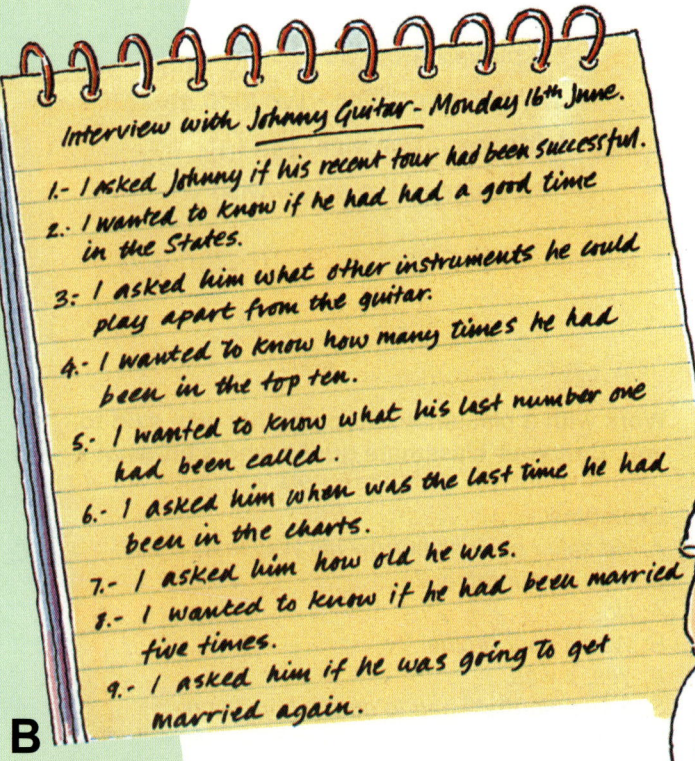

Interview with Johnny Guitar - Monday 16th June.

1.- I asked Johnny if his recent tour had been successful.
2.- I wanted to know if he had had a good time in the States.
3.- I asked him what other instruments he could play apart from the guitar.
4.- I wanted to know how many times he had been in the top ten.
5.- I wanted to know what his last number one had been called.
6.- I asked him when was the last time he had been in the charts.
7.- I asked him how old he was.
8.- I wanted to know if he had been married five times.
9.- I asked him if he was going to get married again.

B

Look at Larry's notes. What do you think Larry actually said in the interview?

Examples
1 I asked Johnny Guitar if his recent tour had been successful. - 'Was your recent tour successful?'
2 I wanted to know if he had had a good time in the States. - 'Did you have a good time in the States?'

🎧 42 Listen to Larry's interview with Johnny Guitar and check your answers.

C

🎧 42 Listen to the interview again. How did Johnny Guitar answer Larry's questions?

Examples

1 He said that it had been very successful.
2 He told Larry that he'd had a great time.

Note:

Direct speech	Reported speech
Was your recent tour successful?	He asked him if his recent tour **had been** successful.
Did you **have** a good time in the States?	I wanted to know if he **had had** a good time in the States.
What other instruments **can** you play apart from the guitar?	I asked him what other instruments he **could** play apart from the guitar

Pilot Politician Tennis player Film director Princess Footballer

TALK TIME

D

These people are on a TV chat show. Look at the questions the interviewer asked them. Find two questions for each person.

Example
The pilot - Can you fly any kind of plane? Which airline do you work for?

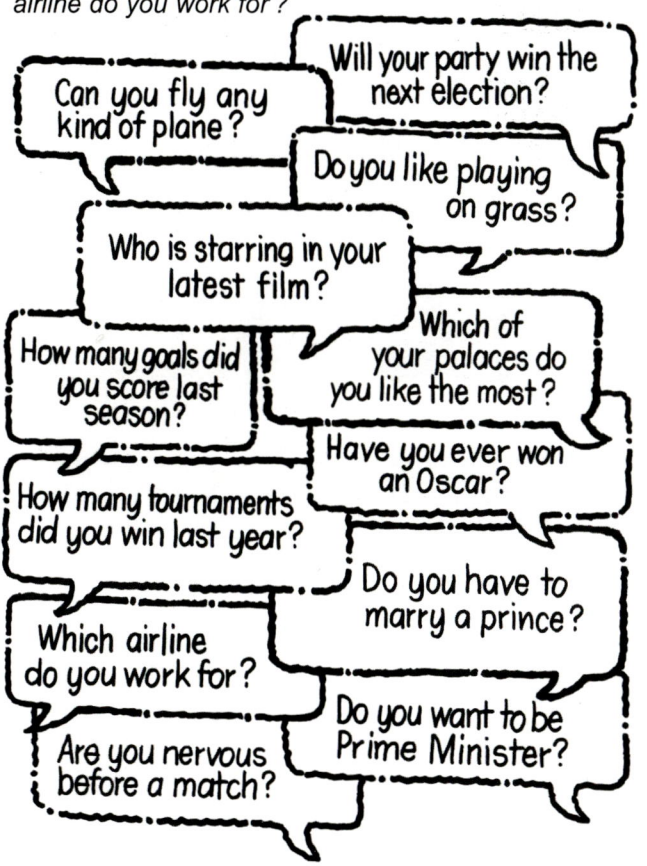

- Can you fly any kind of plane?
- Will your party win the next election?
- Do you like playing on grass?
- Who is starring in your latest film?
- How many goals did you score last season?
- Which of your palaces do you like the most?
- Have you ever won an Oscar?
- How many tournaments did you win last year?
- Do you have to marry a prince?
- Which airline do you work for?
- Do you want to be Prime Minister?
- Are you nervous before a match?

🎧 **43** Listen to the interviews and check your answers.

Now report the questions.

She	asked (him/her)	who/which/how many___.
	wanted to know	if___.

Examples
1 She asked him if he could fly any kind of plane. She wanted to know which airline he worked for.

🎧 **44** Listen and check your answers.

E

Role play
Work with a classmate. Each choose a profession from D. Make sure the profession you choose is different from your classmate's. Write six questions to ask your classmate about his or her profession.

Film Director
1. What is your latest film called?
2. How much did the film cost?
3. Will the film win an Oscar?
4. How many films have you made?
5. Are you rich?
6. Who is your favourite film star?

Student A - Ask your questions. Also, try to ask some follow-up questions. Make notes of your classmate's answers. Student B - Invent answers to your classmates questions.

A: *What's your latest film called?*
B: *Calamity Jane.*
A: *Who plays Calamity Jane?*
B: *Kim Basinger.*
A: *How much did the film cost?*
B: *$30 million.*
A: *That's very cheap. Why did it cost so little?*
B: *...*

Then change roles.

Report back to the rest of class on your interviews.

I asked Andre what his latest film was called. He told me it was called Calamity Jane. I then wanted to know who played Calamity Jane. He told me Kim Basinger. I also asked how much it had cost. He said $30 million....

The true story of a miracle

READING 48

Part One

A
You are going to read about someone called Helen Keller. Here are six important facts about Helen's early life, but they are in the wrong order. Look at pictures 1-6. What is the right order?

- After that, she became a very difficult child to live with.
- In 1882 she almost died of a mysterious illness.
- The director of the Institute asked Annie Sullivan to become Helen's teacher.
- Helen was born in Tuscumbia, Alabama, in 1880.
- Captain Keller asked for help with Helen from an Institute for the Blind.
- Because of the illness, she became blind and deaf.

Now read Part One and check the right order.

1 On 27th June, 1880, a baby girl was born to Captain Arthur Keller and Kate Keller in Tuscumbia, Alabama. The proud parents named their daughter Helen. She was a happy baby. She was also very intelligent. At six months she could even say 'Wah-wah' for water.

2 In January, 1882, Helen almost died of a mysterious illness. Her parents were relieved when the doctor finally told them 'You are very lucky parents. She's going to live.'

3 But shortly after the doctor left, Mrs Keller saw a strange look in her baby's eyes. She called to her 'Helen, Helen.' She then screamed for her husband 'Captain come quickly. Look at Helen.' Before he arrived he heard her cry 'She can't see or hear! My baby is blind and deaf!'

4 Five years later 
Helen's world was a dark and silent place. She became a very difficult child to live with. She ran about the house doing whatever she wanted. She became angry and violent very easily and threw things onto the floor or at other people. She fought with other children and sometimes hurt them.

5 Helen was almost a wild child. No one could control her. The Kellers didn't know what to do. They needed help. In February, 1887, Captain Keller contacted the Perkins Institute for the Blind in Boston. He asked the director of the Institute for help with Helen.

6 The director of the Institute spoke to a young woman called Annie Sullivan. He told Annie about Helen and asked her if she would like to become Helen's teacher. The director explained, 'Helen is a very intelligent child, but she has no language. There's a treasure inside her that needs to be opened. And I think you can open it for her.'

B
Now discuss these questions.

1. Why did Helen become such a difficult child?
2. What did the director think Annie could do for Helen?

C
Read Part Two, and answer these questions.

1. What happened when Annie arrived at the Keller house?
2. How did Annie try to communicate with Helen?
3. How did Helen behave at the dining table that evening?
4. Why did Helen's parents allow Helen to behave like that?
5. What did Annie want to do?

Part Two

1 The Keller House, 2nd March, 1887

Annie Sullivan was excited by the idea of helping a deaf-blind child. She agreed to travel to Tuscumbia and become Helen's teacher. When she arrived at the Keller house, she found a very messy, spoilt little girl. Helen grabbed Annie's suitcase and immediately began pulling everything out of it.

2 Annie took a present for Helen from her suitcase. It was a doll. Then, using a special alphabet, she spelt into Helen's hand, 'D-O-L-L, Doll. I'm going to teach you language, the door to the world for you,' she told Helen.

3 Helen grabbed the doll and threw it violently onto the floor. Annie tried to make her pick it up. But, instead, Helen kicked Annie in the face and knocked out a tooth!

4 At the dining table that evening, Annie found that Helen was allowed to eat with her hands and take food from other people's plates. Captain Keller explained, 'We can't have any peace and quiet unless we give her what she wants.' Annie said, 'That's exactly the point. This child is spoilt.'

5 Annie believed that Helen should learn good manners. She tried to stop Helen from getting out of her dining chair. But Helen fought back. Then Annie said to the family, 'Please leave me alone with her. I can't teach her anything if you just let her do whatever she wants.'

D

In Part Three, Annie begins by saying what happened next on that first evening. As you read Part Three, look at the four pictures below. Which pictures go with which paragraphs?

Part Three

1 I stayed with Helen and asked the family to leave the dining room. Captain Keller was angry with me, but he agreed to go. I forced Helen to sit in a chair and eat from her own plate with a spoon. She was very strong. She kept knocking over her chair and throwing things onto the floor. But finally she sat and ate her food.

2 On that first evening, Mrs Keller wasn't very happy with me. 'Miss Sullivan,' she said, 'I'm not sure about your method of teaching Helen.' 'She ate with a spoon and folded her napkin,' I told her. 'My Helen folded her napkin!' said Mrs Keller. She couldn't believe her ears!

3 The next day, I told Helen's father 'I can't do anything with Helen unless I have her all to myself. I want her to depend on me for her food, her clothes, everything.' Then I asked him if Helen and I could live alone in the guest house in the Kellers' garden. He wasn't happy with the idea, but he agreed. He said that Helen and I could live in the guest house but only for two weeks. 'Two weeks!' I thought. That's a very short time to perform a miracle!'

4 In the guest house, I had complete control over Helen. One day, I remember she wanted a piece of cake. I said, 'OK, Helen, if this is what you want, there's a word for it.' I spelt into her hand, 'C-A-K-E, Cake.' Then I said, 'When you understand that there's a word for everything, the world will be yours.'

5 The two weeks passed. On the last morning Mrs Keller spoke to me. 'Miss Sullivan, your eyes look very tired,' she said. 'Why don't you rest? We're very happy with all that you've done for Helen. She's a different child.' 'She is different,' I said. 'She has manners, but she doesn't have language. She can spell thirteen nouns and five verbs, but she doesn't know what they mean.'

6 Later that day, Helen and I were in the garden. I was thinking. It was my last day, I needed more time. We walked over to the water pump. I began pumping. Then I put Helen's hand under the gushing water. As usual, I spelt the word for her, 'W-A-T-E-R, Water.'

7 Then something happened. In a very strange voice, as if she remembered something from when she was a baby, I heard Helen say, 'Wah-wah.' Then she grabbed my hand and spelt, 'W-A-T-E-R.' I called for her parents.

8 Captain and Mrs Keller came running out of the house. Helen reached for her mother and spelt, 'M-O-T-H-E-R' into her hand, then, 'T-E-A-C-H-E-R.' Next, Helen put her arms around me. She was so happy. She now understood what words were. At last she had a key to language. The world was hers. I held her hand and spelt the words 'I, L-O-V-E, H-E-L-E-N.'

E

Read Part Three again and answer these questions.

1. What did Annie force Helen to do on the first evening?
2. How did Mrs Keller feel about Annie's methods at first?
3. Where did Annie want to live with Helen? Why?
4. Why was Mrs Keller happy on the last morning?
5. How did Annie feel on that morning? Why?
6. What happened later that day?

What was the first word that Helen understood? How was this word also important to her as a baby? Can you remember?

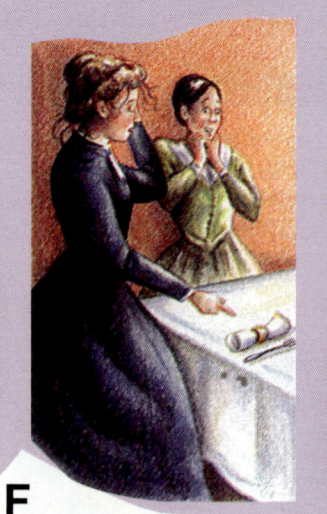

F

What happened to Helen when she grew up? And what happened to Annie? Read this 'Postscript' to the story and find out.

> Helen went on to learn to speak, read and write. In 1904, she graduated from Radcliffe College, one of the best colleges in the United States. She later wrote books, appeared in films, toured foreign countries and became famous all over the world. Helen and Annie stayed together for fifty years, until Annie's death in 1936. Helen died in 1968.

An interview with someone famous

49 PROJECT

Aim:
To write a newspaper article based on an interview.

A

In class: Before you carry out your interview

1 Read Part One. How do you think the Prime Minister answers the questions?

Example
1 - Yes, I do.

2 Read the article. Find the answers to the questions.

Example
1 - She answered that she didn't like living there.

3 Read the captions to the pictures in Part Two. Then answer these questions.

1 What is the name of the Prime Minister of your country?
2 Where does he or she live?
3 What is the name of the parliament in your country?

B

In class: Role play an interview with a famous person

Work with a classmate. Each choose a famous person. Write eight questions to ask your classmate's famous person. Interview each other. Write down your classmate's answers.

C

Out of class: Write a newspaper article based on your interview

Write your newspaper article. Try to find pictures to illustrate your article or make drawings.

You need:
- Some paper
- Glue and scissors
- Some coloured pens

D

In class: Use your newspaper article

Let your classmates read your article. Answer any questions.

MEET THE PRIME MINISTER

Part one — THESE WERE THE QUESTIONS I ASKED THE PRIME MINISTER:

1. Do you like living at 10 Downing Street?
2. What do you like about your job?
3. What don't you like about your job?
4. How many countries have you visited as Prime Minister?
5. Were you a good student at school?
6. What was your best subject at school?
7. What books are you reading?
8. Will you win the next election?

Part two

The Prime Minister

Last week I interviewed the Prime Minister at 10 Downing Street in London. I went into her private office and she kindly asked me to sit down. First, I asked her if she liked living at 10 Downing Street. She answered that she didn't like living there. She said it was more like an office than a home. I then asked her what she liked about her job. She told me that she liked travelling to different countries and that she liked meeting a lot of interesting people. I also wanted to know what she didn't like about her job and she told me that she didn't like having to speak to large groups of people. Next, I asked her how many countries she had visited as Prime Minister and she told me that she had been to sixteen. I then asked her if she had been a good student at school. She smiled and told me she hadn't been a very good student. I also asked her what her best subject at school had been and she told me Science. I wanted to know what books she was reading but she said she hadn't got time to read because she was too busy. Finally, I asked her if she would win the next election and she answered that she was 99% sure she would.

Big Ben and the Houses of Parliament

The most famous door in Britain

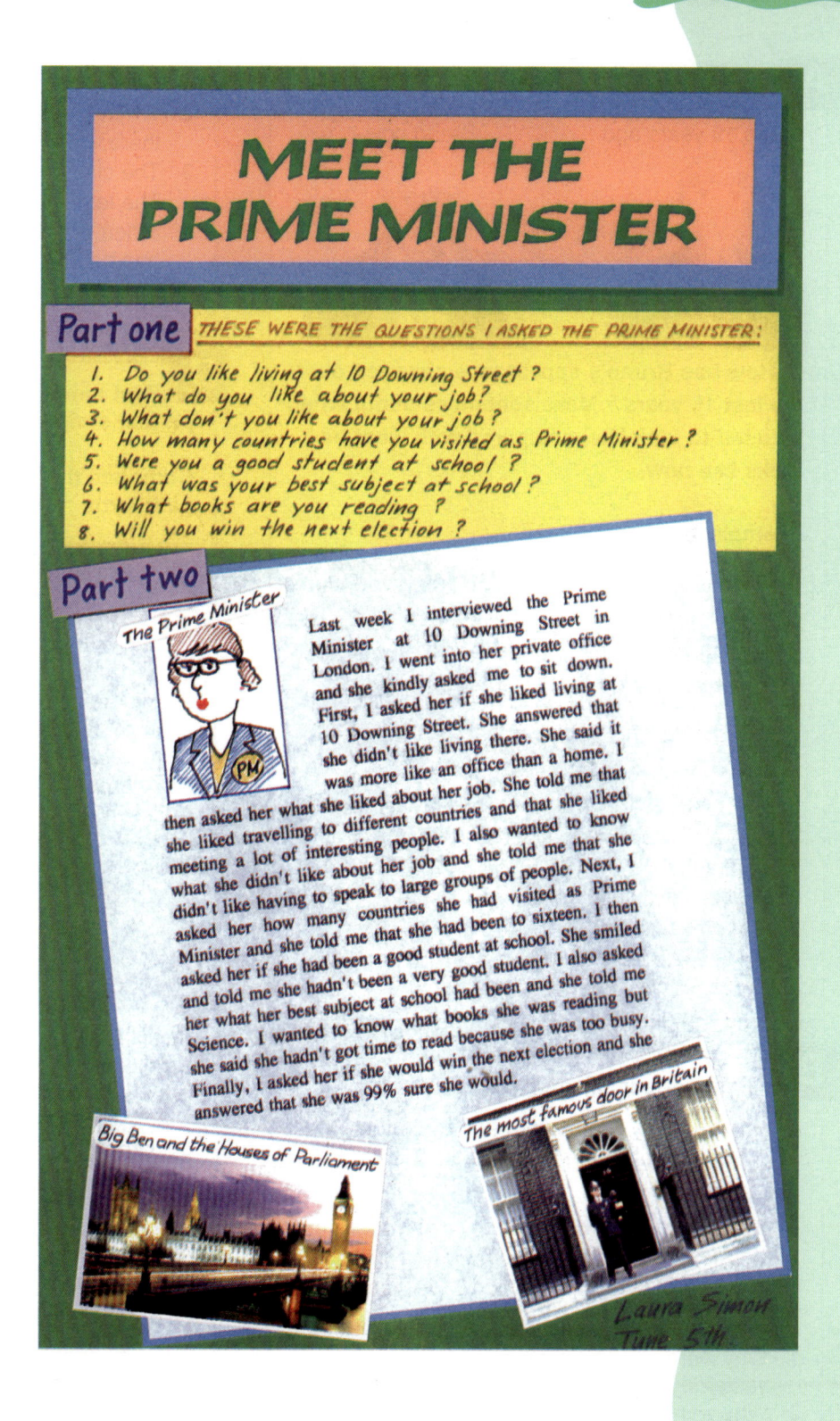

Laura Simon
June 5th.

Consolidation E

50

A Used to (>GR E1)

Bruno 15 years ago   Bruno now

(i) How has Bruno's appearance changed over the last 15 years ? Make sentences about what he used to look like, compared with what he looks like now.

Example
He didn't use to wear glasses, but he does now.

(ii) What did you use to be like when you were a small child ? Make some true sentences. Use some of the words in the box to help you.

> (have) a different hair colour/a different hair style (be) shy/naughty   (suck) my thumb
> (cry) a lot (wear) glasses/a brace on my teeth
> (like/love/hate) certain kinds of food

Examples
I used to have curly hair.
I used to wear a brace on my teeth.
I didn't use to like carrots.

B Past perfect simple (>GR E2)

Think of a way to answer each question. Use: Because and the past perfect simple.

Example
Why were you so worried when I saw you yesterday morning ? - Because I'd had some bad news. Or Because I'd lost my wallet.

1 Why were you so happy when I saw you yesterday morning ?
2 Why were you so upset when I saw you yesterday afternoon ?
3 Why were you so hungry when I saw you yesterday evening ?
4 Why were you so frightened when I saw you last night ?

C Past simple and past perfect simple (>GR E2)

Choose the correct form.

1 We waited in the lift until the door opened, then we walked/had walked out into the corridor.
2 When I looked in my bag, my passport wasn't there. Someone stole/ had stolen it.
3 The classroom was empty when I arrived there. The lesson finished/had finished.
4 When the alarm clock went off, I got out of bed and had/had had a shower.
5 I had breakfast when I had/had had a shower.

D Past simple, past continuous and past perfect simple (>GR E2)

Complete the story. Put the verbs into suitable past form.

I____(not/have) a very good morning yesterday. This____(be) what_____(happen). I____ (leave) home at 9 o'clock and____(catch) the bus into town to do some shopping. At about 9.30 I____(just/get) off the bus and I_____(walk) across the street, when a car____(almost/knock) me over. I____(be) really annoyed. The driver of the car____(not/even/stop) to see if I____(be)

After that, I_____(go) to the bank to get some money. I____: (just/put) my card in the machine and I____(wait) for my cash when an alarm bell ____(go) off. Seconds later, three big security guards____(appear) and____(ask) me what I ____(do). It_____(be) really embarrassing.

Then, at about 11 o'clock, I____(just/finish) doing my shopping and I____(walk) to the bus stop when a jogger_____(suddenly/come) round the corner. He_____(not/look) where he____ (go) and he_____(run) straight into me. It____ (be) terrible. He_____(knock) all the shopping bags out of my hands. There____(be) food everywhere, all over the pavement.

94

E Reported statements (>GR E5)

(i) Kevin met a girl at a party last night. He wanted to make himself sound important and interesting to impress the girl. Look at some of the things that he told her. What were his actual words?

Example
He told her that he was a businessman.
'I'm a businessman.'

He told her that he was a businessman. He said he owned three restaurants in London and that he was thinking of opening another one in the United States. He said he was going to New York on business next week and that he would be there for about a week. He told her that he had been to the United States many times before. He said he enjoyed travelling very much. He told her that he had visited Japan last summer and that he could speak fluent Japanese.

(ii) You and your friends met an Australian girl yesterday. Look at some things that she told you. How can you report these things now?

Example
'My name is Kelly and I come from Sydney.'
She told us her name was Kelly and that she came from Sydney.

'My name is Kelly and I come from Sydney. I'm on holiday at the moment. I arrived in this country last week. I haven't been here before. I like it here very much. I'm a student in Sydney, but I don't like school very much. I'm leaving next summer. I hope to find a job. I've got an older brother. He's an actor in an Australian TV soap opera.'

F Say, tell (>GR E3)

Complete the sentences using the correct form of say or tell.

1 I____my parents that I would be late last night.
2 I____that I would be late last night.
3 Did Marco____where he was going yesterday?
4 Did Marco____you where he was going yesterday?

When do we use *say* and when do we use *tell*? Write two more sentences with *say* and *two* more with *tell*.

G Reported questions (>GR E5)

(i) Francis had an interview for a Saturday job in a supermarket last week. Read what he says about the interview. What were the actual questions that the manager of the supermarket, Mrs Hall, asked him?

Mrs Hall started by asking how old I was, where I lived, what I was studying at college, if I had finished my course at college and if I'd had any part-time jobs before. Then she wanted to know if I had any brothers or sisters, what my hobbies were and what I liked doing in my free time. Then, finally, she asked me if I wanted the job. When I said that I did, she asked me if I could start next Saturday!

(ii) Which question would you ask to which person?

1 'Is it all right to feed the elephants?'
2 'What time is the next bus to London?'
3 'Do I have to take three tablets a day?'
4 'Can you repair my shoes today?'
5 'Have you got any books on James Dean?'
6 'When do you want us to finish the homework?'

| a doctor | a shoe repairer | a bus driver a teacher | a bookseller | a zoo keeper |

Report the questions: I asked the...

1 *I asked the zoo keeper if it was all right to feed the elephants.*

Pronunciation section

Lesson 1: vowel sounds /ɑː/, /eə/, /eɪ/, /aɪ/

● How do we say these sounds? Listen and repeat with the words.

1 /ɑː/ 2 /eə/ 3 /eɪ/ 4 /aɪ/
dark   fair   grey   eyes

● Now write the words in the correct group - 1, 2, 3 or 4.

age hair white glasses straight
quite moustache wears wavy height

Lesson 2: *made of, used for*

● How do we say *made of* and *used for* in the examples below?

1 It's made of glass.
2 Is it made of wood?
3 It's used for writing.
4 Is it used for cutting?

Work with a classmate. Student A – Choose an object from the box below and describe it to your partner. Student B – Guess the object.

Example
A: *It's made of wood. It's used for sitting on.*
B: *Chair*

| dictionary suitcase ~~chair~~ dishwasher ice |
| belt notebook bus calculator telephone |

Lesson 4: adjectives

● Copy the chart. Now listen to the adjectives and write them in the correct column.

two-syllable	three-syllable

● Now look at the adjectives and identify the stressed syllable.

ambitious bad-tempered boring friendly
funny hard-working honest insincere
jealous lazy polite

● Listen and repeat.

Lesson 11: Stress and intonation in questions

● Does the intonation go up or down at the end of these two questions? Listen.

1 Are you going out tonight?
2 Where do you live?

● Listen to eight more questions and mark ↗ or ↘ for the intonation.

Example
1 ↗

● Now listen again and repeat.

Lesson 14: vowel sounds /ʌ/, /ɑː/, /æ/

● How do we say these sounds? Listen and repeat with the words.

1 /ʌ/   2 /ɑː/   3 /æ/
cut   card   cat

● How do we say these words? Write the words in the correct group - 1, 2 or 3.

club can't manners nothing must artist
married lucky heart catch money plan
start aren't had

● Now listen and check.

Lesson 16: *was, were*

● How do we say *was* and *were*? Listen to the examples below. Which one is different in each group? Can you find a rule?

1 She was having a bath. 2 What were you writing?
  Was he watching TV?   Were they going by car?
  Yes, he was.   No, they weren't.

● Underline all the weak forms of *was* (/wəz/) and *were* (/wə(r)/) in the dialogue below.

A: What were you doing at half past eight?
B: I was having dinner.
A: Were you still eating at nine?
B: No, I wasn't. I was leaving the house.
A: Oh, really. Where were you going?
B: I was going to the cinema.

● Listen and check. Now read the dialogue with your partner.

Pronunciation section

Lesson 21: silent letters

● All these words have silent letters. Read the words and underline the letters which are silent.

Example
b<u>u</u>ild

business   climb   should   honest   palm   know
would   write   flight   comb   right   knock

● 📼 Now listen and check.

Lesson 22: rhythm and stress in the present perfect continuous

● Look at the questions below and mark the stress for 2-4.

1 How long have you been learning English?
2 How long have you been living here?
3 How long have you been studying at this school?
4 How long have you been sitting here?

● 📼 Listen and repeat.

● Now ask your partner the questions.

Lesson 24: intonation in offers with *I'll*

● 📼 Listen to these offers. Mark the main stress. Does the intonation go up or down?

1 I'll open the door.
2 I'll make the coffee.

● 📼 Listen to these sentences. Which one is an offer - a or b?

Example
1 a

● Work with your partner. Make offers for the following situations.

| It's hot.   I can't do my homework.   I'm hungry. |
| I haven't got any money. |
| I've got a headache.   I've forgotten my pen. |

Lesson 31: the sound /ʃ/

● The sound /ʃ/ can be spelt in different ways. Underline all the /ʃ/ sounds in these sentences.

1 Short conversations help your English pronunciation.
2 She should ask for permission at the station.
3 The politician was at the official reception.
4 There's a special section in the dictionary.

● 📼 Listen and check. You should have fourteen /ʃ/ sounds. Listen again and repeat.

Lesson 36: pronunciation of *'d*

● 📼 How do we say *'d*? Listen and repeat these sentences.

1 I'd close the door.
2 You'd open the window.
3 He'd phone the police.
4 She'd go down the stairs.

● 📼 Listen to these eight sentences. Which ones use *'d*?

Example
1 Yes

Lesson 37: rhythm and stress in second conditional questions

● 📼 How do we say *would you* in questions? Listen and repeat.

● Read these questions and mark the stress.

1 What would you do if you had a million pounds?
2 Where would you go if you won a free holiday?
3 What places would you visit if you went to London?
4 What would you say if you met your favourite pop star?

● 📼 Listen and repeat. Now ask your partner the questions.

Pronunciation section

Lesson 42: *Used to*

● ▣ How do we say *used to*, *didn't use to*, *never used to*? Listen and repeat.

1 I used to be shy.
2 I didn't use to like school.
3 I never used to eat sweets.

● Copy and complete the chart below. Compare your answers with your partner. How many of your answers are the same?

Example
Student A: I didn't use to be shy.
Student B: I didn't use to be shy. We're the same.

	✓ used to	✗ didn't use to	✗✗✗ never used to
be shy like school eat sweets go to bed early bite my nails have long hair			

Lesson 44: sounds /dʒ/, /j/, /ʌ/

● ▣ How do we say these sounds? Listen and repeat.

1 /dʒ/   2 /j/   3 /ʌ/
   jump   young   under

● How do we say these words? Write the words in the correct group - 1, 2 or 3.

yellow   jealous   usual   umbrella   just   upstairs
year   jogging   ugly   uniform   jeans unlucky

● ▣ Now listen and check.

Pronunciation of word endings

1 Pronunciation: -s/-es

The ending *-s/-es* has three different pronunciations:

-s/-es is pronounced / ɪz / after the sounds
/ tʃ /, / ʃ /, / s /, / z /, / dʒ / and /ʒ/.

watches / tʃɪz /   dishes / ʃɪz /   Alice's / sɪz /
Liz's / zɪz /   fridges / dʒɪz / garages / ʒɪz /

-s/-es is pronounced / s / after unvoiced sounds
(except / tʃ /, / ʃ /, / s /).

stops / ps /   books / ks /   Bert's / ts /

-s/-es is pronounced / z / after voiced sounds
(except / z /, / dʒ /, / ʒ /).

beds / dz /   opens / nz /   Sam's / mz /
goes / əʊz /   lives / vz /   plays / eɪz /
Jenny's / ɪz / cars / ɑz /   Carla's / əz /

2 Pronunciation: -ed

The ending *-ed* has three different pronunciations:

-ed is pronounced / ɪd / after the sounds / t / and / d /.

started / tɪd /   ended / dɪd /

-ed is pronounced / t / after unvoiced sounds (except / t /).

stopped / pt /   looked / kt /   finished / ʃt /
watched / tʃt / danced / st /

-ed is pronounced / d / after voiced sounds (except / d /).

opened / nd /   lived / vd /   stayed / eɪd /
carried / ɪd /   showed / əʊd /   used / zd /
pulled / ld /   remembered / ə(r)d /

Student A activities

Lesson 17 Activity C

Ask your classmate the questions. Check his/her answers.

1 What was Larry doing when the phone rang? (He was running a bath.)
2 What did he do then? (He went to answer it and forgot all about his bath.)
3 What was Larry doing when he dropped his bag? (He was running for the bus.)
4 What did he do then? (He missed the bus and was late for school.)
5 What was Larry doing when he collided with another player? (He was playing basketball.)
6 What did he do then? (He had to have first aid and couldn't play anymore.)

Lesson 27 Activity F

Your classmate is going camping. You are worried about this. Ask your classmate the questions. Check his/her answers.

1 What if it rains all the time? (If it rains all the time, I'll go to a hotel.)
2 What if you can't find a camp site? (If I can't find a camp site, I'll camp in a field.)
3 What if there is a bull in the field? (If there's a bull in the field, I'll climb a tree.)
4 What if the farmer is angry? (If the farmer is angry, I'll give him some money.)
5 What if there are a lot of insects? (If there are a lot of insects, I'll buy a spray.)

Lesson 32 Activity C

1 What is a baker?
a a thing which is used for baking bread
b a place where bread is baked
c a person who bakes bread

2 What is a shoplifter?
a a machine which is used for knocking down buildings
b a person who steals something from a shop
c a person who opens a new shop

3 What is a spade?
a a tool which is used for cutting down trees
b a place where horseshoes are made
c a tool which is used for digging holes in the ground

4 What is a slowcoach?
a a person who is very slow
b a person who lives in an old house
c a bus which is used for traveling long distances

Answers: 1c 2b 3c 4a

Lesson 36 Activity C

Read the situations and ask the questions to your classmate. Write down his/her answers.
1 You are walking alone on a beach when you see someone in the water. This person is calling out for help. What would you do?
a Would you go into the sea and try to rescue the person?
b Would you try to find some other people to help?
2 You are walking in the forest when you meet a bear. The bear begins to run towards you. What would you do?
a Would you climb a tree?
b Would you lie on the ground and not move?
3 Your plane has crashed high in the mountains. You are hundreds of kilometers from civilization. What would you do?
a Would you stay close to the plane?
b Would you try to climb down the mountain?
4 You are lost in a snow storm. You don't know in which direction to walk. What would you do?
a Would you dig a hole and sit in it until it stops snowing?
b Would you carry on walking?

Then tell your classmate the correct answers:

1 - **b** It's best to try to find some other people to help. It can be very dangerous to try to rescue someone on your own.
2 - **b** It's best to lie on the ground and not move. The bear will think you are dead. Bears can climb trees.
3 - **a** It's best to stay close to the plane. Rescuers have got a much better chance of finding the plane than one person on a mountain.
4 - **a** It's best to dig a hole and sit in it until it stops snowing. That's what an Eskimo would do.

Lesson 43 Activity D

You saw your classmate speaking to his/her mother in the street yesterday. Ask your classmate these questions. Find out why he/she said these things.

1 Why did you say 'I'm sorry.'?
2 Why did you say 'I'm really tired.'?
3 Why did you say 'Thanks very much.'?
4 Why did you say 'I'm really depressed.'?
5 Why did you say 'Let's get a taxi.'?

Then change roles.

Your classmate saw you speaking to your mother in the street yesterday. Answer your classmate's questions. Tell him/her why you said the things.

Because she'd lost her comb.
Because I'd seen the film.
Because we hadn't brought an umbrella.
Because I'd forgotten to post an important letter.
Because I hadn't eaten anything all day.

Tapescripts

01 Lesson 1 Activity A
Hello, my name's Mick Malone. I'm a private investigator and I live and work in London. It's 5pm on Friday October 5th and I'm working on the case of a missing person - a young man called Peter Cooper.

02 Lesson 1 Activity B
1 He's quite short and well built. He's got very short, fair hair and brown eyes. He's got freckles.
2 He's tall and well built. He's got quite long, curly hair and blue eyes. He wears glasses.
3 He's quite tall and slim. He's got long, dark hair and blue eyes. He wears glasses.
4 He's short and quite slim. He's got straight, fair hair and green eyes. He's got freckles.

03 Lesson 1 Activity C
Mick: Hello? Mrs Cooper? This is Mick Malone speaking.
Mrs Cooper: Oh, hello, Mr Malone. Thank you very much for phoning.
Mick: Is your son still missing, Mrs Cooper?
Mrs Cooper: Yes, he is. And we're so worried, Mr Malone. Please help us to find him.
Mick: Of course. Can you give me some information about your son, Mrs Cooper. His first name's Peter, isn't it?
Mrs Cooper: That's right, but his friends call him Pete.
Mick: What does Peter look like?
Mrs Cooper: Well, he's quite tall and slim and he's got long, dark hair.
Mick: What about the colour of his eyes?
Mrs Cooper: He's got blue eyes.
Mick: Does he wear glasses?
Mrs Cooper: Yes, he does, but not all the time.
Mick: Can you tell me anything else, Mrs Cooper - anything that will help me find Peter?
Mrs Cooper: Well, we know Peter loves music and he likes going to clubs to listen to bands.
Mick: Do you know the names of the clubs he likes going to?
Mrs Cooper: No, I'm afraid I don't.
Mick: Well, that's all for now, Mrs Cooper. Try not to worry too much. I'll phone you again tomorrow. Goodbye.
Mrs Cooper: Thank you, Mr Malone. Goodbye.

04 Lesson 2 Activity A
1 It's a machine. It's made of metal and plastic. It's used for drying hair.
2 It's long, flat and thin. It's made of metal and it's got a handle. It's a tool used for cutting things.
3 It's rectangular. It's made of leather, plastic or metal. It's used for carrying books and papers.
4 It's round and it's made of metal and glass. It's a thing used for showing direction.
5 It's long, round and thin. It's made of metal and glass. It's used for measuring temperature.

05 Lesson 2 Activity D
A: Is there one in this room?
B: No, there isn't.
C: Do you normally find it outside?
B: Yes, you do.
D: Is it a machine?
B: Yes, it is.
C: Is it big?
B: Yes, quite big.
A: Is it made of metal?
B: Metal, rubber, plastic and glass.
A: Oh, really? I see. Mmm. Has it got wheels?
B: Yes, it has.
C: Four wheels?
B: Yes.
D: Ah, I know! And is it used for getting from one place to another?
B: That's right...

06 Lesson 3 Activity B
I know quite a few people in this street. Can you see the old woman sitting at the newspaper stand? Her name's Meg and she sells newspapers in the street to earn money. She sees a lot of people every day. Perhaps she has seen Peter. And can you see the man coming out of the takeaway? His name's Chris and he drives a taxi. Chris meets a lot of people every day. Perhaps he can help me. And can you see the two young people kneeling outside a cafe? I know them too. Their names are Cathy and Tony. They play music in the street every day to earn money. They like going to clubs in the evening to listen to bands, just like Peter. Perhaps they can help me find him.

07 Lesson 3 Activity C
Mick: Hello Meg.
Meg: Oh, hello Mick. How are things?
Mick: Oh, not bad, thanks.
Meg: Do you want a paper, Mick? I've still got a few left.
Mick: No, thanks, Meg. I'm looking for a boy. He's missing and his parents want me to find him. This is his photo.
Meg: Wait a minute. Let me put on my glasses. Now, let's see. No, I haven't seen him.
Mick: Are you sure?
Meg: Yes, I'm quite sure.
Mick: Okay, Meg. Thanks anyway. See you.
Meg: Yes, bye Mick. Good luck.
Mick: Hi Chris.
Chris: Oh, hi Mick. How are you?
Mick: Fine, thanks. What about you?
Chris: Very well, thank you.
Mick: Chris. I'm looking for this boy. You haven't seen him, have you? This is his photo.
Chris: Let's see. No, sorry, I haven't. But I'll keep an eye out for him.
Mick: Thanks, Chris. Bye.
Mick: Hi Cathy. Hi Tony. How are you?
Cathy: Hi Mick. Fine, thanks. What about you?
Mike: Oh, fine. Cathy, I need some help. I'm looking for this boy. He's really into music and likes going to clubs. You haven't seen him, have you?
Cathy: No, I don't think so. What about you, Tony?
Tony: Let's have a look. Umm. Maybe. We were at the Star Club last night and I think I saw someone like this boy there.

08 Lesson 3 Activity D
It's 9.15pm on Friday, October 5th and I'm at the Star Club in London. I'm with Cathy and her boyfriend Tony. We're looking for Peter Cooper. The club isn't open yet and the other four people you can see work here. I'm going to speak to them. Perhaps they can help me find Peter.

09 Lesson 3 Activity F
A
Mick: Hello. My name's Mick Malone. I'm a private investigator and I'm looking for a missing boy. This is the boy's photograph.
Technician: Let me see. Ah, yes. He's the one who never stops dancing. I often see him here.
B
Mick: What about you? Do you know him?
Cloakroom attendant: Yes. He usually wears a denim jacket and a brightly-coloured T-shirt.
C
Doorman: Let me have a look. Yes, I know him. He's always here early. He's usually the first in the queue when I open the doors at ten o'clock.
D
Barmaid: Can I have a look? Yes, I've seen him here. He usually drinks orange juice with lots of mineral water.

10 Lesson 4 Activity C
1
Tina: Hi. How are you today?
Paul: Oh, er, fine, er, thanks.
Tina: And what can I get you today?
Paul: Oh, er, let's see, er, I'd like a pizza, please.
Tina: And would you like anything to drink?
Paul: Umm, yes, er, a coke.
Tina: A coke and a pizza. Great. That'll be £3.80, please.
Paul: Oh, er, right. Here you are. Er, Tina, are you, er, are you...
Tina: Sorry?
Paul: Are you, er, it's, er, a very nice day today, isn't it?
Tina: Yes, it is, Paul.
Paul: Yes, well, er, goodbye. See you tomorrow then.
Tina: Yes, bye. See you. Hi. How are you today?
Boy: Fine, thanks.
2
Mrs Palmer: Now don't put too much salad in these hamburgers. Tomatoes are very expensive at the moment, you know. I think a half a tomato is plenty.
Kevin: Oh, so do I, Mrs Palmer. Plenty. I'll write that down in my notebook - just half a tomato per hamburger. Thank you. I'll remember that.
Mrs Palmer: What's that notebook for, Kevin?
Kevin: Oh, it's where I write important things about my work.
Mrs Palmer: Umm, that's a very good idea.

Tapescripts

It's nice to see someone taking his job seriously. Oh, yes, and where's Melanie? Why isn't she here helping you?
Kevin: Melanie? Oh, she went to get something from the food store about 45 minutes ago.
Mrs Palmer: What! 45 minutes ago! That's terrible.
Kevin: Yes, and we're so busy too.

3
Rupert: Well, what do you think of my hair?
Andy: Sorry? What did you say?
Rupert: My hair. I had it cut yesterday. Don't you think it looks really great?
Andy: Oh, it's okay.
Rupert: What's the matter with you, Andy? What are you so miserable for? You're not still in love with Tina, are you?
Andy: That's none of your business, Rupert. Leave me alone.
Rupert: Okay, okay. No need to get angry...

4
Sabir: What are you doing in here?
Melanie: Shh! Don't say anything. I'm a tin of tomatoes.
Sabir: You're crazy, Melanie. What are you doing? Are you hiding from Mrs Palmer?
Melanie: That's right. It's really strange but she always wants me to do some work.
Sabir: Well, what about doing some work? We're very busy out there, you know and we all have to work even harder if you're not around.
Melanie: Okay, Sabir. Point taken. Take me to a pizza.

11 Lesson 5 Activity E
Compere: Good Evening and welcome to *What's My Job?* - the quiz game where we try to find out what jobs people do. First, let's welcome our panel - the people who are going to ask the questions. Tonight we have with us actor, Tom Dillon; journalist, Ursula Gray; disc jockey, Riff Greenaway and singer, Martha Vandella. Now the rules of the game are very simple. The panel have twenty questions and the guests can only answer 'Yes' or 'No'. And remember, panel, if you think you know the answer, press your buzzer! Now, here is our first guest this evening. Good evening.
Guest: Good evening.
Compere: All right, now, Tom is going to start. Tom.
Tom: Yes, good evening: Right, er... Can I ask, do you wear a uniform in your job?
Guest: No, not a uniform.
Tom: Not a uniform ... but do you wear special clothes?
Guesf: Yes, I do.
Tom: Do you work outside or inside?
Compere: That's two questions, Tom.
Tom: Oh, I'm sorry. Urn, do you work outside?
Guest: Sometimes, yes.
Compere: Right, thank you, Tom, and now Ursula.
Ursula: When you say you wear special clothes, are they very expensive clothes?
Guest: Yes!
Ursula: I see. Is your job well-paid?
Guest: Oh, yes, very well paid.
Ursula: Do you work unusual hours
Guest: Yes, sometimes.
Compere: Thank you, Ursula, and now Riff.
Riff: Hi there.
Guest: Hello.
Riff: Do you travel in your work?
Guest: Yes, I do.
Riff: Do you work at night?
Guest: Sometimes, yes.
Riff: Do you work in a lot of different places?
Guest: Yes.
Compere: Thanks, Riff. And now it's Martha.
Martha: Do you have to have special qualifications or training to do your job?
Guest: Special training, yes.
Martha: Do you work with other people?
Guest: Yes, I do.
Martha: Ah ... do you work with photographers?
Guesf: Yes.
Martha: Oh, I know ...

12 Lesson 6 Activity B
Officer: Passports, please. Right, thank you.
Harry: Thank you.
Officer: Is this your passport?
Bert: Er, yes, it is.
Officer: Umm. I'd like to ask you a few questions, sir.
Bert: Of course. Go ahead.
Officer: Just a minute. I'll just find your details on the computer. Right, here we are. What's your name?
Bert: Tom Barrymore.
Officer: And where were you born, Mr Barrymore?
Bert: In Glasgow, Scotland.
Officer: And then your family moved to Oxford?
Bert: That's right.
Officer: How old were you when you moved to Oxford, Mr Barrymore?
Bert: How old was I?
Officer: Yes.
Bert: Well, that's a long time ago. Let's think. Er, I was, er, I was ten.
Officer: And how long did you live in Oxford?
Bert: For, er, for three years.
Officer: Three years?
Bert: No, no, for four years. That's right, four years.
Officer: And where do you live now?
Bert: I live in Brighton.
Officer: And how long have you lived in Brighton?
Bert: I've lived there since 1991.
Officer: And where do you work, Mr Barrymore?
Bert: I work for Mario's Restaurant. I'm a waiter.
Announcement: Final call for Mr Bert Dobbs and Mr Harry Woods, passengers on the Malaga flight. Please go immediately to Gate 29.
Harry: Hurry! That's us, Bert.
Bert: Shhh!
Officer: How long have you worked for Mario's, Mr Barrymore?
Bert: Since last April.
Officer: Good. Well, I think that's all, Mr Barrymore.
Bert: Right. Thank you very much. Goodbye.
Harry: Come on Bert, er, Bill. We've got to hurry.
Officer: Oh, just one more question, Mr Barrymore. How long have you been married?
Bert: Married? Er, I've been married for, er, for, er... Well, I've been married for a long time.
Officer: Yes. But how many years?
Bert: Er, that's funny, I can't remember.
Officer: You can't remember?
Bert: No. Six years? Twelve?
Officer: You've been married for nine years.
Bert: Oh, really? Fancy me forgetting that.
Officer: And how many children have you got?
Bert: Children? Er, er, one? Two?
Officer: You can't remember how many children you've got?
Bert: No.
Officer: I think you'd better come with me, sir.
Bert: But what about my plane?
Officer: This way, please.
Harry: Bye, Bert.
Bert: Bye, Harry. Have a nice holiday.

13 Lesson 11 Activities A and B
Ron Clay: Hello. Ron Clay speaking.
Kay Sloane: Oh, hello, Mr. Clay. It's me, Kay Sloane.
Ron Clay: Miss Sloane. Hello, I've been waiting for your call.
Kay Sloane: I've arranged everything, Mr. Clay. I'm coming to London tomorrow.
Ron Clay: Tomorrow. Good.
Kay Sloane: I'm coming by train. I'm leaving Manchester at nine thirty in the evening.
Ron Clay: Right.
Kay Sloane: What about the money, Mr. Clay?
Ron Clay: Don't worry, Miss Sloane, I've arranged to get the money from my bank here in London. I'm going there tomorrow afternoon.
Kay Sloane: All right. So, where shall we meet?
Ron Clay: Do you know the Calypso Club?
Kay Sloane: In Wardour Street? Yes.
Ron Clay: Well, I own the club. Why don't we meet there?
Kay Sloane: All right.
Ron Clay: Fine. What time?
Kay Sloane: What time does the club close?
Ron Clay: Oh, around six in the morning.
Kay Sloane: Okay, I'll be there at five.
Ron Clay: Five. All right. Five am at the Calypso.
Kay Sloane: I'll be there, Mr. Clay.
Ron Clay: Right. Oh, and don't forget to bring the diamonds, Miss Sloane.
Kay Sloane: Don't worry, Mr. Clay. I won't forget. Goodbye.
Ron Clay: Goodbye.

14 Lesson 13 Activity A
May: 770 756
Larry: Hello May. It's Larry,
May: Oh, hi Larry. How are you?
Larry: I'm very well, thanks. And you?

Tapescripts

May: Fine, thank you.
Larry: Er... May, I was wondering. Would you like to go to a disco this evening?
May: I'm afraid I can't this evening, Larry, I have to stay in and study tonight. I've got an exam at college tomorrow.
Larry: Oh, I see. Would you like to go tomorrow evening, then?
May: I'm sorry, but I can't tomorrow, either. I'm going to the cinema with my friend Jackie tomorrow. We're going to see the new Arnold Schwarzenegger film. Have you seen it?
Larry: Yes, I have. It's great.
May: Listen, Larry, What are you doing this Saturday evening?
Larry: Um. This Saturday? Nothing special.
May: Well, let's go to a disco then.
Larry: Okay.
May: So where shall we meet?
Larry: Why don't we meet at your place?
May: All right. What time?
Larry: Eight thirty?
May: Fine, I'll see you here at eight thirty on Saturday, then.
Larry: Yes, see you then. Oh, and good luck in the exam tomorrow.
May: Thanks Larry.
Larry: Bye May.
May: Bye.

15 Lesson 15 Activity B
Speaker 1: A teenaged boy was given six months community service today for credit card fraud and stealing. A report now from Alex McHiggins.

Alex McHiggins: It all began when Karl Thomas and his friends started collecting computer games. As each game costs anything between forty and a hundred pounds, Karl couldn't keep up, the court heard today.

He took his father's credit card and bought a game from a local computer game store. Because Karl is tall and looks older than sixteen, the shop assistant believed it was the boy's own card. Soon he was using the card regularly. Every week he bought one or two games. His father didn't notice what was going on, so Karl started using the card to buy other things. He bought CDs, a new watch, clothes and a new pair of trainers. When the bill came to over two thousand pounds for just one month, his father realised what was happening and stopped him from using the card.

But that didn't stop Karl's shopping! Now instead of using his father's credit card, he started stealing money from other pupils at his school, Parkway High. This continued until one day his teacher caught him stealing money from her handbag. It was then that the school called in the police.

After the court hearing today, Karl, 16, said he was ashamed and very sorry, but that once he started spending, he just couldn't stop. 'I became a "shopping addict", he said, I couldn't live without all the new things.'

16 Lesson 16 Activity B
It was 11.45 at night and I was standing outside the Calypso Club. It was raining hard and I was getting wet, very wet. Suddenly, a large, black car came round the corner and stopped in front of the club. The doorman opened the car door and a man got out. He was big, very big. He was the man I was waiting for.

It was five o'clock in the morning. I was still standing outside the Calypso Club. It was getting light and I was getting tired, very tired. Suddenly, a white taxi came round the corner and stopped in front of the club. The doorman opened the car door and a woman got out. She was beautiful, very beautiful. She was the woman I was waiting for.

17 Lesson 16 Activity D
I waited outside for a few more minutes and then I went into the club. Kay Sloane and Ron Clay were standing in a small room at the back of the club. Sloane was wearing a bright red dress and Clay was wearing a dark blue suit. Clay was taking money out of his briefcase and Sloane was showing him some diamonds. They were the diamonds I was looking for.

18 Lesson 16 Activity E
There were a lot of other people in the club. Three people were sitting at a table. The woman was wearing a long white dress. The man sitting next to her was smoking a cigar and was looking angry. The man on the other side of the table was looking at the woman. She was smiling at him. They were all drinking wine. The barman was drying glasses behind the bar. Two young women were sitting next to each other at the bar. One of the women was wearing a short, black dress and the other woman was wearing a green suit. They were talking to each other. Two men were standing next to them. The man on the left was wearing a light grey suit. The man on the right was looking at a magazine. Three musicians were playing on a small stage. One was singing and playing the guitar and the other two were playing the drums and keyboard. A waitress was coming out of the kitchen. She was carrying an empty tray. A waiter was going into the small room where Kay Sloane and Ron Clay were. He was carrying a bottle of champagne and two glasses on a tray.

19 Lesson 17 Activity B
Male 1: How did you get that black eye, Larry?
Larry: Oh, I had a terrible day yesterday. Everything went wrong for me. In the morning I was running for the bus...
Female: Late as usual.
Larry: That's right. Well, I was running for the bus when I dropped my bag. There were books, papers, pens all over the floor...
Male 2: Oh, no!
Larry: Anyway, I missed the bus and was late for school.
Male 2: Not for the first time, Larry.
Larry: Yes, but what made it worse was I missed the first ten minutes of a really important examination. I felt nervous going into the examination room, I can tell you.
Male 1: But what about the black eye, Larry?
Larry: Oh yes, the eye. Well, in the afternoon I was playing basketball when I collided with another player.
Female: And got a beautiful black eye.
Larry: That's right. I had to have first aid and couldn't play anymore. I felt angry because it was a very important game.
Male 2: Poor Larry. What a horrible day!
Larry: But that's not the end of the story. In the evening...
Male 1: Oh no, Larry. Not something else...
Larry: I'm laughing now but I wasn't laughing yesterday. No, listen. In the evening I was running a bath - you know, a nice relaxing bath after a hard day - when the telephone rang.
Female: A girl.
Larry: No, no, that's not important. Anyway, I went to answer it and forgot all about my bath.
Male 2: Oh, no!
Larry: By the time I got back there was water all over the floor. My father was there. I felt really embarrassed and my father was furious.
Male 2: I bet he was.
Larry: And do you know what date it was yesterday? Friday the thirteenth!
Female: Oh no! You don't believe in that do you.
Larry: Well, all those unlucky things did happen.
Female: But unlucky things always happen to you, Larry.

20 Lesson 17 Activity D
1 This happened when I was ten. I was swimming in the sea when my shorts fell off in the water. I felt really embarrassed and had to find my shorts and put them on under the water.

2 This happened just a few months ago. I was with a friend of mine in a department store and we were going down in a lift when suddenly it stopped between the third and second floors. I felt really scared and so did Pete, my friend. I had to use the emergency phone to get help.

3 This happened when I was about fifteen. I was running with a friend of mine in a park when a dog attacked me. I felt very angry and shouted at it but it wouldn't go away. In the end I had to walk home.

4 This happened a couple of weeks ago. I was working on a computer when I pressed the wrong button. I felt very depressed because I lost the whole document and had to do all the work again.

21 Lesson 22 Activities A and B
I live in London now but I wasn't born here. I was born in Dublin in Ireland but I moved to London from Ireland in 1990. I've been living here ever since and I like

Tapescripts

London a lot. I always wanted to be an investigator even when I was a little boy in Ireland. I got my licence in 1992 two years after I came to London and I have been working as a private investigator since then. The only problem with being a private investigator is the money. I earn very little and can't afford to pay rent for both a flat and an office. So, three weeks ago I moved out of the flat I was living in and came to live here in my office in Soho. I like living here very much. There are a lot of advantages, for example, I don't have to get up early in the morning to travel to work and, if I'm not busy, I can always have a sleep on the sofa. When I moved, I brought my goldfish here with me. Breeding goldfish is a new hobby of mine. A friend of mine gave me two goldfish two months ago. I've only been breeding them for two months and I've already got seven. Another thing I like doing in my free time is playing the saxophone. I bought my first sax when I was fourteen and I've been playing it ever since. I'm not great but I think I make a nice sound. The thing I'm really not good at is driving. I got a provisional driving licence in 1991 and I've been taking driving lessons ever since, but I still haven't passed my test.

22 Lesson 23 Activities A, B and C

Announcer It's 2 o'clock and you're listening to Kate Kelly on Radio 2VR. And now for the weather in the 2VR area this coming weekend. After a cloudy start, Saturday will be sunny and warm, with maximum temperatures of 23 to 24 degrees. The fine weather will continue on Sunday, with temperatures increasing to a maximum of 25 degrees...
Sabir: Did you hear that? The forecast is really good for the weekend. What are you doing, Melanie? Have you got any plans?
Melanie: No, I'm not doing anything special. Maybe I'll go to the beach tomorrow.
Sabir: I've got an idea. Why don't we have a barbecue this weekend?
Kevin: Mmm. That's not a bad idea, Sabir.
Melanie: It's a great idea!
Sabir: So, when shall we have the barbecue?
Melanie: How about having it tomorrow afternoon?
Kevin: Oh, no. I'm working tomorrow afternoon.
Melanie: Well, let's have it on Sunday afternoon, then.
Sabir: Sunday afternoon is fine with me.
Kevin: Yes, all right.
Sabir: Who shall we invite?
Melanie: Let's invite people from work - Tina, Rupert and Andy.
Sabir: Okay. Who else?
Kevin: Why don't we invite Mrs Palmer? I'm sure she'd enjoy it.
Melanie: Oh, no, Kevin! What a terrible idea! Inviting the boss to a barbecue!

23 Lesson 23 Activity D

1
Sabir: How many people shall we invite?
Melanie: Let's invite about ten.

2
Sabir: Where shall we have the barbecue?
Kevin: Why don't we have it out in the country?
3
Sabir: What shall we have to eat?
Melanie: How about having hamburgers, kebabs and salad?
4
Sabir: What shall we have to drink?
Kevin: Let's have Coke and beer.
5
Sabir: When shall we buy the food and drink?
Melanie: Why don't we buy it tomorrow?

24 Lesson 24 Activities A and B

1
Girl: I'll help you carry those things, Andy.
Andy: No, it's okay. I can manage, thanks.
Girl: Are you all right?
Andy: Yes, I'm fine. Just leave me alone, will you?
Girl: All right, all right. I was only trying to help.
2
Girl: Hi Sabir. You look busy. Would you like some help?
Sabir: Oh, yes. That would be great.
Girl: Shall I collect some more wood for the fire? There isn't much left.
Sabir: Oh, yes, thanks. Good idea.
3
Paul: Oh, er, hello there.
Tina: Hi there. How are you?
Paul: I'm, er, fine, thanks. Er, lovely day, isn't it?
Tina: Very nice, yes.
Paul: Would you like, er... would you like me, er...
Tina: Yes?
Paul: Would you like me to do something?
Tina: Oh, if you want to, yes, thanks.
Paul: Er, I'll help you prepare the salad if you like.
Tina: No, it's all right. I've almost finished it, thanks.
Paul: Shall I cut the bread, then?
Tina: Oh, yes please, thanks.
4
Girl: Would you like a kebab, Rupert? They're delicious.
Rupert: Oh, not just now, thanks. I'm fine, thank you. They do look very good though. Perhaps I'll have one later on.
5
Melanie: Hi Kevin. Hi Jackie.
Kevin: Hi, Melanie.
Girl: Hello. How are you?
Melanie: Fine, thanks. Would you like some beer?
Kevin: Oh, yes, please.
Girl: No thanks, Melanie. I'm drinking Coke.
Melanie: Would you like me to get you some more Coke?
Girl: No, I'm fine at the moment, thanks.

25 Lesson 25 Activity C

When we first had the TV, nobody was really interested in it. You see we'd never had a TV before. We live on a farm and my mum and dad thought it would be better if we didn't watch TV. We did lots of other things instead. I went horse riding

two or three evenings a week, played tennis once a week and basketball twice a week. I went swimming once or twice a week, and spent a lot of time reading. I also listened to the radio quite a bit. My friends sometimes laughed at me because they thought it was strange that we didn't have a TV.
Anyway, after a couple of days of just watching anything, my dad bought a TV guide magazine. We used the guide to try to choose the programmes we wanted to watch, but it caused a lot of arguments because we each wanted to watch something different. Often we couldn't decide what to watch, so we ended up not watching anything at all! I wasn't very happy when the TV was taken away again after a month, but now life is just as it was before. I've started watching some programmes at my friend's house. My father still thinks it's better not to have a TV. He says that when we had one, I watched too many stupid programmes. I thought it was quite good, but perhaps after more than a month, I would become bored with it.

26 Lesson 27 Activities A and B
Part One
Bert: This is what we'll do. We'll drive down to Cowslip. We won't go in our car. We'll hire a van. Then, when we get to Cowslip, we'll park in a quiet place near Buttercup Farm. Then we'll go and find Red Runner and bring her back to the van.
Harry: Just a minute, Bert! What if somebody sees us?
Bert: Well, if somebody sees us, er..., er..., we'll say we're lost. Right, now, as soon as she's in the van, we'll drive back to London.
Harry: Just a minute, Bert! What if she won't get into the van?
Bert: Umm. Well, if she won't get into the van, we'll push her in. Then, er, let's see, when we get home, we'll phone Red Runner's owners.
Harry: Just a minute, Bert! Where are we going to keep Red Runner?
Bert: Why, in the flat of course.
Harry: In the flat? What if a neighbour hears her?
Bert: Yes, well, if a neighbour hears her, we'll say it's the TV. Right, so we'll phone Red Runner's owners and I'll say, 'We won't give you Red Runner back until you send us £500,000.'
Harry: Just a minute, Bert! How are they going to send us the money? We can't give them our address, can we?
Bert: Umm. You're right, Harry. We can't. Let me think. Umm. I know! This is what we'll do. We'll drive into the country. As soon as we find a quiet place, we'll stop and put Red Runner into a field. Then we'll wait there until it gets dark. And when it's dark, we'll climb a tree.
Harry: Just a minute, Bert! What if we can't climb it?
Bert: Well, that's easy. If we can't climb the tree, we'll hide behind it. Now, as soon as we're in the tree, I'll phone Red Runner's owners and tell them where to bring the money. We'll stay in the tree until

103

Tapescripts

they arrive with the money.
Harry: Just a minute, Bert! What if they see us in the tree?
Bert: See us in the tree? Well, if they see us in the tree, we'll pretend to be birdwatchers.
Harry: Birdwatchers?
Bert: Yes, birdwatchers. Then, when they leave, we'll climb down the tree and pick up the money. Then we'll drive home in the van, and we'll count the money as soon as we get home.
Harry: Just a minute, Bert! What if it's not all there?
Bert: That's easy. If it's not all there, we won't tell them where Red Runner is.

27 Lesson 27 Activities C and D
Part Two
Harry: What if she gets hungry, Bert?
Bert: If she gets hungry, we'll give her some cornflakes.
Harry: Cornflakes, Bert? But what if she doesn't like cornflakes? And what if she needs some exercise?
Bert: Well, if she needs some exercise, we'll ride her around the flat.
Harry: Around the flat, Bert? Ride a horse around the flat? I don't think that's a very good idea. And anyway, I can't ride a horse and nor can you. And, Bert, what if a friend comes round to our flat?
Bert: Ah, yes, well, er, if a friend comes round to our flat, we'll lock Red Runner in the bathroom.
Harry: In the bathroom, Bert? But what if the friend wants to use the bathroom, Bert? Oh, yes, and what if she starts eating the furniture?
Bert: Eating the furniture?
Harry: Yes, Bert.
Bert: Well, er, er, if she starts eating the furniture, we'll tie her to a chair in the middle of the room.
Harry: But what if she starts eating the chair? And what if she starts kicking us?
Bert: Us?
Harry: Yes, Bert.
Bert: Yes, I see what you mean. Umm, umm. Well, er, if she starts kicking us, we'll give her some sugar lumps. Horses love sugar lumps.
Harry: But sugar lumps aren't very good for horses, Bert. What if she gets ill?
Bert: Ill? Oh, dear. Yes. Well, er, if she gets ill, er, we'll have to call a vet.
Harry: But a vet will recognize Red Runner and will call the police.
Bert: Oh, yes. Umm.

28 Lesson 27 Activity E
Part Three
Harry: Bert?
Bert: Yes, Harry.
Harry: You know the £500,000? What if the police have the numbers of the bank notes?
Bert: Yes, well, it'll be too dangerous to spend the money straight away. We'll have to wait.
Harry: Wait, Bert?
Bert: Yes, we'll have to wait two or three years until it's safe to spend the money.
Harry: But how are we going to pay all these bills, Bert, if we have to wait two or three years until it's safe to spend the money?
Bert: Oh, yes, I see what you mean, Harry. Umm. Perhaps kidnapping Red Runner isn't such a great idea after all.

29 Lesson 31 Activities B and C
1
Sister: Oh, Larry. Sorry to wake you up.
Larry: What?
Sister: Do you think I could leave Tabatha with you for five minutes? I've got to go to the chemist's and Dad's in the bath and Mum's under the car.
Larry: Well, er, yes, that's fine.
Sister: Are you sure? I'll only be ten minutes or so.
Larry: No, that's okay. Don't worry.
Sister: Oh, that's great. I'll be back in half an hour - I promise.
2
Father: Oh, Larry. I'm making some soup for lunch but I've got to go out for half an hour. Can you stir it for me until I get back?
Larry: Yes, all right.
Father: Oh, yes, and your mother wants a cup of tea. She's outside mending the car. Bye.
Larry: Bye.
3
Announcer: Good morning: Welcome to Saturday Sport.
Grandfather: Ah, Larry. Can I change channels? *Bird Life in Britain* is on BBC2.
Larry: Oh, but...
Grandfather: It's my favourite programme, you know.
Larry: Oh, right... well... Yes, go ahead.
Grandfather: Thank you, Larry. Today's programme is all about the breeding habits of birds. I'm sure you'll find it interesting too.
4
Belinda: Larry? You know it's Dad's birthday next week.
Larry: Yes?
Belinda: Well, I've got to buy him a present.
Larry: Yes, Belinda?
Belinda: Well, I haven't got enough. Could I borrow some money?
Larry: How much?
Belinda: Five pounds.
Larry: Five pounds!
Belinda: Yes. Please, Larry. I'll pay you back. Honestly.
Larry: Oh, okay. Help yourself.
5
Mrs Badger: Oh, Larry.
Larry: Oh, hello, Mrs Badger.
Mrs Badger: Are you going into town?
Larry: Yes, that's right.
Mrs Badger: Do you think you could do some shopping for me?
Larry: Er... well, er... Certainly, Mrs Badger.
Mrs Badger: Oh, good. You're so kind. You can take my trolley if you like.
Larry: Oh, good. Thanks very much.
6
Mother: Oh, Larry. Are you going into town?
Larry: Yes. Why?
Mother: Well, Belinda wants to buy a present for your father's birthday. Could you take her with you? The car isn't working and I haven't got time to take her.
Larry: Well, I'm meeting some friends and...
Mother: Oh, come on, Larry. You'd like to meet Larry's friends, wouldn't you, Belinda?
Belinda: Yes, Mum.
Larry: Oh, okay.

30 Lesson 31 Activity D
1
Girl: Oh, Camille. Can I borrow your tennis racket tomorrow morning?
Camille: Oh, I'm sorry, but I'm playing tennis myself tomorrow.
Girl: Oh, I see. Well, thanks anyway.
Camille: Perhaps you could ask Jasmine?
Girl: Yes.
2
Young woman: Oh, excuse me.
Woman: Yes.
Young woman: Could I have a look at your magazine?
Woman: Yes, of course. Here you are.
3
Girl: Vince.
Vince: Yes.
Girl: Could you tell me the answer to the second question?
Vince: No, I'm afraid not. I don't know the answer myself.
Girl: Oh.
4
Young man: Oh, Mr Cooper.
Mr Cooper: Yes.
Young man: Do you think I could you use your phone? It's just a local call.
Mr Cooper: Certainly. Please, go ahead.
Young man: Thanks very much.

31 Lesson 33 Activity A
Belinda: Yuk!
Larry: What?
Belinda: You're not wearing that brown sweater to school, are you?
Larry: Yes, I am.
Belinda: Well then, I wouldn't wear that shirt.
Larry: Why not?
Belinda: Because it's blue, Larry. Brown doesn't go with blue: everyone knows, that. I'd wear yellow with that sweater, if I were you.
Larry: Well, you're not me and anyway I haven't got time to talk about this now. I'm late.
Grandfather: Late again, Larry?
Larry: Yes.
Grandfather: No, time for breakfast, I suppose?
Larry: No.
Grandfather: Tut, tut. You should go to bed earlier, Larry. You don't get enough sleep at night. People need eight hours sleep every night.
Larry: That's not the problem, Granddad. I just don't hear my alarm clock in the morning.
Grandfather: You don't need an alarm clock when you sleep enough. Take me, for example, I go to bed at nine and I wake up without an alarm clock. And another thing, Larry, you shouldn't go out without

Tapescripts

having breakfast in the morning. Breakfast is the most important meal of the day, you know. I always have a good breakfast.
Larry: Yes, Granddad.

Larry: Hic... hic. Oh, no. This is really ... hic... embarrassing. Sorry, about this, hic, oh, dear, hic, this is terrible, hic. What do you think I should do? Hic.
May: Why don't you try drinking from the other side of the glass?
Larry: Hic. How? Like this?
May: That's right. Well?
Larry: Hic.
May: Umm. Why don't you try holding your breath for a minute?

32 Lesson 35 Activity E

1 Have you met Paul's older brother, Guido? He's really nice. Everyone likes him. He's very friendly and is always helping people. He's also got a very good sense of humour. He can be really funny sometimes. He's also very good-looking and wears great clothes.

2 Martina never says much. It's sometimes difficult to know what she's thinking. She doesn't make new friends very easily. I think she's a bit shy, actually. She's an excellent chess player. When she leaves school, she hopes to go to university and study computer science.

3 I'm not sure how old Emmy is. I think she's about 17. She's tall and she's got short, blonde hair. She's not exactly unfriendly, but she seems to enjoy her own company. When she leaves school, she wants to do a course at art college. She doesn't show her feelings very easily, especially with people she doesn't know very well.

4 Imran? He's a workaholic! He never stops. He says he wants to be a millionaire before he's thirty. I think he works too hard, actually. I mean, he gets angry very easily. And you never see him laugh or smile. He's 'Mr Perpetual Motion'. He can't sit still for five minutes! He's always on the move. And he finds it really difficult to wait for anything for very long.

33 Lesson 36 Activities A and B

Expert: **1** I'd set off the fire alarm first because the most important thing to do is warn other people in the building.
2 I'd go out in the corridor and try to go downstairs. It's important to try to get out of the building.
3 I'd crawl along the corridor. At head height the air may be full of poisonous gases.
4 I'd go up the stairs to the roof. Never use a lift - the lift shaft can very quickly fill with smoke.
5 I'd open the window and shout for help. You'll probably kill yourself jumping. You're better off in the room.
6 I'd tell someone from the emergency services. They can help this person better than you can.

34 Lesson 37 Activity A

Interviewer: Where do you live, Hanna?
Hanna: I live in London.
Interviewer: Where would you live if you could live anywhere in the world?
Hanna: I'd live in San Francisco.
Interviewer: Why San Francisco?
Hanna: Well, I've been there a couple of times. I think it's a very exciting place and I've got some good friends there.
Interviewer: And who would you meet if you could meet a famous person from the past?
Hanna: Umm, that would be wonderful, let me think... If I could meet somebody from the past, I'd meet Mahatma Gandhi.
Interviewer: Why Gandhi?
Hanna: Well, he's a hero of mine. And I'd like to tell him about the problems of the world today and get his advice.
Interviewer: Concerning the problems of the world - what would you change about the world if you had the power to change something?
Hanna: I'd stop people killing each other because they have a different religion or a different colour or because they come from a different place. You know, stupid reasons like that.
Interviewer: What would you change about your personality if you could change something?
Hanna: Oh, I'd like to change a lot of things... I'd like to be more calm. I'm a very nervous sort of person and I envy people who are calm and relaxed.
Interviewer: And what would you change about the way you look if you change something?
Hanna: Well, I wouldn't mind having smaller feet. But they're not such a problem. As for the rest, I certainly wouldn't want plastic surgery!
Interviewer: Hanna, the last question - what would you buy if you had a lot of money?
Hanna: Oh, I'd buy a house next to the sea. There's nothing more relaxing than listening to the sound of the sea.

35 Lesson 43 Activity B

Somebody had opened the drawer of my desk and had emptied the wastepaper bin. Perhaps this person had wanted to find some information. But, more strangely, somebody had switched off the light in the bathroom and had closed the window. Why had somebody done that? Also, why had somebody washed the three mugs on my desk and taken the poster off the wall? I just couldn't understand it. Then I had an even bigger shock. I saw that the person or people who had been in my office had stolen the aquarium from the top of the filing cabinet! I just couldn't understand it. Who had been in my office? Why had they stolen my seven goldfish? Then I noticed that somebody had left a note on the screen of my computer. I took the note off the screen and read it.

36 Lesson 44 Activity B

I had just come out of the post office and was posting a letter. A young woman was cycling across the road junction when she was knocked down by a lorry. The lorry was turning right into North Street. It was the lorry driver's fault. The traffic lights were still green for the young woman.

I had just got off the bus and was waiting to cross the road. A young woman on a bike was turning right into North Street when she was knocked down by a lorry. The lorry was also turning right and hit the young woman's bike from behind. It was the lorry driver's fault. The traffic light had just changed to red for the lorry driver.

I had just sat down on a bench opposite the bank and was taking a magazine out of my bag. A young woman was turning right into South Street when she was knocked down by a lorry. The lorry was turning right into North Street. It was the girl's fault. The traffic lights were red for her and green for the lorry driver.

37 Lesson 45 Activity F

When Andrew arrived at the house, it was dark. He tried to switch on the lights, but there was no electricity. He wanted to leave then, but he didn't want his friends to laugh at him. He found a candle and lit it. Then he walked into the dining room. He started looking at an old oil painting on the wall. As he was looking at the painting, he noticed a strange mark on the ceiling. He couldn't see the mark very well and moved closer to get a better look. Just then, he heard footsteps outside the door. Suddenly there was a sickening scream, followed by the sound of a man laughing. It was a terrifying laugh. Andrew couldn't breathe.

He tried to get out of the room, but found, to his horror, that the door was now locked. He wanted to turn round, but before he could move, he felt two icy-cold hands go round his neck. Then everything went black...

The next morning, Andrew's friends found him lying on the dining room floor. There were large bruises on his neck and scratches all over his face. He was unconscious, but he wasn't dead. His friends took him to a hospital in Edinburgh.

Andrew was unconscious for another twenty-four hours. Then he came to and slowly opened his eyes. A doctor examined him and told him that he needed to stay in bed and rest. Later that day, the police visited Andrew in the hospital. They wanted to know why he had been in the house, how long he had been there and what had happened. Andrew told them all he could.

That evening, two policemen arrived at the house. They had a police dog with them. They started looking around. When they were in the dining room, they noticed the old oil painting. The dog suddenly became excited and started jumping up at the wall. The policemen took a close look at the wall, but they couldn't see anything there.

Tapescripts

Then the dog started barking angrily. In the end, the policemen decided to make a hole and see if there was anything inside the wall. Half an hour later, they found something hidden there. It was a large metal box. They opened it. Inside the box, there were hundreds of old gold coins.

38 Lesson 45 Activity H
So who had hidden the gold coins inside the wall? And where had the coins come from? The police looked back over their records and discovered that the coins had been stolen from a museum in Edinburgh in 1947 by a man called Frank McKay. McKay had been arrested by the police. However, before they had caught him, he had been in the house and hidden the coins there. McKay died in prison some years later. He had always refused to tell anyone where the coins were.

Was there really a ghost in the old house? Some people believe there was. They say it was the ghost of Frank McKay, trying to protect his gold coins. No one is really sure, of course, but one thing is certain. After the coins had been taken from the house, the ghost was never heard of again.

39 Lesson 46 Activity B
1
Mother: Judy, you can't wear your new top to school, you know.
Judy: Why can't I?
Mother: It's cold.
Judy: Oh, Mum!
Mother: You'll be too cold.
2
Judy: You look really down, Dominique. What's the matter?
Dominique: I've finished with Peter.
Judy: Oh, no! Really?
Dominique: Yes, I saw him kissing another girl.
Judy: Oh, that's terrible.
3
Mr Winters: Well, can't anybody answer that question? Mark? David? Judy?
Judy: No, sorry, Mr Winters.
Mr Winters: No? Honestly! You're the worst class in the school. You must work harder.
4
Judy: Hi Glen.
Glen: Oh, hi Judy. How are you?
Judy: Oh, I'm fine, thanks.
Glen: Listen, Judy. I may have a party at the weekend.
Judy: Oh, great. Where - at your place?
Glen: Yes, I think so. Look, I'll phone you about it on Thursday - okay?
5
Isabelle: Oh, hi Judy. How are you?
Judy: Oh, I'm fine. Oh, no! Look at the time. I'm sorry, Isabelle, I'm in a hurry and I have to catch a bus.
Isabelle: Oh, right. See you, then.
Judy: Yes, see you. Bye.
6
Mother: You look happy, Judy. What's happened?
Judy: Oh, nothing. I'm going to my room, Mum. I've got lots of homework to do.

40 Lesson 46 Activity C
1 My optician said my eyes were fine. He told me that I didn't need to wear glasses.
2 My dentist said that I needed a filling. He told me it wouldn't hurt.
3 My doctor said that I had an ear infection. She told me I had to take antibiotics three times a day.
4 My sports teacher said that I played very well. She told me she was putting me into the school team.
5 Granddad said that grandma was very ill. He told me she'd had to go into hospital and that she might have to have an operation.
6 My maths teacher said she'd marked the examination. She told me I'd done very well and that I'd got 92%!
7 My best friend, Dominique, said she couldn't come to the disco with me on Friday. She told me that she had to go out with her parents.

41 Lesson 47 Activity A
Producer: Well, how did the interview go, Larry?
Larry: Umm. Well, it started off okay. I asked Johnny Guitar if his recent tour had been successful and he seemed pleased to talk about the tour.
Producer: Good. And then?
Larry: Well, then I wanted to know if he'd had a good time in the States.
Producer: Yes.
Larry: And I asked him what other instruments he could play apart from the guitar. And then I wanted to know how many times he'd been in the top ten.
Producer: Good.
Larry: And I wanted to know what his last number one had been called.
Producer: Right. And what did you ask him then?
Larry: Well, he didn't seem to like my next question.
Producer: No? Why not?
Larry: Well, I asked him when was the last time he had been in the charts.
Producer: Well, that's okay. What's wrong with that?
Larry: Well, he said it'd been ten years ago.
Producer: Oh, right.
Larry: Yes, and then I made a big mistake.
Producer: A mistake?
Larry: Yes, well, I asked him how old he was.
Producer: Oh, dear.
Larry: Yes, well he didn't seem to want to answer that question. And then I made things worse.
Producer: Worse?
Larry: Yes, then I wanted to know if he'd been married five times.
Producer: Oh.
Larry: Yes, well, he didn't like that question very much either, but he did answer it.
Producer: Right. Well, it was good he answered.
Larry: Yes, but then he didn't like my next question at all.
Producer: What was that?
Larry: I asked him if he was going to get married again.
Producer: What did he say? *Larry:* Er, well he got a bit angry, I'm afraid, and asked me if I wanted to be kicked out of the room.

42 Lesson 47 Activities B and C
Larry: Testing. Testing. Testing. Right, Johnny. I think that's fine. Good. Right. Johnny Guitar. I know you've just returned from the States. Was your recent tour successful?
Johnny: Yes, it was. It was very successful. We had ten gigs altogether and we were sold out at every one of them.
Larry: Oh, that's very good. And, er, did you have a good time in the States?
Johnny: I had a great time.
Larry: And what other instruments can you play apart from the guitar, Johnny?
Johnny: Well, I can play the keyboards, of course, and I can play the trumpet.
Larry: The trumpet. Really? That's very interesting. I see. Great. Johnny, how many times have you been in the top ten?
Johnny: Oh, lots and lots of times. I've had eight songs in the top ten and that includes two number ones, of course.
Larry: Oh, that's very good. And what was your last number one called?
Johnny: Don't you remember?
Larry: Er, no.
Johnny: That's it. 'Don't you remember?'
Larry: Oh, right. When was the last time you were in the charts, Johnny?
Johnny: Yes, well, er, well, it was seven, no, eight, er, no, it was ten years ago.
Larry: Oh, right. That's quite a long time ago. Er, how old are you, Johnny?
Johnny: Look. Is that at all important? Are you trying to say I'm getting too old for the music business or what?
Larry: Oh, no, Johnny. Not at all. Let me see. What else. Ah, yes. I read this in the newspapers and I wondered if it was true - have you been married five times, Johnny?
Johnny: Er, well, yes, I have.
Larry: Five times! Really! That's a lot. And are you going to get married again?
Johnny: Look, who do you think you are? You work for some stupid little student radio station, don't you? Get out or do you want me to kick you out of the door?
Larry: Oh, no, thank you. I'm just leaving now. Thank you for the interview. Good bye.
Johnny: Get out!

43 Lesson 47 Activity D
1
Interviewer: Can you fly any kind of plane?
Pilot: Yes, any kind of commercial plane.
Interviewer: Which airline do you work for?
Pilot: I work for Virgin Airlines.
2
Interviewer: Will your party win the next election?
Politician: Yes, I'm sure we will.
Interviewer: Do you want to be Prime Minister?
Politician: Of course. Every politician wants to be Prime Minister.

Tapescripts

3
Interviewer: Do you like playing on grass?
Tennis player: No, I prefer hard courts.
Interviewer: How many tournaments did you win last year? *Tennis player:* Three.

4
Interviewer: Who is starring in your latest film?
Film director: Kim Basinger.
Interviewer: Have you ever won an Oscar?
Film Director: No, I haven't, but perhaps next year.

5
Interviewer: Which of your palaces do you like the most?
Princess: Balmoral in Scotland.
Interviewer: Do you have to marry a prince?
Princess: No, of course not.

6
Interviewer: How many goals did you score last season?
Footballer: Sixteen.
Interviewer: Are you nervous before a match?
Footballer: Yes, always.

44 Lesson 47 Activity D
1 – She asked him if he could fly any kind of plane.
She wanted to know which airline he worked for.
2 – She asked him if his party would win the next election.
She wanted to know if he wanted to be prime minister.
3 – She asked her if she liked playing on grass.
She wanted to know how many tournaments she had won last year.
4 – She asked him who was starring in his latest film.
She wanted to know if he had ever won an Oscar.
5 – She asked her which of her palaces she liked the most.
She wanted to know if she had to marry a prince.
6 – She asked him how many goals he had scored last season.
She wanted to know if he was nervous before a match.

Lesson 2 Activity C

a a screwdriver **b** a lawn-mower
c a saw **d** a plastic ruler
e a compass **f** a dishwasher
g a hairdryer **h** a paper hole punch
i a thermometer
j a leather briefcase

Lesson 43 Activity B

Read the note that Mick found stuck on his computer screen. Who is Mrs Parker?

Dear Mr Malone,

I came into your office this afternoon because I noticed you had left a window open. This is a very dangerous thing to do. Please close all windows before you go out in future.

I would like to remind you to switch off lights before you leave the office – electricity is very expensive! Also, please don't put posters on the wall – they make marks on the wallpaper.

I also noticed your office was very dirty. I washed the three very dirty mugs I found on your desk and emptied your wastepaper basket.

While I was in your office, I thought I would look for the rent you owe me. I couldn't find it, however. Can I remind you that you owe me £145. I will come to your office at 1 o'clock tomorrow. Please let me have the rent then and clean your office thoroughly before I get there.

Yours sincerely,
N. Parker (Mrs)
PS I have taken your aquarium. As you know, you are not allowed to keep pets in my building. Please find your goldfish a new home.

Student B activities

Lesson 27 Activity F

You are going camping. Your classmate is worried about this. Answer your classmate's questions.

If there are a lot of insects I'll buy a spray.
If there is a bull in the field, I'll climb a tree.
If it rains all the time, I'll go to a hotel. I
f the farmer is angry, I'll give him some money.
If I can't find a camp site, I'll camp in a field.

Lesson 32 Activity C

1 What is a florist?
a a person who makes wooden floors
b a person who sells flowers from a shop
c a thing which is used for repairing wooden floors

2 What is a screwdriver?
a a person who does crazy things
b a person who is learning to drive
c a tool which is used for turning screws

3 What is a scarf?
a a thing which is worn around the neck in cold weather
b a person who sells fish from a shop
c a place where you can pay to wash your clothes in a machine

4 What is a bookworm?
a a place where very old books are sold
b a worm which eats books
c a person who loves reading books

Answers: 1b   2c   3a   4c

Lesson 36 Activity C

Read the situations and ask questions to your classmate. Write down his/her answers.

5 You are lost in the jungle and are trying to find a village or a town. You come to a river. What would you do?
a Would you follow the river downstream?
b Would you follow the river upstream?

6 You are in a lifeboat in the middle of the ocean. You have got some food but you haven't got any water. You are very thirsty. What would you do?
a Would you eat something?
b Would you not eat anything?

7 You have been bitten on the leg by a poisonous snake. You are a long way from the nearest hospital. What would you do?
a Would you suck the poison out of your arm?
b Would you tie a cloth very tightly around your leg above the bite?

8 You see somebody getting a powerful electric shock from a hairdryer. You want to help this person. What would you do?
a Would you knock the hairdryer out of the person's hand with a stick?
b Would you throw some water over the person?

Then tell your classmate the correct answers:

1 - **a** It's best to follow the river downstream. There's more chance of finding a village or a town downstream than upstream.

2 - **b** It's best not to eat anything. You use water in your body when you digest the food. This water is more important than food. You can live a long time without food, but not very long without water.

3 - **b** It's best to tie a cloth around your leg above the bite. It's very dangerous to take the poison into your mouth.

4 - **a** It's best to use a stick to knock the hairdryer out of the person's hand. Water would probably kill the person getting the shock.

Lesson 43 Activity D

Your classmate saw you speaking to your mother in the street yesterday. Answer your classmate's questions. Tell him/her why you said the things.

Because she'd bought me some chocolate.
Because I'd forgotten her birthday.
Because we'd missed the bus.
Because I hadn't passed a test at school.
Because I hadn't slept very well.

Then change roles.

You saw your classmate speaking to his/her mother in the street yesterday. Ask your classmate these questions. Find out why he/she said these things.

1 Why did you say 'I'm really hungry.'?
2 Why did you say Ten really annoyed.'?
3 Why did you say 'I hope it doesn't rain.'?
4 Why did you say 'You can borrow mine.'?
5 Why did you say 'I don't want to go to the cinema.'?

Reference Grammar: Contents

A

Lessons 1-10

- **A1** Present simple
- **A2** Present simple passive
- **A3** *For* (purpose)
- **A4** *-ing* clauses
- **A5** Present continuous
- **A6** Present continuous and present simple
- **A7** *One, ones*
- **A8** Past simple
- **A9** Past simple of the verb *be*
- **A10** Present perfect simple
- **A11** *For* and *since*
- **A12** Present simple, past simple and present perfect simple
- **A13** Infinitive

B

Lessons 11-20

- **B1** Present continuous for the future
- **B2** *By bus, by car* etc
- **B3** *Will*
- **B4** *May*
- **B5** Invitations
- **B6** *Must*
- **B7** *Have to*
- **B8** *Can*
- **B9** Past continuous
- **B10** Past continuous and past simple
- **B11** *Like* and *would like*

C

Lessons 21–30

- **C1** *Too many, too much, not enough*
- **C2** *Should*
- **C3** Present perfect continuous
- **C4** Suggestions
- **C5** Offers
- **C6** Present simple for the future after *when, as soon as, until* and *if*
- **C7** *When* and *if*
- **C8** *If* sentences

D

Lessons 31-40

- **D1** Infinitive and *-ing* form
- **D2** Requests
- **D3** Relative clauses with *which, who* and *where*
- **D4** Advice
- **D5** Past simple passive
- **D6** *If* sentences

E

Lessons 41-50

- **E1** Used to
- **E2** Past perfect simple
- **E3** *Say* and *tell*
- **E4** Reported statements
- **E5** Reported questions

Irregular verbs
page 120

109

Reference Grammar

A Lessons 1-10

A1 Present simple

▶ **Affirmative**

| I/you/we/they | **play** |
| he/she/it | **plays** |

Negative

| I/you/we/they | **do not (don't)** | **play** |
| he/she/it | **does not (doesn't)** | |

Question

| **do** | I/you/we/they | **play?** |
| **does** | he/she/it | |

▶ We use the present simple to talk about:

– things which happen repeatedly – for example, every day, usually or sometimes.

*I **walk** to school every day.*
***Do** you usually **go** to school on Saturdays?*
*My grandmother sometimes **plays** basketball.*

– facts which are generally true.

*A vegetarian **doesn't eat** meat.*
*Kangaroos **live** in Australia.*

A2 Present simple passive

▶ *am/is/are* + past participle

*A saw **is used** for cutting things.*
*Those cars **are made** in Italy.*

Compare:

Active   *We **use** a saw for cutting things.*
Passive *A saw **is used** for cutting things.*

The object of an active verb (eg *a saw*) becomes the subject of a passive verb.

▶ We use the passive when we are not interested in who does something.

*Football **is played** all over the world.*
*Those T-Shirts **are made** of cotton.*

In these sentences, we are interested in *football* and *those T-shirts*, not who plays football or who makes those T-shirts.

A3 *For* (purpose)

We can use *for* + an *-ing* form to talk about the purpose of a thing.

*A compass is used **for showing direction**.*
*What's the name of the machine used **for mixing food**?*

A4 *-ing* clauses

We can use an *-ing* clause like an adjective, to give more information about a noun.

*The boy **wearing the dark glasses** is my brother.*
*Do you know those people **waving at us**?*

Wearing the dark glasses gives more information about *the boy*. *Waving at us* gives more information about *those people*.

A5 Present continuous

▶ *am/is/are* + verb.*-ing*

Affirmative

I	**am ('m)**	
you/we/they	**are ('re)**	**playing**
he/she/it	**is ('s)**	

Negative

I	**am not ('m not)**	
you/we/they	**are not (aren't)**	**playing**
he/she/it	**is not (isn't)**	

Question

am	I	
are	you/we/they	**playing?**
is	he/she/it	

▶ We use the present continuous to talk about:

– something which is happening at the moment we speak.

*I**'m going** home now. Goodbye.*
*Look outside! It**'s raining**.*
*Jim and Liz are in the living room. They**'re playing** chess.*

– something which is happening around now, but not necessarily at the moment we speak.

*I**'m taking** driving lessons at the moment. (But perhaps I'm not taking a driving lesson exactly at the moment I speak.)*

Reference Grammar

A6 Present continuous and present simple

Present continuous	Present simple
Jim is in the kitchen. He's having dinner.	Jim has dinner at 7.00 every evening.
Do you usually go to bed so early?	Are you going to bed now?
A librarian works in a library.	Liz is in her office. She's working.

We use the present continuous to talk about something which is happening at the moment we speak.

We use the present simple to talk about something which happens repeatedly (eg *every day, usually*) or for facts which are generally true.

A7 One, ones

We can use *one* instead of repeating a singular noun.

Who is that girl – the **one** talking to Andy? (= the girl talking to Andy)

We can use *ones* instead of repeating a plural noun.

Who are those girls – the **ones** talking to Andy? (= the girls talking to Andy)

We only use *one* and *ones* in place of countable nouns (*girl* = singular countable; *girls* = plural countable).

A8 Past simple

▶ The form of the past simple is the same for all persons (*I, you, he, she, we* etc).

Affirmative

I/you/he/she/it we/they	played went

Many verbs are regular. The past simple of regular verbs ends in *-ed*, eg *played*.

Some verbs have irregular past simple forms, eg *go → went*. For a list of irregular verbs, see page 120.

Negative

I/you/he/she/it we/they	did not (didn't)	play go

Question

did	I/you/he/she/it we/they	play? go?

▶ We use the past simple to talk about a definite time in the past, eg *yesterday, last night, in 1980*.

My friend and I **played** tennis yesterday.
I **didn't go** out last night. I **stayed** at home.
My grandparents **went** to Africa in 1980.

A9 Past simple of the verb *be*

▶ was/were

Affirmative

I/he/she/it	was
you/we/they	were

Negative

I/he/she/it	was not (wasn't)
you/we/they	were not (weren't)

Question

was	I/he/she/it?
were	you/we/they?

▶ We use the past simple to talk about a definite time in the past, eg *yesterday, last night, in 1980*.

I **was** at home **yesterday**, I **wasn't** at school.
Where **were** you **last night**? – We **were** at the cinema.
My grandparents **were** in Africa **in 1980**.

A10 Present perfect simple

▶ have/has + past participle

Affirmative

I/you/we/they	have ('ve)	played
he/she/it	has ('s)	been

Many verbs are regular. The past participle of regular verbs ends in *-ed*, eg *played*.

Some verbs have irregular past participle forms, eg *be → been*. For a list of irregular verbs, see page 120.

Negative

I/you/we/they	have not (haven't)	played
he/she/it	has not (hasn't)	been

Question

have	I/you/we/they	played?
has	he/she/it	been?

▶ The present perfect connects the past and the present. We use the present perfect to talk about:

– something which started in the past and continues up to the present.

I've had my Apex computer **for a year**. (I still have the computer now.)
Eva **has been** ill **since Monday**. (She is still ill now.)

111

Reference Grammar

– experiences in our lives, up to the present.

Have you ever **been** to Disneyland? (in your life, up to now)
I've never **played** golf. (in my life, up to now)

– past actions, when we can see the result of the actions in the present.

The bus **has left**. (The bus isn't here now.)
My father **has grown** a moustache. (He has a moustache now.)

A11 For and since

▶ We can use *for* to talk about a length of time in the past, present or future.

I had my old job **for five years**.
Peter always reads in bed **for half an hour** before he goes to sleep.
Liz will be in Paris **for a few days** next week.

▶ We often use *for* and *since* with the present perfect to say how long something has continued up to the present. Compare:

I've been here **for** three days.

TUESDAY   WEDNESDAY   THURSDAY

I've been here **since** Tuesday.

▶ We use *for* + a length of time (eg *for three days*), and *since* + the starting point (eg *since Tuesday*).

More examples:

for + length of time	since + starting point
for two hours / a month / ten years	since six o'clock / April / 1984

A12 Present simple, past simple and present perfect simple

When we talk about something which has continued up to the present, we use the present perfect, not the present simple.

I've **been** ill since Monday. (Not: I'm ill since Monday.)

When we talk about something which finished in the past, we use the past simple, not the present perfect.

I **was** ill last week, but I'm better now. (Not: I've been ill last week.)

A13 Infinitive

After the verbs *would like* and *hope* we use the *to* infinitive verb form, eg *to learn, to go*.

I **would like to learn** another foreign language.
Do you **hope to go** to university when you leave school?

We can also use the *to* infinitive after the verb *be* (*am/is/are* etc).

My big ambition **is to travel** round the world.

B Lessons 11-20

B1 Present continuous for the future

We can use the present continuous to talk about something which we have already arranged to do in the future.

I'**m meeting** a friend tomorrow. (I have arranged to meet a friend tomorrow.)

What **are** you **doing** this evening? (What have you arranged to do this evening?)

Paul **is having** a party on Saturday. (Paul has arranged to have a party on Saturday.)

B2 By bus/by car etc

We use *by bus/by car/by train/by plane* etc (without *the*), to talk about how we travel.

Maggie usually goes to school **by bus**.
We're going to London **by car**.

But we say *on foot* (= walking).

Paul usually goes to school **on foot**.

Reference Grammar

B3 Will

▶ The form of *will* is the same for all persons (*I, you, he, she, we* etc).

Affirmative

I/you/he/she/it we/they	will ('ll)	play

Negative

I/you/he/she/it we/they	will not (won't)	play

Question

will	I/you/he/she/it we/they	play?

▶ We use *will* to talk about what we think or know will happen in the future.

I'll be in London next Monday.
We won't be at home this evening.
In the future, people will live on the moon.

We often use *think* with *will*.

I think I'll play tennis at the weekend.
I don't think England will win the next World Cup.
Do you think you'll come to the party?

B4 May

We use *may* to say that perhaps something will happen in the future.

I may be rich one day. (= Perhaps I will be rich.)
It may rain tomorrow. (= Perhaps it will rain.)

After *may*, we use the infinitive without *to*, eg *be, rain*.

B5 Invitations

We use *would like to* to invite people to do things.

Would you like to go to a disco this evening?
Would you like to come to my party?

After *would like*, we use the *to* infinitive verb form, eg *to go, to come*.

B6 Must

We use *must* when we think something is necessary.

You've got a bad cold. You must stay in bed today.

We use *must* to talk about the present or future.

It's late. We must go now.
I haven't got much money. I must go to the bank later.

To talk about the past, we use *had to* (see B7).

I had to go to the bank yesterday.

We use *mustn't* to tell someone not to do something.

You mustn't leave all your clothes on the floor.

After *must* and *mustn't*, we use the infinitive without *to*, eg *leave, go, stay*.

B7 Have to

▶ We use *have to* when something is necessary.

In England, children have to start school when they are five.

The difference between *must* and *have to* is small:

– Use *must* when **you** think that something is necessary.

You must be home by eleven. (I want you to do that.)

– Use *have to*, for example, when a law or another person says that something is necessary.

You have to be eighteen to vote in England. (That is the law.)
I have to be home by eleven. (My parents want me to do that.)

▶ We use *don't/doesn't have to* when something is not necessary.

We don't have to hurry. We've got plenty of time.

There is a big difference in meaning between *mustn't* and *don't/doesn't have to*.

You've got a bad cold. You mustn't go to school today. (= Do not go to school today.)
You're on holiday. You don't have to go to school today. (= It is not necessary to go to school.)

▶ We use *had to* to talk about the past.

I had to clean my room yesterday.
We missed the bus, so we had to walk home last night.

B8 Can

We use *can* to ask for and give permission.

Can I use your dictionary? – *Of course you can.*
You can borrow some of my CDs if you like.

We can wear any clothes we like at our school.
I can't do whatever I want at home.

Reference Grammar

B9 Past continuous

▶ was/were + verb -ing

Affirmative

| you/we/they | were | playing |
| I/he/she/it | was | |

Negative

| you/we/they | were not (weren't) | playing |
| I/he/she/it | was not (wasn't) | |

Question

| were | you/we/they | playing? |
| was | I/he/she/it | |

▶ We use the past continuous to talk about something which was in the middle of happening at a past time.

7.45   8.00   8.15

Past ─────────────── Present

What **were** you **doing** at 8 o'clock last night? – I **was having** dinner.

B10 Past continuous and past simple

▶ Compare

Past continuous	Past simple
I **was watching** a video.	I **watched** a video.
(= I was in the middle of watching it.)	(= I started and finished watching it.)

▶ We often use the past continuous and past simple together in a sentence:

Past continuous		Past simple
I **was having** dinner	when	the doorbell **rang**.
Tom **was swimming** in the sea	when	he **saw** a shark.
We **were playing** tennis	when	the storm **started**.

The past continuous describes a background activity. The past simple describes something which happened in the middle of this background activity.

▶ When we tell a story, we often use the past continuous for a background scene, and the past simple for the main actions.

I **was sitting** in my hotel room. It **was getting** late and I **was beginning** to feel tired. Suddenly, I **heard** a strange noise outside in the corridor. I **got up** and **walked** over to the door …

B11 Like and would like

▶ After the verb *like*, we can use the *-ing* form or the *to* infinitive, normally without much difference of meaning.

Do you **like meeting**/**to meet** new people?

In British English, we often use *like* with the *-ing* form to say we 'enjoy' something.

I **like going** to discos. (= I enjoy going.)

▶ After the verb *would like*, we always use the *to* infinitive.

Would you **like to go** to a disco this evening?
I **would like to meet** you tomorrow.

C Lessons 21–30

C1 Too many, too much, not enough

We use *too many* before plural countable nouns and *too much* before uncountable nouns.

We bought **too many eggs**. (plural countable)
There's **too much milk** in this coffee. (uncountable)

We use *enough* before plural countable nouns and uncountable nouns.

We haven't got **enough eggs**.
There isn't **enough milk** in this coffee.

C2 Should

We use *should* to talk about what we think is good or right.

You worry too much. You **should relax** more.
You **shouldn't tell** lies. You **should tell** the truth.
There isn't enough public transport in this town. There **should be** more buses.

After *should*, we use the infinitive without *to*, eg *relax*, *tell*, *be*.

Reference Grammar

C3 Present perfect continuous

▶ *have/has been* + verb *-ing*

Affirmative

| I/you/we/they | have ('ve) | been playing |
| he/she/it | has ('s) | |

Negative

| I/you/we/they | have not (haven't) | been playing |
| he/she/it | has not (hasn't) | |

Question

| have | I/you/we/they | been playing? |
| has | he/she/it | |

▶ We use the present perfect continuous to talk about something which started in the past and has been continuing up to the present.

Past ———————————————— Present

Present perfect continuous
He has been sitting there for two hours.

More examples:

*I've been learning English since 1991.
How long has Mick been playing the saxophone?*

C4 Suggestions

▶ We can use *shall* to ask for a suggestion.

What/Where etc **shall we** (+ infinitive)?

*What shall we do today?
Where shall we go?*

▶ We can make suggestions in these ways:

Let's (+ infinitive).   (Let's = Let us)

*Let's watch a video.
Let's go to the cinema.*

Why don't we (+ infinitive)?

*Why don't we stay at home?
Why don't we go for a walk?*

How about (+ *-ing*)?

*How about going for a swim?
How about playing tennis?*

C5 Offers

▶ We can use *would like* to offer something to someone.

Would you like ...?

*Would you like a Coke?
Would you like something to eat?*

▶ We can offer to do something for someone in these ways:

Would you like me to (+ infinitive)?

*Would you like me to help you?
Would you like me to close the window?*

Shall I (+ infinitive)?   (= Do you want me to?)

*Shall I help you?
Shall I carry your bag?*

I'll (+infinitive).   (I'll = I will)

*I'll help you.
I'll lend you some money if you like.*

C6 Present simple for the future after *when*, *as soon as*, *until* and *if*

We use the present simple to talk about the future in clauses after *when*, *as soon as*, *until* and *if*.

I'll buy a newspaper	when	I go shopping.
We'll have dinner	as soon as	we get home.
I won't go out	until	it stops raining.
What will you do	if	you fail your exam?

In sentences like these, we do not use *will* after *when*, *as soon as*, *until* and *if*.

I'll speak to Julia when I see her. (Not: ... ~~when I will see her.~~)
We'll play tennis if the weather is fine. (Not: ... ~~if the weather will be fine.~~)

C7 *When* and *if*

We use *when* for things we are sure will happen.

I'll speak to Julia when I see her. (I am sure I will see Julia.)

We use *if* for things we are not sure will happen.

I'll speak to Claudia if I see her. (I am not sure I will see Claudia.)

115

Reference Grammar

C8 *If* sentences

> **If** it **rains,** we**'ll stay** at home.
> **If** you**'re** cold, **I'll close** the window.
> **If** you **don't study** hard, you **won't pass** the exams.

if + present simple, + *will* + infinitive without *to*

This structure is often called the 'first conditional'.

▶ We use this structure when it is possible that the situation in the *if* clause will happen in the future or is true now.

If it **rains, we won't play** tennis. (Perhaps it will rain, perhaps it won't.)
If you **are** cold, **I'll close** the window. (Perhaps you are cold, perhaps you aren't.)

D Lessons 31–40

D1 Infinitive and *-ing* form

▶ After the verb *want*, we use the *to* infinitive verb form.

I **want to play** tennis today.
Do you **want to do** the shopping?

After *want*, we often use an object, eg *Maria*, *me* and the *to* infinitive.

I **want Maria to play** tennis with me today.
Do you **want me to do** the shopping?

After *want*, we do not use *that* ... For example, we do not say ~~Do you want that I do the shopping~~?

▶ We use the *-ing* form after prepositions, eg *to*, *about*, *before*.

I'm looking forward **to going** on holiday next week.
How **about playing** tennis tomorrow?
I switched off the lights **before leaving** home.

D2 Requests

▶ We use *can* and *could* to ask for permission to do something.

Can I **use** your pen?
Could I **look** at your magazine?
Do you think I **could borrow** your Walkman?

▶ We use *can* and *could* to ask someone to do something for us.

Can you **help** me?
Could you **open** the door for me?
Do you think you **could lend** me your Walkman?

D3 Relative clauses with *which*, *who* and *where*

▶ We can use *which*, *who* and *where* in defining relative clauses. These clauses identify the thing, person or place we mean.

The train **which goes to Paris** *leaves from platform 3.*
(**which goes to Paris** identifies *the train* we mean)
The woman **who owns the hairdresser's** *is Greek.*
(**who owns the hairdresser's** identifies *the woman* we mean)
The cafe **where we had lunch** *is very nice.* (**where we had lunch** identifies *the cafe* we mean)

▶ We use *which* for things (eg *the train*), *who* for people (eg *the woman*) and *where* for places (eg *the café*).

We can use *that* instead of *who* and *which*.

The train **that goes to Paris** *leaves from platform 3.*
The woman **that owns the hairdresser's** *is Greek.*

▶ We use *which*, *who*, *that* and *where* in place of *it*, *he*, *she* etc.

Where is the book **which** *was on this table?* (Not: ~~Where is the book which it was on this table?~~)
I like the postman **who** *delivers our mail.* (Not: ~~I like the postman who he delivers our mail.~~)

D4 Advice

We can give advice in these ways:

> **You should(n't)** (+ infinitive).

I'm cold. – *You* **should put on** *a sweater.*
You're always tired. You **shouldn't work** *so hard.*

> **I would(n't)** (+ infinitive) **(if I were you).**

What colour should I paint my room? – **I'd paint** *it white.*
I **wouldn't lend** *John any money* **if I were you.**

> **Why don't you** (+ infinitive)?

I've got a headache. – **Why don't you take** *an aspirin?*
I need some money. – **Why don't you ask** *your parents to lend you some?*

Reference Grammar

D5 Past simple passive

▶ was/were + past participle

| A fire | was | started | in the Zap Club yesterday. |
| Two people | were | injured | in the fire. |

Compare:

Active Someone **started** a fire in the Zap Club.
Passive A fire **was started** in the Zap Club.

The object of an active verb (eg *a fire*) becomes the subject of a passive verb.

▶ We use the passive when we cannot say who (or what) did something.

A fire was started in the Zap Club yesterday. (We do not know who started it.)

The money was stolen last night. (We do not know who stole it).

We also use the passive when we are not interested in who (or what) did something.

A new motorway was opened yesterday. (We are interested in the new motorway, not who opened it.)

D6 If sentences

If I **had** enough money,	I'**d buy** a new Walkman.
If I **didn't feel** so tired,	I'**d go** jogging with you.
If Paul **knew** my address,	he'**d write** to me.

if + past simple, + *would* + infinitive without *to*

This structure is often called the 'second conditional'.

▶ We use this structure to talk about:

– unreal present or future situations.

*If I **had** enough money, I'**d buy** a new Walkman.* (But I haven't got enough money.)
*If I **didn't feel** so tired, I'**d go** jogging with you.* (But I feel tired.)

– unlikely present or future situations.

*If Paul **knew** my new address, he'**d write** to me.* (He probably doesn't know my new address).
*If I **won** a lot of money, I'**d travel** round the world.* (I probably won't win a lot of money).

▶ In this structure, we often use:

– *were* instead of *was* in the *if* clause.

*If I **were** older, I'd buy a car.*
*If the weather **were** nicer, we'd go camping.*

– *could* instead of *would* in the other clause.

*If I had enough money, I **could** buy some new trainers.*
(= I would be able to buy some new trainers.)

E Lessons 41–50

E1 Used to

▶ The form of *used to* + infinitive is the same for all persons (*I, you, he, she, we* etc).

| I
He
They
etc | used to | **eat** meat.
live in Liverpool.
be slim. |

▶ We use *used to* + infinitive to talk about:

– things which happened repeatedly in the past, but are now finished.

*I **used to eat** meat, but I became a vegetarian two years ago.*
*Carmen **used to smoke**, but she stopped last year.*

– things which were true in the past, but are not true now.

*John **used to be** slim, but he isn't any more.*

We only use *used to* to talk about the past. When we talk about such things in the present, we use the present simple.

*I never **eat** meat nowadays.*
*Maria **smokes** 20 cigarettes a day.*
*John **is** fat now.*

The negative of *used to* is normally *didn't use to* or *never used to*.

*I **didn't use to** be interested in tennis, but I am now.*
*Tina **never used to** like jazz, but she does now.*

We form questions with *did ... use to*.

***Did** you **use to suck** your thumb when you were a child?*

E2 Past perfect simple

▶ The form of the past perfect simple is the same for all persons (*I, you, he, she, we,* etc).

had + past participle

Affirmative

| I/you/he/she/it
we/they | had | played
gone |

Many verbs are regular. The past participle of regular verbs ends in -ed, eg *played*.

Some verbs have irregular past participle forms, eg *go* → *gone*. For a list of irregular verbs, see page 120.

Reference Grammar

Negative

| I/you/he/she/it we/they | had not (hadn't) | played gone |

Question

| had | I/you/he/she/it we/they | played? gone? |

▶ When we talk about the past, we sometimes want to refer back to an earlier past.

Earlier Past ─────── Past ─────── Present

When David arrived home, his parents had gone to bed.

We use the past perfect (eg *his parents had gone to bed*) to talk about something which had happened before the past time we are talking about (eg *when David arrived home*).

More examples:

When I looked in my pocket, my wallet had disappeared.
I was upset when I saw you yesterday because I had just had some bad news.

E3 Say and tell

▶ After *tell*, we normally use a personal object (eg *Paul, me*) to say who was told. We normally use *say* without a personal object.

| say + something | tell + someone + something |

I said that I was angry.   *I told Paul that I was angry.*
You said you had some money.   *You told me you had some money.*

▶ If we want to put a personal object with *say*, we use *to*.

I said to Paul that I was angry.

E4 Reported statements

▶ When we report what someone said, we can use direct speech or reported speech:

My name is Sid.

Direct speech   The man said, 'My name is Sid'.
Reported speech The man said that his name was Sid.

In direct speech, we give the exact words the person said and we use quotation marks (' … ' or " …").

In reported speech, we change some of the words the person said and we do not use quotation marks.

▶ When the reporting verb is in the past (eg *the man said, you told me*), the tense in reported speech normally 'moves back':

Speaker's words	**Reported speech**
'*I am leaving.*'	He said he **was** leaving.
'*We are French.*'	They told us they **were** French.
'*I work in a bank.*'	She said she **worked** in a bank.
'*Peter has gone.*'	You told me Peter **had gone**.

Verbs already in the past, either do not change or they change into the past perfect.

'*I arrived late.*'   I said I **arrived** late./
                     I said I **had arrived** late.

Verbs already in the past perfect, do not change.

'*I had finished.*'   You said you **had finished**.

Note the past form of the modal verbs: *can → could; will → would; shall → should; may → might*.

'*I can swim.*'   She said she **could** swim.
'*I may be late.*'   He said he **might** be late.

The modal verbs *could, would, should* and *might* do not change in reported speech.

'*You should relax.*'   He said I **should** relax.

Must either does not change or it changes to *had to*.

'*I must go.*'   He said he **must** go./
                He said he **had to** go.

We often use *that* before a reported speech clause.

*You said **that** you had finished.*
*They told us **that** they were French.*

We can leave out *that* after *said* and *told*, especially in an informal style.

E5 Reported questions

▶ The tense in a reported question normally 'moves back' (in the same way as in a reported statement).

Speaker's words	Reported speech
'Where **is** Ken?'	We asked where Ken **was**.
'When **can** we meet?'	I asked when we **could** meet.

In reported questions, the word order is the same as in statements (eg *Ken was, we could meet*), and we do not use question marks (?).

In reported questions, we do not use *do*, *does* or *did*.

'What **do** you **want**?'	They asked what I **wanted**.
'Where **does** Tom **live**?'	I asked where Tom **lived**.
'What **did** you **say**?'	He asked what I said.

▶ When there is no question word (*what*, *where*, etc), we can use *if* to introduce a reported question.

Speaker's words	Reported speech
'Are you tired?'	They asked **if** I was tired.
'Do you like jazz?'	She asked **if** I liked jazz.

▶ After *ask*, we often use a personal object (eg *Maria*, *me*) to say who was asked.

I asked **Maria** when we could meet.
She asked **me** if I liked jazz.

Reference Grammar

Irregular verbs

Infinitive form	Past tense	Past participle
be	was/were	been
beat	beat	beaten
become	became	become
begin	began	begun
bite	bit	bitten
blow	blew	blown
break	broke	broken
bring	brought	brought
build	built	built
burn	burnt*	burnt*
buy	bought	bought
catch	caught	caught
choose	chose	chosen
come	came	come
cost	cost	cost
cut	cut	cut
do	did	done
draw	drew	drawn
dream	dreamt*	dreamt*
drink	drank	drunk
drive	drove	driven
eat	ate	eaten
fall	fell	fallen
feed	fed	fed
feel	felt	felt
fight	fought	fought
find	found	found
fly	flew	flown
forget	forgot	forgotten
freeze	froze	frozen
get	got	got
give	gave	given
go	went	gone
grow	grew	grown
have	had	had
hear	heard	heard
hide	hid	hidden
hit	.hit	hit
hold	held	held
hurt	hurt	hurt
keep	kept	kept
know	knew	known
learn	learnt*	learnt*
leave	left	left
lend	lent	lent
let	let	let
lie	lay	lain
light	lit	lit
lose	lost	lost
make	made	made
mean	meant	meant
meet	met	met
pay	paid	paid
put	put	put
read /riːd/	read /red/	read /red/
ride	rode	ridden
ring	rang	rung
run	ran	run
say	said	said
see	saw	seen
sell	sold	sold
shake	shook	shaken
send	sent	sent
shine	shone	shone
shoot	shot	shot
show	showed	shown
shut	shut	shut
sing	sang	sung
sit	sat	sat
sleep	slept	slept
smell	smelt*	smelt*
speak	spoke	spoken
spell	spelt*	spelt*
spend	spent	spent
stand	stood	stood
steal	stole	stolen
swim	swam	swum
take	took	taken
teach	taught	taught
tear	tore	torn
tell	told	told
think	thought	thought
throw	threw	thrown
understand	understood	understood
wake	woke	woken
wear	wore	worn
win	won	won
write	wrote	written

* These forms can also be regular:

burned, dreamed, learned, smelled, spelled.

Reference Grammar

Index

A
advice D4
as soon as C6

B
by bus, *by car* etc B2

C
can
   permission B8, D2
   requests D2
conditional sentences
   first conditional C8
   second conditional D6
could
   requests D2
   conditional D6

D
did A8, E5
direct speech and reported speech E4
do, does A1, E5
don't have to and *mustn't* B7

E
-ed pronunciation page 98
enough, not enough C1

F
first conditional C8
for eg *a machine for mixing food* A3
for and *since* A11
future
   present continuous B1
   will B3
   present simple C6

H
had to B6, B7
have to B7
how about C4

I
if
   if with the present simple for the future C6
   when and *if* C7
   if sentences C8, D6
   if in reported questions E5
infinitive after certain verbs A13, B11, D1

-ing clauses eg *a man wearing a hat* A4
-ing form after certain verbs B11, D1
invitations B5

L
let's C4
like and *would like* B11

M
many, too many C1
may B4
much, too much C1
must B6
   must and *have to* B7
   mustn't and *don't have to* B7

N
not enough C1

O
offers C5
on foot, by bus, by car etc B2
one, ones A7

P
passive
   present simple passive A2
   past simple passive D5
past continuous B9
past continuous and past simple B10
past perfect simple E2
past simple A8
past simple of the verb *be* A9
past simple and past continuous B10
past simple passive D5
permission B8, D2
prepositions *-ing* form after prepositions D1
present continuous A5
present continuous and present simple A6
present continuous for the future B1
present perfect continuous C3
present perfect simple A10
present simple A1
present simple for the future C6, C8
present simple, past simple and present perfect simple A12
present simple and *used to* E1
present simple passive A2
pronunciation of *-ed* and *-s/-es* endings page 98

R
relative clauses D3
reported questions E5
reported speech and direct speech E4, E5
reported statements E4
requests D2

S
-s/-es pronunciation page 98
say and *tell* E3
second conditional D6
shall C4, C5
should C2, D4
since and *for* A11
suggestions C4

T
tell and *say* E3
that
   relative pronoun D3
   in reported speech E4
too many C1
too much C1

U
until C6
used to E1

W
want to, want someone to D1
was, were A9
when eg *when I get home* C6, C7
which, who, where
   relative pronouns D3
why don't we C4
will B3, C5
would D4
would like
   would like C5
   would like and *like* B11
   would like to B5
   would like me to C5

Wordlist

Lesson 1

build /bɪld/
case /keɪs/
curly /kɜːli/
description /dɪsˈkrɪpʃn/
feature /ˈfiːtʃə(r)/
find out /faɪnd aʊt/
freckles /ˈfreklz/
height /haɪt/
help /help/
missing /ˈmɪsɪŋ/
office /ˈɒfɪs/
other /ˈʌðə(r)/
private investigator /ˈpraɪvɪt ɪnˈvestɪɡeɪtə(r)/
quite /kwaɪt/
short /ʃɔːt/
slim /slɪm/
so /səʊ/
still /stɪl/
straight /streɪt/
tall /tɔːl/
tell /tel/
too much /tuː ˈmʌtʃ/
try /traɪ/
wavy /ˈweɪvi/
well built /ˌwel ˈbɪlt/
worried /ˈwʌrɪd/
worry /ˈwʌri/

Lesson 2

compass /ˈkʌmpəs/
cut (v) /kʌt/
direction /dɪˈrekʃn/
dry (v) /draɪ/
find /faɪnd/
flat /flæt/
glass /ɡlɑːs/
hairdryer /ˈheədraɪə(r)/
handle /ˈhændl/
heavy /ˈhevi/
inside /ɪnˈsaɪd/
lawn-mower /ˈlɔːnməʊə(r)/
leather /ˈleðə(r)/
leg /leɡ/
measure (v) /ˈmeʒə(r)/
normally /ˈnɔːməli/
outside /aʊtˈsaɪd/
paper hole punch /ˈpeɪpə ˈhəʊl pʌntʃ/
place /pleɪs/
plastic /ˈplæstɪk/
rectangular /rekˈtæŋɡjʊlə(r)/
round /raʊnd/
rubber /ˈrʌbə(r)/
ruler /ˈruːlə(r)/
saw /sɔː/
screwdriver /ˈskruːdraɪvə(r)/
temperature /ˈtemprətʃə(r)/
thermometer /θəˈmɒmɪtə(r)/
tool /tuːl/
wheel /wiːl/
wood /wʊd/
wool /wʊl/

Lesson 3

anyway /ˈeniweɪ/
barmaid /ˈbɑːmeɪd/
be into /bɪ ˈɪntə/
boyfriend /ˈbɔɪfrend/
brightly-coloured /ˌbraɪtlɪˈkʌləd/
bus stop /ˈbʌs stɒp/
called (to be) /kɔːld/
change (v) /tʃeɪndʒ/
cloakroom /ˈkləʊkruːm/
coat /kəʊt/
come out of /kʌm ˈaʊt əv/
count /kaʊnt/
denim /ˈdenɪm/
doorman /ˈdɔːmən/
earn /ɜːn/
few (quite a) /fjuː/
fine /faɪn/
get on /ɡet ˈɒn/
helmet /ˈhelmɪt/
keep an eye out /kiːp ən ˈaɪ aʊt/
kneel /niːl/
let /let/
let's see /lets ˈsiː/
light (v) /laɪt/
lock /lɒk/
look for /lʊk fə(r)/
maybe /ˈmeɪbiː/
mineral water /ˈmɪnərəl ˌwɔːtə(r)/
need /niːd/
newspaper stand /ˈnjuːspeɪpə(r) ˌstænd/
observant /əbˈzɜːvənt/
operate /ˈɒpəreɪt/
pavement /ˈpeɪvmənt/
perhaps /pəˈhæps/
plug (n) /plʌɡ/
pm /ˈpiːem/
queue /kjuː/
sell /sel/
serve /sɜːv/
sound /saʊnd/
stand /stænd/
sure /ʃɔː(r)/
takeaway /ˈteɪkəˌweɪ/
technician /tekˈnɪʃn/
yet /jet/

Lesson 4

ambitious /æmˈbɪʃəs/
angry /ˈæŋɡri/
assistant manager /əˌsɪstənt ˈmænɪdʒə(r)/
bad-tempered /ˌbædˈtempəd/
be sorry for (someone) /bɪ ˈsɒri fə(r) (ˈsʌmwʌn)/
bit /bɪt/
boring /ˈbɔːrɪŋ/
boss /bɒs/
busy /ˈbɪzi/
character /ˈkærəktə(r)/
crazy /ˈkreɪzi/
cruel /krʊəl/
either /ˈaɪðə(r)/
food store /fuːd stɔː(r)/
friendly /ˈfrendli/
get angry /ɡet ˈæŋɡri/
great /ɡreɪt/
half /hɑːf/
hard-working /ˌhɑːdˈwɜːkɪŋ/
hate /heɪt/
hide /haɪd/
hold /həʊld/
honest /ˈɒnɪst/
idea /aɪˈdɪə/
in love with /ɪn ˈlʌv wɪð/
insincere /ˌɪnsɪnˈsɪə(r)/
jealous /ˈdʒeləs/
just /dʒʌst/
knife /naɪf/
lazy /ˈleɪzi/
mean /miːn/
menu /ˈmenjuː/
minute /ˈmɪnɪt/
mirror /ˈmɪrə(r)/
miserable /ˈmɪzrəbl/
moment /ˈməʊmənt/
notebook /ˈnəʊtbʊk/
order (n) /ˈɔːdə(r)/
per /pə(r)/
plenty /ˈplenti/
point taken /ˌpɔɪnt ˈteɪkn/
rebellious /rɪˈbelɪəs/
rude /ruːd/
salad /ˈsæləd/
save (money) /seɪv/
seriously /ˈsɪərɪəsli/
shy /ʃaɪ/
smile /smaɪl/
sociable /ˈsəʊʃəbl/
staff /stɑːf/
star /stɑː(r)/
strange /streɪndʒ/
take (an order) /teɪk/
tin /tɪn/
upset /ʌpˈset/
vain /veɪn/
weather /ˈweðə(r)/
write down /raɪt ˈdaʊn/

Lesson 5

'A' Level /ˈeɪ levl/
accept /əkˈsept/
addition /əˈdɪʃn/
advertising /ˈædvətaɪzɪŋ/
alternatively /ɔːlˈtɜːnətɪvli/
apply for /əˈplaɪ fɔː(r)/
assist /əˈsɪst/
assistant /əˈsɪstənt/
attend /əˈtend/
biology /baɪˈɒlədʒi/
briefly /ˈbriːfli/
Bristol /ˈbrɪstəl/
buzzer /ˈbʌzə(r)/
career /kəˈrɪə(r)/
chemistry /ˈkemɪstri/
client /ˈklaɪənt/
clinic /ˈklɪnɪk/
company /ˈkʌmpəni/
compere /ˈkɒmpeə(r)/
computer programmer /kəmˌpjuːtə(r) ˈprəʊɡræmə(r)/
computer science /kəmˌpjuːtə(r) ˈsaɪəns/
customer /ˈkʌstəmə(r)/
Dear Sir or Madam /ˌdɪə(r) sɜː(r) ɔː(r) ˈmædəm/
department /dɪˈpɑːtmənt/
depend /dɪˈpend/
design /dɪˈzaɪn/
diploma /dɪˈpləʊmə/
disc jockey /ˈdɪsk ˌdʒɒki/
emergency /ɪˈmɜːdʒənsi/
examine /ɪɡˈzæmɪn/
fashionable /ˈfæʃnəbl/
flexi-time /ˈfleksɪˌtaɪm/
flexible /ˈfleksəbl/
formal /ˈfɔːml/
general knowledge /ˌdʒenrəl ˈnɒlɪdʒ/
generally /ˈdʒenrəli/
grade /ɡreɪd/
graduate /ˈɡrædʒʊət/
hairdresser /ˈheədresə(r)/
however /haʊˈevə(r)/
increase /ɪnˈkriːs/
insurance /ɪnˈʃʊərəns/
interview /ˈɪntəvjuː/
invite /ɪnˈvaɪt/
journalist /ˈdʒɜːnəlɪst/
junior /ˈdʒuːnɪə(r)/
local /ˈləʊkl/
look forward to /lʊk ˈfɔːwəd tu/
low /ləʊ/
mainly /ˈmeɪnli/
maths /mæθs/
medical school /ˈmedɪkl ˌskuːl/
model (v) /ˈmɒdl/
national /ˈnæʃnəl/
occasionally /əˈkeɪʒənəli/
on your own /ɒn jɔː(r) ˈəʊn/
operation /ˌɒpəˈreɪʃn/
opportunity /ˌɒpəˈtjuːnəti/
outpatients /ˈaʊtpeɪʃnts/
panel /ˈpænl/
patient /ˈpeɪʃnt/
perm (v) /pɜːm/
physics /ˈfɪzɪks/
prepare /prɪˈpeə(r)/

122

Wordlist

press /pres/
press conference /ˈpres ˌkɒnfərəns/
private /ˈpraɪvɪt/
promotion /prəˈməʊʃn/
public relations /ˌpʌblɪk rɪˈleɪʃnz/
qualification /ˌkwɒlɪfɪˈkeɪʃn/
quickly /ˈkwɪkli/
quiz /kwɪz/
radio station /ˈreɪdiəʊ ˌsteɪʃn/
recently /ˈriːsəntli/
requirement /rɪˈkwaɪəmənt/
research /rɪˈsɜːtʃ/
rise /raɪz/
salary /ˈsæləri/
salon /ˈsælɒn/
science /ˈsaɪəns/
section /ˈsekʃn/
send /send/
senior /ˈsiːnɪə(r)/
shampoo /ʃæmˈpuː/
show (n) /ʃəʊ/
special /ˈspeʃl/
specific /spəˈsɪfɪk/
spend (time) /spend ˈtaɪm/
style (n) /staɪl/
subject /ˈsʌbdʒɪkt/
suit (v) /suːt/
surgeon /ˈsɜːdʒən/
surgery /ˈsɜːdʒəri/
surgical /ˈsɜːdʒɪkl/
system /ˈsɪstəm/
train (v) /treɪn/
trainee /treɪˈniː/
training /ˈtreɪnɪŋ/
training course /ˈtreɪnɪŋ ˌkɔːs/
uniform /ˈjuːnɪfɔːm/
university /ˌjuːnɪˈvɜːsɪti/
unusual /ʌnˈjuːʒl/
useful /ˈjuːsfl/
varied /ˈveərɪd/
voluntary /ˈvɒləntri/
well paid /ˌwel ˈpeɪd/
Yours faithfully /ˌjɔːz ˈfeɪθfəli/

Lesson 6

Berlin /bɜːˈlɪn/
borrow /ˈbɒrəʊ/
detail /ˈdiːteɪl/
fancy /ˈfænsi/
final call /ˌfaɪnl ˈkɔːl/
flight /flaɪt/
gate (in airport) /geɪt/
Germany /ˈdʒɜːməni/
Glasgow /ˈɡlɑːzɡəʊ/
immediately /ɪˈmiːdɪətli/
immigration officer /ˌɪmɪˈɡreɪʃn ˈɒfɪsə(r)/
Just a minute /ˌdʒʌst ə ˈmɪnɪt/
lose /luːz/
married /ˈmærɪd/
memorise /ˈmeməraɪz/
mine /maɪn/
move (house) /muːv/
New York /nuː ˈjɔːk/
Oxford /ˈɒksfəd/
passenger /ˈpæsɪndʒə(r)/
pencil case /ˈpensl keɪs/
problem /ˈprɒbləm/
San Francisco /ˌsæn frænˈsɪskəʊ/
Scotland /ˈskɒtlənd/
since /sɪns/
so much /ˌsəʊ ˈmʌtʃ/
Sydney /ˈsɪdni/
that's funny /ˌðæts ˈfʌni/
this way /ˌðɪs ˈweɪ/
United Nations /juːˌnaɪtɪd ˈneɪʃnz/
year /jɪə(r)/

Lesson 7

a few weeks time /ə fjuː wiːks ˈtaɪm/
ambition /æmˈbɪʃn/
amongst /əˈmʌŋst/
Birmingham /ˈbɜːmɪŋəm/
both /bəʊθ/
Britain /ˈbrɪtn/
business /ˈbɪznɪs/
choose /tʃuːz/
enough /ɪˈnʌf/
experience /ɪkˈspɪərɪəns/
fashion /ˈfæʃn/
finishing line /ˈfɪnɪʃɪŋ ˌlaɪn/
footballer /ˈfʊtbɔːlə(r)/
get married /ˌɡet ˈmærɪd/
hope /həʊp/
including /ɪnˈkluːdɪŋ/
interest /ˈɪntrəst/
international /ˌɪntəˈnæʃnəl/
long distance /ˌlɒŋ ˈdɪstəns/
marathon /ˈmærəθən/
Mexico /ˈmeksɪkəʊ/
musician /mjuːˈzɪʃn/
Nepal /nəˈpɔːl/
Olympics /əˈlɪmpɪks/
over /ˈəʊvə(r)/
own (adj) /əʊn/
own (v) /əʊn/
perfect /ˈpɜːfɪkt/
professional /prəˈfeʃənl/
race /reɪs/
raise /reɪz/
rich /rɪtʃ/
runner /ˈrʌnə(r)/
space /speɪs/
store (n) /stɔː(r)/
travel /ˈtrævl/
unemployed /ˌʌnɪmˈplɔɪd/
whatever happens /wɒtevə(r) ˈhæpnz/

Lesson 8

advantage /ədˈvɑːntɪdʒ/
Antarctica /ænˈtɑːktɪkə/
area /ˈeərɪə/
as soon as /əz ˈsuːn əz/
breed /briːd/
breeding ground /ˈbriːdɪŋ ˌɡraʊnd/
calendar /ˈkælɪndə(r)/
chick /tʃɪk/
emperor penguin /ˌempərə(r) ˈpeŋɡwɪn/
enemy /ˈenəmi/
even so /ˌiːvn ˈsəʊ/
fall /fɔːl/
female /ˈfiːmeɪl/
group /ɡruːp/
hardly /ˈhɑːdli/
hatch /hætʃ/
ice /aɪs/
icy /ˈaɪsi/
improve /ɪmˈpruːv/
incubate /ˈɪŋkjʊbeɪt/
inhospitable /ˌɪnhɒˈspɪtəbl/
instead /ɪnˈsted/
keep alive /ˌkiːp əˈlaɪv/
lay (an egg) /leɪ/
line /laɪn/
male /meɪl/
mate /meɪt/
middle /ˈmɪdl/
move /muːv/
must /məst/; strong form /mʌst/
nest /nest/
once more /ˌwʌns ˈmɔː(r)/
only /ˈəʊnli/
predator /ˈpredətə(r)/
protect /prəˈtekt/
return /rɪˈtɜːn/
safe /seɪf/
season /ˈsiːzn/
shelter /ˈʃeltə(r)/
snowstorm /ˈsnəʊstɔːm/
South Pole /ˌsaʊθ ˈpəʊl/
stomach /ˈstʌmək/
storm /stɔːm/
such /sʌtʃ/
survive /səˈvaɪv/
take turns /ˌteɪk ˈtɜːnz/
together /təˈɡeðə(r)/
tucked away /ˌtʌkd əˈweɪ/
until /ənˈtɪl/
vegetation /ˌvedʒɪˈteɪʃn/
weigh /weɪ/
while /waɪl/
wind /wɪnd/
without /wɪˈðaʊt/

Lesson 9

aluminium /ˌæljʊˈmɪnɪəm/
amount /əˈmaʊnt/
cardboard box /ˌkɑːdbɔːd ˈbɒks/
container /kənˈteɪnə(r)/
crush /krʌʃ/
dirty /ˈdɜːti/
elastic /ɪˈlæstɪk/
energy /ˈenədʒi/
full /fʊl/
glue /ɡluː/
item (of clothing) /ˈaɪtəm/
load /ləʊd/
material /məˈtɪərɪəl/
notice (n) /ˈnəʊtɪs/
packaging /ˈpækɪdʒɪŋ/
planet /ˈplænɪt/
plastic bag /ˈplæstɪk ˌbæɡ/
pollution /pəˈluːʃn/
pull out /ˌpʊl ˈaʊt/
recycle /ˌriːˈsaɪkl/
reduce /rɪˈdjuːs/
remind /rɪˈmaɪnd/
reuse /ˌriːˈjuːs/
sew /səʊ/
single /ˈsɪŋɡl/
somewhere /ˈsʌmweə(r)/
string /strɪŋ/
washing machine /ˈwɒʃɪŋ məˌʃiːn/
way /weɪ/

Lesson 10

break /breɪk/
corner /ˈkɔːnə(r)/
feel /fiːl/
flat (n) /flæt/
foreign /ˈfɒrən/
Rome /rəʊm/
tired /ˈtaɪəd/
wave /weɪv/
World Cup /ˌwɜːld ˈkʌp/

Lesson 11

bring /brɪŋ/
by /baɪ/
everything /ˈevrɪθɪŋ/
go out /ˌɡəʊ ˈaʊt/
Manchester /ˈmæntʃɪstə(r)/
relative /ˈrelətɪv/

Lesson 12

believe /bɪˈliːv/
broken /ˈbrəʊkən/
curved /kɜːvd/
exciting /ɪkˈsaɪtɪŋ/
fate /feɪt/
get older /ˌɡet ˈəʊldə(r)/
head /hed/

Wordlist

health /helθ/
heart /hɑːt/
intelligence /ɪnˈtelɪdʒəns/
lucky /ˈlʌkɪ/
may /meɪ/
middle-aged /ˌmɪdl ˈeɪdʒd/
palm /pɑːm/
palmist /ˈpɑːmɪst/
palmistry /ˈpɑːmɪstrɪ/
possible /ˈpɒsəbl/
shine /ʃaɪn/
successful /səkˈsesfl/
top /tɒp/
unlucky /ʌnˈlʌkɪ/
weak /wiːk/

Lesson 13

already /ɔːlˈredɪ/
decide /dɪˈsaɪd/
I'm afraid I can't /aɪm əˌfreɪd aɪ ˈkænt/
my place /maɪ pleɪs/
stay in /steɪ ˈɪn/
wonder /ˈwʌndə(r)/

Lesson 14

apology /əˈpɒlədʒɪ/
appearance /əˈpɪərəns/
bad language /ˌbæd ˈlæŋgwɪdʒ/
certain /ˈsɜːtn/
chore /tʃɔː(r)/
complain /kəmˈpleɪn/
girlfriend /ˈgɜːlfrend/
good manners /ˌgʊd ˈmænə(r)s/
horror movies /ˈhɒrə(r) ˌmuːviːz/
late-night /ˌleɪtˈnaɪt/
nearly /ˈnɪəlɪ/
politeness /pəˈlaɪtnəs/
something else /ˌsʌmθɪŋ ˈels/
story /ˈstɔːrɪ/
tidy /ˈtaɪdɪ/
true /truː/
untidy /ʌnˈtaɪdɪ/

Lesson 15

absolutely /ˈæbsəluːtlɪ/
aerobics /eəˈrəʊbɪks/
afford /əˈfɔːd/
allow /əˈlaʊ/
almost /ˈɔːlməʊst/
ashamed /əˈʃeɪmd/
bill /bɪl/
calorie /ˈkælərɪ/
carrier bag /ˈkærɪə ˌbæg/
CD /siː ˈdiː/
choc-aholic /ˈtʃɒkəhɒlɪk/
collect /kəˈlekt/
comfort /ˈkʌmfət/
community service /kəˌmjuːnətɪ ˈsɜːvɪs/
competition /ˌkɒmpəˈtɪʃn/
continue /kənˈtɪnjuː/
cost /kɒst/
court /kɔːt/
credit card /ˈkredɪt ˌkɑːd/
cuddly /ˈkʌdlɪ/
delicious /dɪˈlɪʃəs/
elegant /ˈelɪgənt/
enjoy /ɪnˈdʒɔɪ/
experiment /ɪkˈsperɪmənt/
face /feɪs/
fan /fæn/
fattening /ˈfætnɪŋ/
forever /fəˈrevə(r)/
fraud /frɔːd/
fridge /frɪdʒ/
from time to time /frəm ˈtaɪm tʊ ˈtaɪm/
handbag /ˈhændbæg/
hopefully /ˈhəʊpflɪ/

horrible /ˈhɒrəbl/
industry /ˈɪndəstrɪ/
jogging /ˈdʒɒgɪŋ/
keep up /kiːp ˈʌp/
last (v) /lɑːst/
mad /mæd/
realise /ˈrɪəlaɪz/
regularly /ˈregjʊləlɪ/
report /rɪˈpɔːt/
rucksack /ˈrʌksæk/
set /set/
several /ˈsevrəl/
soft drink /ˌsɒft ˈdrɪŋk/
sports kit /ˈspɔːts kɪt/
swap /swɒp/
sweet shop /ˈswiːt ʃɒp/
team /tiːm/
teenage /ˈtiːneɪdʒ/
trendy /ˈtrendɪ/
use /juːz/

Lesson 16

bright /braɪt/
get wet /get ˈwet/
suit /suːt/
take out of /teɪk ˈaʊt əv/
wet /wet/

Lesson 17

all over the floor /ɔːl ˌəʊvə(r) ðə ˈflɔː(r)/
annoyed /əˈnɔɪd/
anymore /enɪˈmɔː(r)/
attack /əˈtæk/
bet /bet/
black eye /ˌblæk ˈaɪ/
button /ˈbʌtn/
collide /kəˈlaɪd/
damaged /ˈdæmɪdʒd/
department store /dɪˈpɑːtmənt ˌstɔː(r)/
depressed /dɪˈprest/
document /ˈdɒkjʊmənt/
else /els/
embarrassed /ɪmˈbærəst/
furious /ˈfjʊərɪəs/
go wrong /ɡəʊ ˈrɒŋ/
happen /ˈhæpən/
hurt /hɜːt/
miss (the bus) /mɪs/
nervous /ˈnɜːvəs/
poor /pɔː(r)/
relaxing /rɪˈlæksɪŋ/
repair shop /rɪˈpeə(r) ʃɒp/
ring /rɪŋ/
run (a bath) /rʌn/
scared /skeəd/
shorts /ʃɔːts/
whole /həʊl/
worse /wɜːs/

Lesson 18

ability /əˈbɪlətɪ/
accurately /ˈækjərətlɪ/
astonish /əˈstɒnɪʃ/
Atlantic /ətˈlæntɪk/
author /ˈɔːθə(r)/
automatic /ˌɔːtəˈmætɪk/
bend /bend/
bridge /brɪdʒ/
claim /kleɪm/
clairvoyance /kleəˈvɔɪəns/
connection /kəˈnekʃn/
contact /ˈkɒntækt/
control /kənˈtrəʊl/
crash /kræʃ/
crime /kraɪm/
cross (v) /krɒs/
describe /dɪsˈkraɪb/

disappear /ˌdɪsəˈpɪə(r)/
downstairs /ˌdaʊnˈsteəz/
drawing /ˈdrɔːɪŋ/
Dutch /dʌtʃ/
engineer /ˌendʒɪˈnɪə(r)/
extra-sensory perception /ˌekstrəˈsensərɪ pəˈsepʃn/
fail /feɪl/
finger /ˈfɪŋgə(r)/
float /fləʊt/
hearing (sense of) /ˈhɪərɪŋ/
iceberg /ˈaɪsbɜːg/
impressive /ɪmˈpresɪv/
injury /ˈɪndʒərɪ/
journey /ˈdʒɜːnɪ/
lifeboat /ˈlaɪfbəʊt/
magic /ˈmædʒɪk/
maiden voyage /ˌmeɪdn ˈvɔɪɪdʒ/
mind (n) /maɪnd/
modern /ˈmɒdn/
Netherlands /ˈneðələndz/
object (n) /ˈɒbdʒɪkt/
on board /ˌɒn ˈbɔːd/
politics /ˈpɒlətɪks/
power /ˈpaʊə(r)/
predict /prɪˈdɪkt/
process /ˈprəʊses/
professor /prəˈfesə(r)/
prove /pruːv/
psychic trance /ˌsaɪkɪk ˈtrɑːns/
psychokinesis /ˌsaɪkəʊkɪˈniːsɪs/
recent /ˈriːsnt/
remarkable /rɪˈmɑːkəbl/
remarkably /rɪˈmɑːkəblɪ/
same /seɪm/
sight /saɪt/
similar /ˈsɪmɪlə(r)/
simple /ˈsɪmpl/
sink /sɪŋk/
smell (sense of) /smel/
solve /sɒlv/
Southampton /saʊˈθæmtən/
spoon /spuːn/
state /steɪt/
taste /teɪst/
technology /tekˈnɒlədʒɪ/
touch (sense of) /tʌtʃ/
trance /trɑːns/
treat /triːt/
trick /trɪk/
unsinkable /ʌnˈsɪŋkəbl/
wreck /rek/

Lesson 19

belt /belt/
boxing /ˈbɒksɪŋ/
competitor /kəmˈpetɪtə(r)/
court (n) /kɔːt/
fencing /ˈfensɪŋ/
horse race /ˈhɔːs reɪs/
ice hockey /ˈaɪs hɒkɪ/
jockey /ˈdʒɒkɪ/
kick /kɪk/
lacrosse /ləˈkrɒs/
last (v) /lɑːst/
literature /ˈlɪtrətʃə(r)/
pelota /pəˈlɒtə/
pentathlon /penˈtæθlən/
riding /ˈraɪdɪŋ/
shooting /ˈʃuːtɪŋ/
ski jumper /ˈskiː ˌdʒʌmpə(r)/
squash /skwɒʃ/
wrestling /ˈreslɪŋ/

Lesson 20

be unfit /bɪ ʌnˈfɪt/
breakdown /ˈbreɪkdaʊn/
burn (yourself) /bɜːn/
camp site /ˈkæmp saɪt/

Wordlist

card /kɑːd/
factory /fæktərɪ/
ill /ɪl/
ladder /lædə(r)/
lie /laɪ/
own /əʊn/
pay /peɪ/
postman /pəʊstmən/
prefer /prɪˈfɜː(r)/
sunny /sʌnɪ/
too many /tuː ˈmenɪ/
warm /wɔːm/

Lesson 21

bottle bank /bɒtl bæŋk/
cycle lane /saɪkl ˌleɪn/
doorway /dɔːweɪ/
entertainment /entəteɪnmənt/
graffiti /grəˈfiːtiː/
library /laɪbrərɪ/
lighting /laɪtɪŋ/
litter bin /lɪtə(r) bɪn/
noise /nɔɪz/
pedestrian /pɪˈdestrɪən/
pedestrian crossing /pɪˌdestrɪən ˈkrɒsɪŋ/
public /pʌblɪk/
relax /rɪˈlæks/
road /rəʊd/
rubbish /rʌbɪʃ/
safely /seɪflɪ/
traffic /træfɪk/
transport /trænspɔːt/
underground /ʌndəgraʊnd/
zone /zəʊn/

Lesson 22

Barcelona /bɑːsɪˈləʊnə/
driving licence /draɪvɪŋ ˌlaɪsns/
Dublin /dʌblɪn/
free-time /friːˈtaɪm/
goldfish /gəʊldfɪʃ/
hobby /hɒbɪ/
Ireland /aɪələnd/
penfriend /penfrend/
postcard /pəʊstkɑːd/
provisional /prəˈvɪʒnl/
rent /rent/
saxophone /sæksəfəʊn/
Soho /səʊhəʊ/
test /test/

Lesson 23

beer /bɪə(r)/
cloudy /klaʊdɪ/
degree /dɪˈgriː/
forecast /fɔːkɑːst/
kebab /kɪˈbæb/
maximum /mæksɪməm/

Lesson 24

exercise /eksəsaɪz/
explain /ɪkˈspleɪn/
give a hand /gɪv ə hænd/
glass (n) /glɑːs/
headache /hedeɪk/
lend /lend/
loud /laʊd/
manage /mænɪdʒ/
throw away /θrəʊ əˈweɪ/

Lesson 25

argument /ɑːgjʊmənt/
attitude /ætɪtjuːd/
awkward /ɔːkwəd/
cartoon /kɑːˈtuːn/

cause /kɔːz/
confused /kənˈfjuːzd/
dad /dæd/
documentary /dɒkjʊˈmentrɪ/
each /iːtʃ/
end up /end ˈʌp/
farm /fɑːm/
game show /geɪm ʃəʊ/
go horse riding /gəʊ ˈhɔːsˌraɪdɪŋ/
guide /gaɪd/
impressed /ɪmˈprest/
join in /dʒɔɪn ˈɪn/
left out /left ˈaʊt/
lonely /ləʊnlɪ/
main /meɪn/
nowadays /naʊədeɪz/
occupy /ɒkjʊpaɪ/
pleased /pliːzd/
popular /pɒpjʊlə(r)/
soap opera /səʊp ɒprə/
someone else /sʌmwʌn ˈels/
spare time /speə ˈtaɪm/
suggest /səˈdʒest/
TV-addict /tiːviː ˈædɪkt/
wildlife programme /waɪldlaɪf ˌprəʊgræm/
worst /wɜːst/

Lesson 26

address /əˈdres/
be worth /biː ˈwɜːθ/
champion /tʃæmpɪən/
hire /haɪə(r)/
kidnap /kɪdnæp/
lane /leɪn/
mile /maɪl/
owe /əʊ/
owner /əʊnə(r)/
pound /paʊnd/
straight away /streɪt əˈweɪ/
van /væn/

Lesson 27

bank note /bæŋk nəʊt/
birdwatcher /bɜːdwɒtʃə(r)/
bull /bʊl/
camp (v) /kæmp/
cornflakes /kɔːnfleɪks/
farmer /fɑːmə(r)/
insect /ɪnsekt/
lost /lɒst/
mean (v) /miːn/
neighbour /neɪbə(r)/
pretend /prɪˈtend/
push /pʊʃ/
recognise /rekəgnaɪz/
spray (n) /spreɪ/
sugar lump /ʃʊgə(r) ˌlʌmp/
tie (v) /taɪ/
vet /vet/

Lesson 28

admire /ədˈmaɪə(r)/
anniversary /ænɪˈvɜːsərɪ/
as well as /əz ˈwel əz/
back (n) /bæk/
bandit /bændɪt/
bury /berɪ/
cavalry /kævlrɪ/
Cheyenne /ʃaɪˈæn/
coffin /kɒfɪn/
Deadwood /dedwʊd/
death /deθ/
draw (a gun) /drɔː/
entertainer /entəˈteɪnə(r)/
epidemic /epɪˈdemɪk/
fire /faɪə(r)/
follow /fɒləʊ/

funeral /fjuːnərəl/
gambler /gæmblə(r)/
gold /gəʊld/
grow /grəʊ/
gunfighter /gʌnfaɪtə(r)/
hard /hɑːd/
historian /hɪˈstɔːrɪən/
kill /kɪl/
labourer /leɪbərə(r)/
miner /maɪnə(r)/
mountain lion /maʊntɪn ˌlaɪən/
mule /mjuːl/
murder /mɜːdə(r)/
nickname /nɪkneɪm/
nurse (v) /nɜːs/
poker /pəʊkə(r)/
real /rɪəl/
reason /riːzn/
rector /rektə(r)/
reputation /repjʊˈteɪʃn/
rider /raɪdə(r)/
risk /rɪsk/
saloon bar /səˈluːn ˌbɑː(r)/
saloon keeper /səˈluːn ˈkiːpə(r)/
scout /skaʊt/
shot (n) /ʃɒt/
sick /sɪk/
smallpox /smɔːlpɒks/
South Dakota /saʊθ dəˈkəʊtə/
St Louis /seɪnt ˈluːɪ/
stage (n) /steɪdʒ/
stage coach /steɪdʒ kəʊtʃ/
stage show /steɪdʒ ʃəʊ/
tour /tʊə(r)/
trouble /trʌbl/
well known /wel ˈnəʊn/
West /west/
whisky /wɪskɪ/
wild /waɪld/
wish /wɪʃ/

Lesson 29

amusement arcade /əˈmjuːzmənt ɑːˌkeɪd/
atmosphere /ætməsfɪə(r)/
busker /bʌskə(r)/
discount /dɪskaʊnt/
environmentally friendly /ɪnvaɪərəˌmentəlɪ ˈfrendlɪ/
food poisoning /fuːd ˌpɔɪznɪŋ/
hairdressers /heə(r)dresə(r)z/
kick out /kɪk ˈaʊt/
mug (v) /mʌg/
price /praɪs/
product /prɒdʌkt/
reasonable /riːznəbl/
repair /rɪˈpeə(r)/
selection /sɪˈlekʃn/
skin cream /skɪnkriːm/

Lesson 30

be surprised /biː səˈpraɪzd/
cheap /tʃiːp/
coach /kəʊtʃ/
driving test /draɪvɪŋ ˌtest/
housework /haʊswɜːk/
junk food /dʒʌŋk fuːd/
neither have I /naɪðə(r) (h)əv ˈaɪ/
pass (an exam) /pɑːs/
result /rɪˈzʌlt/

Lesson 31

certainly /sɜːtnlɪ/
channel /tʃænl/
habit /hæbɪt/
help yourself /help jəˈself/
honestly /ɒnɪstlɪ/
promise /prɒmɪs/
soup /suːp/

Wordlist

stir /stɜː(r)/
tennis racket /ˈtenɪs ˌrækɪt/
trolley /ˈtrɒli/
wake up /ˈweɪkʌp/

Lesson 32

add up /æd ˈʌp/
alcohol /ˈælkəhɒl/
bake (v) /beɪk/
baker /ˈbeɪkə(r)/
bookworm /ˈbʊkwɜːm/
chatterbox /ˈtʃætəˌbɒks/
cut down /kʌt ˈdaʊn/
dig /dɪg/
distance /ˈdɪstəns/
extremely /ɪkˈstriːmli/
ground /graʊnd/
hang /hæŋ/
horseshoe /ˈhɔːsʃuː/
knock down /nɒk ˈdaʊn/
neck /nek/
pensioner /ˈpenʃənə(r)/
position /pəˈzɪʃn/
scarf /skɑːf/
screw /skruː/
shoplifter /ˈʃɒplɪftə(r)/
slowcoach /ˈsləʊkəʊtʃ/
spade /speɪd/
steal /stiːl/
teetotaller /tiːˈtəʊtlə(r)/
vegetarian /ˌvedʒɪˈteərɪən/
wardrobe /ˈwɔːdrəʊb/

Lesson 33

alarm clock /əˈlɑːm klɒk/
embarrassing /ɪmˈbærəsɪŋ/
go with /gəʊ wɪð/
granddad /ˈgrændæd/
hiccups /ˈhɪkʌps/
hold your breath /həʊld jɔː(r) ˈbreθ/
ink /ɪŋk/
opinion /əˈpɪnɪən/
part-time /pɑːtˈtaɪm/
sheep /ʃiːp/
side /saɪd/
suppose /səˈpəʊz/

Lesson 34

blow open /bləʊ ˈəʊpən/
chemical /ˈkemɪkl/
clear /klɪə(r)/
damage /ˈdæmɪdʒ/
emergency services /ɪˌmɜːdʒənsɪ ˈsɜːvɪsɪz/
evacuate /ɪˈvækjʊeɪt/
farmland /ˈfɑːmlænd/
fire /faɪə(r)/
firefighter /ˈfaɪəfaɪtə(r)/
flood /flʌd/
fume /fjuːm/
helicopter /ˈhelɪkɒptə(r)/
injure /ˈɪndʒə(r)/
involve /ɪnˈvɒlv/
motorway /ˈməʊtəweɪ/
poisonous /ˈpɔɪzənəs/
rescue /ˈreskjuː/
robber /ˈrɒbə(r)/
rush hour /ˈrʌʃ aʊə(r)/
scene /siːn/
security guard /sɪˈkjʊərətɪ ˌgɑːd/
shoot /ʃuːt/
south west /saʊθ ˈwest/
square /skweə(r)/
vehicle /ˈvɪəkl/

Lesson 35

active /ˈæktɪv/
actually /ˈæktʃʊlɪ/
approach /əˈprəʊtʃ/
artistic /ɑːˈtɪstɪk/
bedding /ˈbedɪŋ/
brain /breɪn/
budgie /ˈbʌdʒɪ/
carefully /ˈkeəflɪ/
cautious /ˈkɔːʃəs/
check-up /ˈtʃekʌp/
choice /tʃɔɪs/
colourful /ˈkʌləfl/
constant /ˈkɒnstənt/
creative /kriːˈeɪtɪv/
creature /ˈkriːtʃə(r)/
especially /ɪˈspeʃəlɪ/
everywhere /ˈevrɪweə(r)/
exactly /ɪgˈzæktlɪ/
feelings /ˈfiːlɪŋz/
hamster /ˈhæmstə(r)/
helpful /ˈhelpfl/
ideal /aɪˈdɪəl/
impatient /ɪmˈpeɪʃnt/
independent /ˌɪndɪˈpendənt/
leader /ˈliːdə(r)/
logical /ˈlɒdʒɪkl/
look after /lʊkˈɑːftə(r)/
millionaire /ˌmɪljəˈneə(r)/
mouse /maʊs/
perpetual motion /pəˌpetʃʊəl ˈməʊʃn/
personality /ˌpɜːsəˈnælətɪ/
pet /pet/
possibility /ˌpɒsəˈbɪlətɪ/
properly /ˈprɒpəlɪ/
rabbit /ˈræbɪt/
rat /ræt/
regular /ˈregjʊlə(r)/
relaxed /rɪˈlækst/
reserved /rɪˈzɜːvd/
routine /ruːˈtiːn/
sense of humour /sens əv ˈhjuːmə(r)/
shape /ʃeɪp/
stick insect /ˈstɪk ˌɪnsekt/
suitable /ˈsuːtəbl/
take care of /teɪk ˈkeər əv/
talkative /ˈtɔːkətɪv/
therefore /ˈðeəfɔː(r)/
tropical fish /ˌtrɒpɪkl ˈfɪʃ/
unfriendly /ʌnˈfrendlɪ/
unhappy /ʌnˈhæpɪ/
vaccination /ˌvæksɪˈneɪʃn/
workaholic /ˌwɜːkəˈhɒlɪk/

Lesson 36

air /eə(r)/
bear /beə(r)/
better off /ˈbetər ˈɒf/
call out /kɔːl ˈaʊt/
civilisation /ˌsɪvəlaɪˈzeɪʃn/
crawl /krɔːl/
downstream /ˌdaʊnˈstriːm/
electric shock /ɪˌlektrɪk ˈʃɒk/
fire alarm /ˈfaɪər əˌlɑːm/
fire extinguisher /ˈfaɪə(r) ɪkˌstɪŋgwɪʃə(r)/
flame /fleɪm/
forest /ˈfɒrɪst/
gas /gæs/
jungle /ˈdʒʌŋgl/
lift shaft /ˈlɪft ʃɑːft/
powerful /ˈpaʊəfl/
put out /pʊt ˈaʊt/
rescuer /ˈreskjʊə(r)/
set off /set ˈɒf/
smoke /sməʊk/
towards /təˈwɔːdz/
trap /træp/

upstream /ˈʌpstriːm/
warn /wɔːn/

Lesson 37

aid /eɪd/
cheat /tʃiːt/
concerning /kənˈsɜːnɪŋ/
envy /ˈenvɪ/
hero /ˈhɪərəʊ/
kiss /kɪs/
manager /ˈmænɪdʒə(r)/
plastic surgery /ˌplæstɪk ˈsɜːdʒərɪ/
religion /rɪˈlɪdʒən/
shoplift /ˈʃɒplɪft/

Lesson 38

ancestors /ˈænsestə(r)z/
apart /əˈpɑːt/
arithmetic /əˈrɪθmətɪk/
barn /bɑːn/
belief /bɪˈliːf/
buggy /ˈbʌgɪ/
Canada /ˈkænədə/
celebration /ˌselɪˈbreɪʃn/
common /ˈkɒmən/
community /kəˈmjuːnətɪ/
destroy /dɪˈstrɔɪ/
dialect /ˈdaɪəlekt/
electricity /ɪˌlekˈtrɪsətɪ/
escape /ɪˈskeɪp/
evil /ˈiːvl/
face-to-face /ˈfeɪstəˈfeɪs/
friendliness /ˈfrendlɪnəs/
generation /ˌdʒenəˈreɪʃn/
German /ˈdʒɜːmən/
God /gɒd/
greedy /ˈgriːdɪ/
horse-drawn /ˈhɔːs drɔːn/
huge /hjuːdʒ/
kindness /ˈkaɪndnəs/
lead (v) /liːd/
living (n) /ˈlɪvɪŋ/
mains /meɪnz/
mistake /mɪˈsteɪk/
neighbourliness /ˈneɪbə(r)lɪˌnəs/
North America /nɔːθ əˈmerɪkə/
obey /əˈbeɪ/
occasion /əˈkeɪʒn/
oil lamp /ˈɔɪlæmp/
Pennsylvania /ˌpensəlˈveɪnɪə/
religious persecution /rɪˌlɪdʒəs pɜːsɪˈkjuːʃn/
rule /ruːl/
social event /ˌsəʊʃl ɪˈvent/
tractor /ˈtræktə(r)/
traditional /trəˈdɪʃənl/
treatment /ˈtrɪːtmənt/
wedding /ˈwedɪŋ/
well (n) /wel/
worship /ˈwɜːʃɪp/

Lesson 39

addictive /əˈdɪktɪv/
ashtray /ˈæʃtreɪ/
ban /bæn/
breath /breθ/
confident /ˈkɒnfɪdənt/
drug /drʌg/
lung /lʌŋ/
nicotine /ˈnɪkətiːn/
nuclear weapon /ˌnjuːklɪə(r) ˈwepən/
racism /ˈreɪsɪzəm/
sexual discrimination /ˌsekʃʊəl dɪˌskrɪmɪˈneɪʃn/
short of breath /ˈʃɔːt əv ˈbreθ/
sophisticated /səˈfɪstɪkeɪtɪd/
tax /tæks/
tobacco /təˈbækəʊ/
unemployment /ˌʌnɪmˈplɔɪmənt/

Wordlist

vivisection /ˌvɪvɪˌsekʃn/
world-wide /wɜːldˈwaɪd/

Lesson 40

Australian /ɒsˈtreɪliən/
cheque book /tʃek bʊk/
completely /kəmˈpliːtli/
contaminate /kənˈtæmɪneɪt/
cough /kɒf/
fight /faɪt/
launderette /ˌlɔːndəˈret/
luckily /ˈlʌkɪli/
Moscow /ˈmɒskəʊ/
nuclear reactor /ˌnjuːklɪə rɪˈæktə(r)/
power station /ˈpaʊə(r) ˌsteɪʃn/
puncture /ˈpʌŋktʃə(r)/
radiation /ˌreɪdɪˈeɪʃn/
spare wheel /ˌspeə(r) ˈwiːl/
tie (n) /taɪ/

Lesson 41

block capitals /blɒk ˈkæpɪtlz/
clarinet /ˌklærəˈnet/
divorced /dɪˈvɔːst/
enclose /ɪnˈkləʊz/
grateful /ˈɡreɪtfl/
high school /ˈhaɪ skuːl/
mechanic /mɪˈkænɪk/
pen pal /ˈpen pæl/
physical education /ˈfɪzɪkl ˌedʒʊˈkeɪʃn/
put in touch /ˌpʊt ɪn ˈtʌtʃ/
regarding /rɪˈɡɑːdɪŋ/
sign /saɪn/
type /taɪp/

Lesson 42

bite (your nails) /baɪt/
Crete /kriːt/
fashion model /ˈfæʃn ˌmɒdl/
get travel sick /ˌget ˈtrævl sɪk/
occasional /əˈkeɪʒənl/
put on weight /ˌpʊt ɒn ˈweɪt/
salsa /ˈsælsə/
track suit /ˈtræksuːt/
travel guide /ˈtrævlɡaɪd/

Lesson 43

aquarium /əˈkweərɪəm/
drawer /drɔː(r)/
filing cabinet /ˈfaɪlɪŋ ˌkæbɪnət/
mark (n) /mɑːk/
mug /mʌɡ/
screen /skriːn/
shock /ʃɒk/
strangely /ˈstreɪndʒli/
thoroughly /ˈθʌrəli/

Lesson 44

bench /bentʃ/
fault /fɔːlt/
hit /hɪt/
junction /ˈdʒʌŋkʃn/
parking meter /ˈpɑːkɪŋ ˌmiːtə(r)/
pram /præm/
raincoat /ˈreɪnkəʊt/
teenager /ˈtiːneɪdʒə(r)/

Lesson 45

angrily /ˈæŋɡrəli/
bang /bæŋ/
bark /bɑːk/
blood /blʌd/
breathe /briːð/
bruise /bruːz/

brush (v) /brʌʃ/
candle /ˈkændl/
ceiling /ˈsiːlɪŋ/
coin /kɔɪn/
drip /drɪp/
Edinburgh /ˈedɪnbrə/
excited /ɪkˈsaɪtɪd/
foolish /ˈfuːlɪʃ/
footstep /ˈfʊtstep/
icy cold /ˌaɪsi ˈkəʊld/
motionless /ˈməʊʃnlɪs/
move into /muːv ˈɪntə/; strong form /muːv ˈɪntuː/
move out of /muːv ˈaʊt əv/
museum /mjuːˈzɪəm/
notice (v) /ˈnəʊtɪs/
oil painting /ˈɔɪl peɪntɪŋ/
prison /ˈprɪzn/
refuse /rɪˈfjuːz/
reply /rɪˈplaɪ/
rush /rʌʃ/
scratch (n) /skrætʃ/
scream /skriːm/
shake /ʃeɪk/
sickening /ˈsɪkənɪŋ/
terrifying /ˈterɪfaɪɪŋ/
unconscious /ʌnˈkɒnʃəs/

Lesson 46

antibiotic /ˌæntɪbaɪˈɒtɪk/
ear /ɪə(r)/
filling /ˈfɪlɪŋ/
infection /ɪnˈfekʃn/
mark (v) /mɑːk/
optician /ɒpˈtɪʃn/
politician /ˌpɒlɪˈtɪʃn/
tournament /ˈtɔːnəmənt/

Lesson 47

airline /ˈeəlaɪn/
altogether /ˌɔːltəˈɡeðə(r)/
apart from /əˈpɑːt frəm/
charts /tʃɑːts/
commercial /kəˈmɜːʃl/
election /ɪˈlekʃn/
film director /ˈfɪlm dɪˌrektə(r)/
gig /ɡɪɡ/
grass /ɡrɑːs/
keyboard /ˈkiːbɔːd/
match /mætʃ/
palace /ˈpælɪs/
pilot /ˈpaɪlət/
prime minister /ˌpraɪm ˈmɪnɪstə(r)/
prince /prɪns/
princess /prɪnˈses/
producer /prəˈdjuːsə(r)/
score /skɔː(r)/
seem /siːm/
sold out (tickets) /səʊlˈdaʊt/
testing /ˈtestɪŋ/
trumpet /ˈtrʌmpɪt/

Lesson 48

arm /ɑːm/
arrangement /əˈreɪndʒment/
as usual /əz ˈjuːʒl/
because of /bɪˈkɒz əv/
behave /bɪˈheɪv/
blind /blaɪnd/
Captain /ˈkæptɪn/
communicate /kəˈmjuːnɪkeɪt/
complete /kəmˈpliːt/
cry /kraɪ/
deaf /def/
director /dɪˈrektə(r)/
doll /dɒl/
even /ˈiːvn/

fold /fəʊld/
force /fɔːs/
grab /ɡræb/
guest house /ˈɡest haʊs/
gush /ɡʌʃ/
hear /hɪə(r)/
illness /ˈɪlnɪs/
institute /ˈɪnstɪtjuːt/
knock out /ˌnɒk ˈaʊt/
knock over /ˌnɒk ˈəʊvə(r)/
manners /ˈmænəs/
mention /ˈmenʃn/
messy /ˈmesi/
method /ˈmeθəd/
miracle /ˈmɪrəkl/
mysterious /mɪˈstɪərɪəs/
napkin /ˈnæpkɪn/
noun /naʊn/
peace /piːs/
perform /pəˈfɔːm/
piece /piːs/
plate /pleɪt/
point (n) /pɔɪnt/
proud /praʊd/
pump (v) /pʌmp/
relieved /rɪˈliːvd/
repeat /rɪˈpiːt/
shortly after /ˈʃɔːtli ˈɑːftə/
silent /ˈsaɪlənt/
spoilt /spɔɪlt/
unless /ənˈles/
violent /ˈvaɪələnt/
violently /ˈvaɪələntli/
voice /vɔɪs/
water pump /ˈwɔːtə(r) pʌmp/

Lesson 49

parliament /ˈpɑːləmənt/

Lesson 50

alarm bell /əˈlɑːm bel/
bookseller /ˈbʊk ˌselə(r)/
brace /breɪs/
businessman /ˈbɪznɪsmən/
fluent /ˈfluːənt/
Japanese /ˌdʒæpəˈniːz/
naughty /ˈnɔːti/
shoe repairer /ˈʃuː ˌrɪpeərə(r)/
suck /sʌk/
thumb /θʌm/
wallet /ˈwɒlɪt/
zoo keeper /ˈzuː ˌkiːpə(r)/

Macmillan Education

Between Towns Road, Oxford OX4 3PP

A division of Macmillan Publishers Limited

Companies and representatives throughout the world

ISBN 0 435 29236 6

Text ©Colin Granger, Digby Beaumont 1993
Design and illustration © Macmillan Publishers Limited 1998

First published 1993

All rights reserved; no part of this publication may be reproduced, stored in a retrieval system, transmitted in any form, or by any means, electronic, mechanical, photocopying, recording, or otherwise, without the prior written permission of the publishers.

Designed by KAG Design Ltd, Basingstoke Cover illustration by Threefold Design

Illustrated by: Sophie Allsopp pp.56-57; John Gilkes pp.19, 37, 55, 73, 93; Donald Harley pp.52-54, 82-83; Geoff Jones pp.66-67; KAG Design Ltd, Basingstoke pp.13, 16, 18, 25, 35, 46; Paul McCaffrey pp.40-41; Colin Mier pp.60; Mark Olroyd pp. 4, 6-7, 22, 30-31, 42-43, 80-81; Oxford Illustrators pp.47, 74-75; John Richardson pp.8-9, 44, 45; Jacky Rough pp.69, 94-95; Paul Russell pp.24, 32-33, 58-59, 61, 88-89; Paul Sullivan p.85; Russell Webb p.21; Tracy Wilson pp.90-92; Celia Witchard pp.12, 48-49, 50-51; John York pp.23, 26-27, 86-87.

The publishers would like to thank the following for their kind permission to reproduce copyright material: Enterprise Holidays, Mars Confectionary, Pepsi Cola, Qualcast, Zanussi.

The authors and publishers would like to thank the following for permission to reproduce their photographs: Action Plus pp.37, 73; All Sport p.55; Andes Press Agency p.14; Animal Photography/Sally Anne Thompson & R.T.Willbie p.64; Ardea Londo p.64; Art Directors p.10; ASAP p.14; Britstock IFA pp.14, 15, 78; Bubbles Photo Library p.78; Camera Press London p.75; Mary Evans Picture Library pp.34, 35, 36; Greg Evans International p.14;Glasgow Herald pp.62, 63; The Ronald Grant Archive p.68; Impact Photos p.14; The Image Bank p.70; Images Colour Library Limited p.34; The Hulton Deutsch Collection pp 34, 62; Lupe Cunha p.78; Natural History Photographic Agency p.16; Oxford Scientific Films pp.16, 17; The Photographers Library p.10; Pictor International, London pp. 37, 47, 55, 77, 93; Rex Features Limited pp.14, 62, 68, 72; Spectrum Colour Library p.55; Still Pictures Environmental Picture Library/Mark Edwards pp.19, 73; The Telegraph Colour Library p.71; ZEFA p15.

Commissioned photography by Simon Chapman p.40; Paul Freestone pp.5, 10, 11, 19, 29, 34, 55, 68, 73; Chris Honeywell pp. 15, 47, 68, 73, 76, 77, 84 and Alexander MacIntyre p.79. We would like to thank the following for their co-operation: Flaggs, Oxford; Freuds, Oxford; Partners, Oxford; Exeter College, Oxford; Cherwell Radio at The Churchill Hospital, Oxford; Gosford School 6th Form Centre, Kidlington; Swan School, Oxford; Mr and Mrs Chapman, Richard Gill, Sam Laverty, John Major, Dawn Treadwell and Aileen Welch.

The authors and publishers would like to thank Patricia Lodge and Beth Wright-Watson for the Skills section, Pilar Garcia Ramos and Bienvenido Hernandez for their contributions to the projects, David King for the pronunciation section and Margot Gramer for her contribution to the Helen Keller Story.

Printed and bound in Romania by Infopress S.A.

2007 2006 2005 2004
14 13 12